KU-175-466

THE
ENGLISH
CASTLE

THE
ENGLISH
CASTLE

François Matarasso

CASSELL

First published in the UK 1995 by
Cassell plc
Wellington House,
125 Strand
LONDON
WC2R 0BB

Hardback edition Published 1993

Copyright text and illustrations © François Matarasso 1993 and 1995

All rights reserved. No part of this book may be reproduced or
transmitted in any form or by any means, electronic or mechanical,
including photocopying, recording or any information storage and
retrieval system, without prior permission in writing from the copyright
holder and Publisher.

Distributed in the United States
by Sterling Publishing Co., Inc.
387 Park Avenue South, New York, NY 10016-8810

Distributed in Australia
by Capricorn Link (Australia) Pty Ltd
2/13 Carrington Road, Castle Hill, NSW 2154

British Library Cataloguing in Publication data for this title is available
upon request from the British Library Biblographic Services.

ISBN 0-34753-1

Typeset by August Filmsetting, Haydock, St Helens

Printed and bound in Great Britain by The Bath Press, Avon

Contents

For my mother

Item, donne a ma povre mere
Pour saluer nostre Maistresse
(Qui pour moi eut douleur amere
Dieu le set, et mainte tristesse)
Autre chastel n'ai, ne fortresse
Ou me retraie corps et ame
Quant sur moi court male destresse
Ne ma mere la povre femme.

François Villon

Preface

According to Bernard of Chartres, we are like dwarfs on the shoulders of giants, able to see further than them only because we use their own height as a platform. He was referring to the debt owed by medieval writers to their Greek and Roman predecessors, but the metaphor is apt for much of human endeavour – and certainly for this book. For more than a hundred years, men and women have sought to understand the truth about castles: they have excavated and observed, measured, drawn and, most of all, written. It is only because of their work, which ranges from comprehensive volumes to slim but no less erudite pamphlets, that a book such as this is possible, and it is a pleasure to record my indebtedness to those giants both here and in the bibliography. But if their research has provided knowledge and facts, what I have done with them, the ordering and interpretation, remains my responsibility. Omissions are different, however, and I know that I have not been able to do justice to all the castles which could claim a place in a book of this sort: to those readers who fail to discover a favourite in the following pages, I apologize, and plead the limitations of space.

Many people have helped me over the years I have been engaged in this work, including the owners or guardians of many castles; those who have patiently endured tortuous expositions of ideas; and those who have shared long journeys and cold tramps through weeds and nettles in search of obscure ruins: they all know who they are. I wish, however, particularly to record my debt to M. J. Fazan and to Caroline Davidson, both of whom provided invaluable help. My mother helped make this book possible in many ways, commenting on its numerous drafts and providing occasional translations. I must also thank Carol, who sometimes found more to admire in the view than in the ruin, and Ziggy and Laurence, who generally did not, for their patience.

François Matarasso

Introduction

The bones of the kingdom, that is, the king's fortresses.

WILLIAM OF NEWBURGH, 1198

Castles are an essentially paradoxical form of architecture. At the most basic level they seek to fulfil the diametrically opposed functions of secure fortress and comfortable home, but high levels of security are incompatible with spacious, airy buildings, and vice versa. The English medieval castle – the castle as far as this book is concerned – is perhaps architecturally unique in attempting to serve *two* basic purposes. No other building, be it church, palace, school, hospital or conference centre, works in this way; even the most complex serves only one end.

The function of an airport is to get people on and off aeroplanes. This job is greatly complicated by secondary needs, such as security, transport to and from the site, and feeding and entertaining waiting passengers, but these are consequent upon the primary function, which they assist rather than inhibit. With castles, everything pulls in opposite directions. A multiplication of gates and portcullises will make the entrance hard to force, but then it becomes tiresomely inconvenient for the owner to get in, so a small postern door is built which, in turn, may provide a weak point during a siege. Thus the tug of war between the demands of military strength and those of domestic convenience pulls to and fro.

There is duality even within the castle's two functions. Its military role, for example, was both defensive and offensive: it controlled land, preventing its seizure by enemy troops, but it also acted as a base from which to threaten or occupy neighbouring territory. It was never merely a passive instrument of defence. It was also, in military terms, one arm of a double weapon, for without its mounted knights, whose horses allowed them to ride the land for 16 kilometres (10 miles) around and whom it protected when they were unarmed, at rest and vulnerable, the castle was nothing. The castle's domestic nature was similarly fragmented, for within the walls it was home to its lord, his family and retainers, church, storehouse and granary, administrative centre and court of law, while in its shadow were farms, orchards and pastures, and in many cases, the local market and economic centre too.

The final paradox of the castle's nature is intangible: the relationship between its appearance and its actual strength. It was designed to impress and to underline the status and power of its owner, not for reasons of vanity but because, then as now, power has to be seen to be believed. To have one or more strong castles, built of the stone that only the wealthiest could afford, not only conferred military strength but the political power that came with it, and throughout the Middle Ages the first act of a rising knight was to build (or improve) a castle to drive home his elevated rank in society. We now have more complex, but not always more subtle, ways of demonstrating power; however, in the fourteenth century there was no more effective symbol than the castle, and the manifestation of power can often become its substance.

It will be seen that the essentially contradictory nature of the castle, with all its complexities, allows no room for absolutes. Take, for example, the notion of impregnability. There can be no such thing as an impregnable castle since its strength depends on the numbers and morale of the opposed forces, on the weapons and food at their disposal, and on the length of time each side is able to continue the struggle. The best that can be said is that a castle, if stoutly defended, would be extremely difficult and costly to take by assault; in the end, though, every fortress must fall when its supplies have been exhausted.

The two castles which did most to defeat the French invasion of 1215 were the barely finished and very sophisticated fortress of Dover and the old-fashioned and frankly, crude castle of Lincoln: what mattered most was not their design, but the courage and luck of the defenders, the tide of events elsewhere, and the belief or otherwise of the assailants in their ability to conquer – in short, the human factors. This is often neglected when castles are discussed: they were not intellectual exercises developed in the abstract, but buildings with purpose and value, so it is crucial that an appreciation of their physical form is not divorced from an understanding of their functions and of the aspirations and lives of their builders and occupants.

It is this dynamic tension which makes the medieval castle so interesting, for the solutions sought by different men, at different times and places, create an extraordinary variety of forms, styles and ideas. The basic home/fortress dichotomy is only the principal of a host of greater and lesser factors which influenced castle design. The status of the builder, his financial resources, the availability of different building materials and skilled craftsmen to work them, the choice of site, the security of the region, the power of the king, the time available for construction and the experience of the designer: all these and other factors had their part to play in shaping the final creation.

Different reasons, equally complex, have dictated which castles have survived, and consequently how we view them. Since their construction, most, including all those built of timber, have disappeared, leaving only bumps on the ground. The survival of one rather than another (Kenilworth, say, instead of Nottingham) is the merest accident of history.

From his seven surviving plays, it is possible to gain an idea of the world view of Sophocles, but if the hundred-odd which have been lost were discovered, they might present a quite different story. The same is true of castles. Although, as this book attempts to do, it is possible to describe and analyse the development of the English medieval castle, it is essential to remember that the picture might look very different if all those which have been destroyed could stand before us entire.

It is also important not to apply contemporary beliefs in the nature and value of material progress to medieval buildings, such as castles. We see progress in terms of the abandonment of old ideas and styles for newer and better ones, and we tend to judge our ancestors in a similar way. Thus architectural historians have created a convincing picture of the stylistic and structural evolution of ecclesiastical buildings during the Middle Ages. Churches and fortresses, however, are built for very different reasons and it would be wrong to look for such a smooth progression in the architecture of castles. New ideas, and new stylistic idioms for articulating them, certainly emerged, but they complemented rather than replaced existing ways of thinking and building. Maybe soldiers are naturally conservative or, perhaps, as even today's grim wars suggest, ways of attacking and defending do not change drastically; whatever the reason, the medieval castle builder appears reluctant to abandon ideas tested in the rigours of battle.

The keep, for example, is fundamental to the castles of the eleventh and twelfth centuries, but there are fewer examples from the thirteenth and fourteenth. This might be thought to imply an abandonment of the idea, but a closer examination shows this not to be the case. First of all, since most castles already had twelfth-century keeps, there was clearly no purpose in replacing them. Secondly, a small number of keeps was built throughout these years, generally – as at Southampton in the 1360s – when an old keep fell into disrepair. Thirdly, the *idea* of the keep, the prominent final refuge, was often applied to other buildings, such as gatehouses or rampart towers, in new castles with no actual keep.

So a picture of the development of castle architecture, which described a steady acceptance of new ideas and styles in place of what had gone before, would be misleading. It would be more accurate to suggest that new developments were added to a stock of existing ideas without necessarily discrediting them, in much the same way as graphic designers add new typefaces to their range of choices without discarding old ones. Round towers have certain military advantages over rectangular ones, but their introduction did not cause the abandonment of the latter, whose ease of construction, furnishing and use still had a value.

These matters are further complicated by the changing nature of the buildings themselves, for what was a strong castle in the eleventh century, had it remained unimproved, would have been no more than a fortified manor to the larger, more professional, armies of the fourteenth century. Unlike a church, which does not become more or less a church if it receives a grand new nave or loses a lady chapel, many sites were truly castles for only part of their lives, either because they were left alone or, paradoxically, because they were updated. Windsor was less a castle after Edward III had spent £50,000 on it than before, because almost all the money had gone on the domestic quarters; Nottingham Castle is a nineteenth-century house which merely occupies the site of one of the greatest fortresses of the Middle Ages.

Most of the time, because we do not understand them, we look at things without seeing them. A petrochemical engineer, noticing an oil refinery from the train, will understand what he sees, but to the rest of us it is just a maze of pipes, storage tanks, chimneys and ladders; we recognize it for what it is, but no more. This book is for those who recognize a castle but want to know more about its purpose, its location, its design and its inhabitants – who want to understand it. Like the scene of a crime, a castle will tell its story to eyes which know what to look for; everything once had a reason, however complex or contradictory, but only the discerning eye will discover it. The following pages try to draw together some of the paradoxes into a pattern of art, artifice and brute force, which, if it is to be both convincing and attractive, has all the faults of hindsight. We look back, see some things, miss others, and try to find some meaning which may, in truth, be quite different from that perceived by our ancestors.

Map of England
showing principal castles

A Note on the Illustrations

All the illustrations have been drawn specially for this book, but the plans are based on published sources, and I am grateful to the following for permission to use plans originally published by them: English Heritage, CADW (Welsh Historic Monuments), the National Trust, Friends of Lincoln Archaeological Research and Excavation, Derek Renn and John Baker Ltd for plans from *Norman Castles in Britain*, Dalesman Books, Historic Tours (Wales), the Society of Antiquaries of Newcastle upon Tyne, William Heinemann Ltd. and B.T. Batsford Ltd. for the plan of Queensborough Castle from *English Medieval Castles* by R. Allen Brown. Although every effort has been made to trace copyright holders of original plans, this has not always been possible. My apologies are offered to any copyright holder I have not been able to trace.

The following conventions have been adopted. Slopes are indicated by lines of decreasing thickness, with the thickest part of the line being the top of the slope. Black lines indicate standing walls, hollow lines indicate foundations; occasionally, for the sake of clarity, foundations have been shown in black. Water is indicated by wavy shading; other shading indicates a feature generally explained in the captions.

Drawings show the castles as they are – with the exception of Exeter and Framlingham where later alterations have been removed.

———1———
Colonizing England

Behind the bland façades of Exeter's post-war high street, hidden and apparently uncherished, stand the remains of one of Britain's very earliest castles. A rocky outcrop in the north-east corner of the old city was walled around in hard, red volcanic rock to form a citadel from which the Norman administration of the city was to be conducted. Today the State continues to administer the law from the same spot and access to the interior of Rougemont Castle is denied by porters as officious as their Norman predecessors.[1] They stand in the shadow of a tall gate tower, built on the orders of the Conqueror himself in about 1068, after he had crushed the rebellious citizens. Exeter, of course, preserves traces of its history much older than this; what makes the castle special is that it underlines the extent to which we, our culture and our institutions, are the children of our past. Here, where the same business has been conducted for almost a millenium, an unbroken chain links us with our Norman and Anglo-Saxon predecessors.

Exeter's story really begins two years earlier, on a Thursday late in September 1066. On that day 5,000 Normans, Bretons and other French soldiers of fortune, under the command of William of Normandy, landed on the Sussex coast by the ruins of a Roman fort, known as Pevensey. A fortnight later they met the forces of the elected English king, Harold Godwinsson, outside Hastings and routed them, killing Harold and scattering his troops. The Normans certainly had luck on their side: Harold and his troops reached Hastings by forced marches from Yorkshire, where they had defeated a Norwegian force only three weeks before. Moreover, Harold had been unable to call on the fyrd, the country's defence force, since he had already done so in the spring, and its period of service had been exhausted.

But if the Normans had luck, they also had superior military power with which to hammer it home: Duke William and his battle-hardened knights fought on horseback, using stirrups to hold them secure while they charged with lowered lances. The stirrup enabled a rider to add the weight of the horse's charge to his own strength, to collide with an opponent without being unseated.[2] France had seen the development of the heavy cavalry charge as a decisive factor in warfare, but Harold's housecarls (his personal bodyguards) always fought on foot, with the traditional tactics of hand-to-hand warfare. The fight was inevitably uneven.

Harold raised his standard beside a grey apple tree on the brow of a hill, disposing his forces in a long line across the London road, shields and spears to the front. William was left with the valley below, organizing his troops into three divisions, each of which was composed of archers, foot-soldiers and mounted knights. At first it

Exeter Castle, the eleventh-century gatehouse. The entrance, which is now blocked, has been left open in the drawing to give a better idea of the tower's original appearance.

appeared that the English shield-wall might combine with the rising ground to break the Norman charge; indeed the left flank began to falter and, as William was suddenly nowhere to be seen, to turn. Rashly the English pushed them down the hill, losing their advantage. At that critical moment William reappeared – his horse had been cut down – and rallied his troops. They faced their enemies and, on the flat ground, mounted knights destroyed the English foot-soldiers; this accidental manoeuvre was repeated intentionally with equal success. Norman archers were shooting into the sky so that their arrows rained down on the English, forcing them to raise their shields and weaken the wall they had made. When Harold was struck, some said by an arrow, others by a lance, the English lost heart, fell back, and were routed.

French knights had taken victory from soldiers used to fighting on foot, and whose passive courage had been unable to withstand the charging war-horses. The power of the knight, both military and symbolic, forms an arc which rises in the eighth and ninth centuries, reaches its zenith in the two or three centuries after Hastings, and dips as a result of the social changes of the later Middle Ages. Anglo-Saxon England, culturally and socially distanced from the Continent, had not accepted the new weapon and, at Hastings, paid the price for its conservatism.

But one battle did not give England to the Normans. William had defeated an army, not a nation, and his movements after Hastings reflect that fact. Leaving garrisons in earthwork castles at Pevensey and Hastings, he went to Dover where the ancient hilltop fort was briefly held against him.[3] After gaining control of the port and securing his communications with Normandy, William was able to move towards London, the powerful heart, if not yet the capital, of England. His army stopped at Canterbury, where they met no resistance and again raised a castle. A tentative move against London proved to William that he could not yet risk a full assault. Instead, he took his troops on a long march through Surrey and Berkshire (where, at Wallingford, they crossed the Thames); like molehills, earth and timber castles marked their progress to Little Berkhampsted in Hertfordshire. This relentless isolation of London from the rest of the country appears to have convinced the remaining Anglo-Saxon establishment that further resistance was futile: the nobles and important citizens came to Berkhampstead to submit. An advance party of Normans entered London to prepare a castle for their lord and, on Christmas Day 1066, William was crowned in Westminster Abbey.

It had taken William almost three months since the killing of Harold to succeed him as King of England. It would be years more before the English were reconciled to the Norman nobility; the conquest begun at Hastings took William most of his remaining years to consolidate. The task would be accomplished by knights and, for they were inextricably linked, by castles. The castle was essential to the knight because, while armed and mounted he was almost unstoppable, at rest both he and his horse were extremely vulnerable: the castle existed to protect both from sudden attack (remembering that a war-horse might cost £20 in 1066, or enough for the lesser gentry to live on for a year). If the knights won the field at Hastings, the castles from which they rode enabled them to keep it.

The origins of the castle appear to lie in northern France, an outcome of the chaos which followed the death of Charlemagne in 814. The great empire he had forged in western Europe splintered under the combined pressures of an internal vacuum and external attack; the power of the centre ebbed as that of local leaders, ready and able to protect their people, grew. Throughout the ninth century a particularly terrible struggle was engaged with the Vikings who sailed out of Scandinavia. They struck the coastal areas of northern Europe with ferocity and, thanks to their ships, without warning; the only answer was to be always on guard, and so people began to fortify their settlements.

The medieval castle begins with the ditches which local chieftains dug around their farms. If the spoil from such a ditch was banked on the inner edge, the scarp confronting an attacker became quite impressive; crowned with a palisade of tree trunks, it became a serious obstacle. The hall, in which the local chief and his people lived communally, could stand safely within such an enclosure, alongside the other essential buildings of the settlement. These first castles, or ringworks, seem to have become common over northern continental Europe in the century or two before the Norman Conquest.

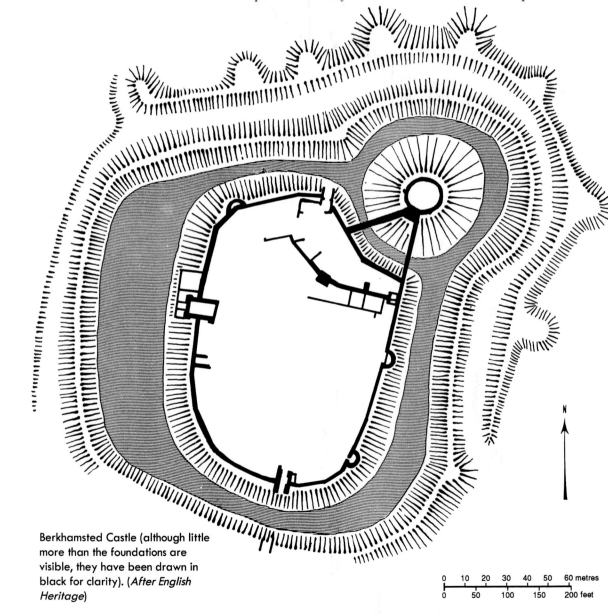

Berkhamsted Castle (although little more than the foundations are visible, they have been drawn in black for clarity). (*After English Heritage*)

0	10	20	30	40	50	60 metres
0		50		100	150	200 feet

The appearance of the stirrup had, as already noted, been followed by that of the mounted knight who formed the aggressive arm of the castle's strength. The castle became the secure base from which a cavalry force could defend the surrounding countryside and resist Viking incursions. It was also the home of a war-lord, whose authority, delegated from the king perhaps through a count or duke, rested on his ability to protect the local population. The central element of feudalism (the concept of land granted by a superior in return for military service) was formed, and the link between mounted knight, feudal society and castle sealed.

Anglo-Saxon England had also suffered the depredations of the Vikings, but here, after initial set-backs, central authority was able to regroup and take the offensive against them. The fortifications built by the English monarchs were communal, and the surviving traces are those of fortified towns, or burhs, not of private castles. The distinction can be seen at Wallingford, an Anglo-Saxon town fortified by an earthen rampart, with the Thames running along its eastern side; only a quarter of it is taken up by William the Conqueror's castle, and the difference in area of the fortified town and castle underlines the private nature of the Norman castle.

In France the crown had been obliged to cede a large tract of land to the Vikings. During the tenth century the Duchy of Normandy was formed and, though external attacks petered out, the Norsemen failed to make comfortable neighbours. Castle and knight found employment in civil warfare, as local war-lords struggled to increase their power. King and barons attempted, never with much success, to prevent the construction of unauthorized castles, or at least to limit their strength, but by 1066 northern France was dotted with private fortresses. Some, like Langeais, or William's own castle at Rouen, were already provided with stone buildings which made them safe from fire, but the majority depended on ditches, ramparts and palisades. In plan they were basically enclosures, though they might have had more than one bailey.[4] When the motte, that characteristic element of the medieval earthwork castle, developed is not known: the ringwork castles probably had watch-towers from quite an early stage, and it was a short step to build such a tower on an artificial hillock which both raised it and made it much less vulnerable.

The Anglo-Saxon nobility seem to have lived in wooden halls, perhaps secured by a moat and fence but of little military strength – the antecedent of the manor-house rather than the castle. Ordericus Vitalis, the twelfth-century historian, believed that their lack of castles prevented the English from resisting the invasion of 1066, and it is not difficult to agree with him. The castle, as brought to England by the Normans, had been developed and refined in the crucible of continental-European warfare; new to Britain it might have been, but a century or more of bitter experience had made the Normans understand it, respect it and believe in it; and they were very good at building and using it.

In the months and years that followed William's coronation, castles rose in towns and villages from Devon to Durham. The first priority was evidently to quieten potentially troublesome centres of population, and most county towns soon found themselves dominated by a royal fortress maintained by the king's constable. Thus did the citizens of Exeter find themselves overlooked by an uncomfortable new neighbour.

The castle, built by William after the siege, occupied a rocky knoll in the northern corner of the city, making use of the existing Roman walls on two sides; it was only necessary to prevent access from the city by a ditch and stone wall to create a simple rectangular bailey. What makes Rougemont Castle so important is that it preserves two towers and a wall which probably date from 1068. Of these, the most important and impressive survivor is the gatehouse. The triangular-headed windows above the gate-arch suggest that the tower was built by local masons, still using styles and techniques with which they were familiar. However, the design of the structure is Norman. It is a rectangular tower, projecting boldly from the line of the wall, with a gate passage running through the ground level, above which were two further floors. Such a tower was a not uncommon form of defence at the most vulnerable point of the castle's perimeter, but the designer at Exeter had more imagination than most: he brought the side walls forward and linked them with a high arch in front of the gate itself; behind this arch was a wooden platform accessible from a door high in the tower itself. This ingenious structure allowed the defenders to attack, from above, any soldiers attempting to force the gate itself; an aggressive defence was clearly intended.

The knight's approach to castle-building was essentially prag-matic. Where good defences existed, as at Exeter, they would be used; on less-promising sites, like Huntingdon (raised by William shortly after Exeter), a basic motte-and-bailey plan was chosen. At Exeter, where stone was readily available, it was used from the begin-ning; elsewhere timber was the only sensible material since speed was required. The royal castles erected for William in the early years of the Norman colonization reflect this diversity. The castle built in London, begun even before William's coronation with the expressed purpose of intimidating the 'huge and brutal populace', was set between the Roman wall and the Thames.[5] A ditch, its inner edge built up into a rampart and crowned with a palisade, was cut north from the river and then across to the wall, creating a large enclosure in the south-eastern corner of the city.

An expedition into the north of England following the subjugation of Devonshire led to the foundation of a number of castles with vary-ing plans. At Warwick, a simple motte and bailey was laid out, pro-tected on one side by a precipitous cliff and the River Avon. Nottingham offered an unoccupied sandstone hill rising steeply above the Trent and a little way from the Saxon town: this was laid out as an upper and lower ward with rock-cut ditches, but no motte. At York, a spit of land between the confluence of the Rivers Ouse and Foss provided the site for another motte-and-bailey castle with extensive water defences (which proved troublesome in later years). At Lincoln, through which William passed on his return to the south, the walls of its Roman founders were re-used. Once again, a corner of the city was occupied: a castle in such a position commanded both town and country, and avoided the risk of being cut off by a turbulent populace. This time the construction of a motte-and-bailey castle

```
0    10   20   30   40   50   60 metres
|----|----|----|----|----|----|
0      50      100     150    200 feet
```

London Castle. Site plan about 1070, showing the White Tower built against the Roman wall, with the Thames to the south. (*After English Heritage*)

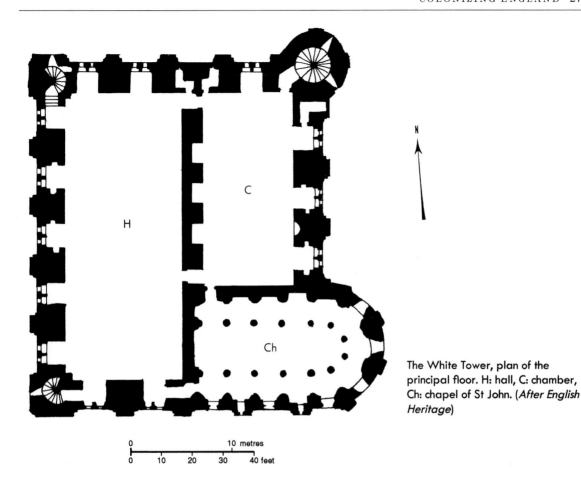

N

The White Tower, plan of the principal floor. H: hall, C: chamber, Ch: chapel of St John. (*After English Heritage*)

```
0                 10 metres
0   10   20   30   40 feet
```

caused the destruction of 166 houses and the occupation of one-quarter of the city. The Roman wall was too dilapidated to be of much use, so it was buried in a huge bank made from the spoil of ditches; a motte was built on the southern, and most precipitous, part of the site, and it too was ditched. Sadly, the ground outside the walls was sold in the seventeenth century, and the ditches filled and built on; as a result, the visual impact of the walls today is less impressive than it once was.

Within three or four years of the Conquest, royal castles existed, in addition to those already mentioned, at Hereford, Worcester, Gloucester, Cambridge, Norwich, Oxford, Colchester, Stafford, Winchester and many other places. The havoc and resentment caused by the intrusion of these castles can easily be imagined: not only did they cause the destruction of large parts of the town – 27 houses in Cambridge, 51 in Shrewsbury and 81 inside the burh of Norwich, with another 17 outside – but the inhabitants themselves were conscripted as ditchers and loggers to assist in their construction. The defeated population was obliged to help make permanent the colonization of England; the process begun on a hillside outside Hastings was enforced by the castles of William I.

The White Tower of London, from the south; the only remaining Norman windows are on the top left-hand side.

Power, wealth and the passage of time are great distorters; like an enormous skein of Chinese whispers, they encourage us to weave fact with fear and fantasy in the creation of a tapestry of myth in which the ignorant, malevolent or merely manipulative seek to twist the pattern their own way. The Tower of London occupies, like Stonehenge, a most extraordinary position in the national psyche, a position whose grip is so tenacious that it is risky to attempt the separation of truth from trifle. Yet, in the very first rank of British castles, its story is pivotal so, like a long-drowned hulk raised dripping from the waters, its medieval character must be exhumed and the accretions of centuries chipped away to reveal the bones of the castle and of the government at whose heart it lay.

It did not long remain the simple enclosure established late in 1066: its importance meant not only that it had to be very strong but also that it had to be seen to be so. William began its development as a symbol of kingship with the construction of a stone tower large enough to accommodate the royal household, and strong enough to protect it. By 1077, work on the huge keep – the tower which has given its name to the whole castle – had begun under the direction of Gundulf, the Norman Bishop of Rochester. His overseeing of the operations at London must be seen in the context of the times: when stone was rarely used for buildings other than churches, the clergy, who were usually literate and numerate, became involved in their design and construction. It is impossible to know the extent to which Gundulf was responsible for the actual design of the White Tower, although it is tempting to see his hand in its stately form; certainly it has a quality more usual in the ecclesiastical than in the military architecture of the period. Comparison with the contemporary keep of Colchester – surely inspired by London, but undertaken by a lesser designer – confirms the high regard in which the architect of the White Tower must be held, whoever he was.

The White Tower, (the name comes from the later custom of white-washing it), is of exceptional importance, both architecturally and as a reflection of the Norman feudal society which had become the government of England. It has no direct antecedent (unless we take into account the vanished keep William's grandfather built at Rouen in Normandy), but there are some buildings which point the way to it. At Doué-la-Fontaine and Langeais in France there are the remains of small stone keeps which date from between 950 and 1000. They consisted of a hall raised over a ground-floor room which, being inaccessible from outside, served as a basement.[6] The defensive advantages of a hall raised above ground are obvious but, as so often in the Middle Ages, the link between the real purpose of the castle and the idea of lordship become blurred, so that first-floor halls are found (for instance at Kenilworth in 1380) with no conceivable defensive purpose. But in 1077, King William's hall in London was built over a basement for very good defensive reasons. The entrance was high in the southern face of the keep, well out of reach of battering rams, and it was reached by a wooden stair which could be withdrawn in time of danger.

Built of yellow-brown rubble, with freestone dressings from Caen in Normandy (since renewed), the keep rises 28 metres (90 feet) to the parapet, and higher at the angle turrets; its walls are 6 metres (15 feet) thick at the base, and cover an area roughly 33 by 36 metres (107 by 118 feet). It originally contained three floors: a basement, the entrance floor above it, and then the principal floor, twice the height of those below, and with a gallery running through the thickness of the wall half-way up. (The worst damage suffered by the keep in later centuries has been the subdivision of this space to create a new, fourth floor at gallery level). Above the main apartment was the roof: the walls were built up to protect it from missiles and behind crenellated parapets was a wall-walk from which soldiers could survey castle and city. Turrets rose at the four corners of the keep; they, too, originally had crenels, not the silly caps they now wear. The tower was not rectangular but had a large apsidal extension to accommodate the chapel of St John. Each floor was divided by cross-walls into three parts, corresponding on the principal floor to the hall, chamber and chapel. A spiral stair gave access to the floors above and below. All the windows have been altered (except for four pairs at gallery level in the southern wall): they were originally mere slits below the level of the main floor.

Several times taller than the wooden houses of the city at its feet, the tower must have been awesome to Londoners, as dominantly alien as a high-rise block in a country village. Much care must have been spent on this foremost royal house, and inside it would have been equally impressive. The comforts of the age were provided: latrines, evacuating outside the building, were built into the thickness of the walls, and there were fireplaces at first- and second-floor levels. The walls themselves were plastered and painted: thin reddish lines imitating ashlar were characteristic of the period, but there may have been more complex paintings or wall-hangings. Furniture was basic, probably not much more than trestle-tables and benches, wooden

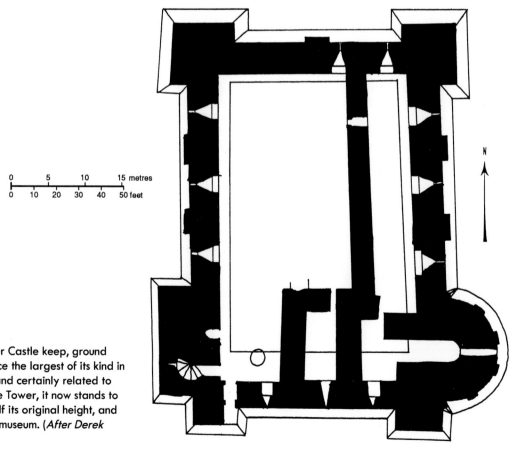

0   5   10   15 metres
0   10   20   30   40   50 feet

N

Colchester Castle keep, ground plan. Once the largest of its kind in Europe, and certainly related to the White Tower, it now stands to about half its original height, and houses a museum. (*After Derek Renn*)

chests, and a bed for William and Queen Matilda. Chairs were rare at the time, and were symbols of authority; the throne was probably no more than a carved and painted wooden chair.

Architecturally speaking, the impressiveness of the building lies in the way it balances, to the highest standard of comfort then available, the roles of fortress, home and centre of government. The basement provided secure storage for valuable foodstuffs and arms, while its well ensured that the occupants of the keep would be able to withstand a long siege. The sheer walls, with their small openings, were sufficient to guard against assault, yet the hall and gallery were high enough to be well-lit without risk. And the division of the principal floor into three rooms – hall, chamber and chapel – mirrored exactly the organization of the king's household and, since they were identical, of the new feudal government of England.[7]

The chapel was under the authority of the chancellor, who kept the great seal which gave authority to the king's writs; the highest-paid official, he regulated all administrative work, which fell naturally to the literate clerics of the chapel. The king's business was conducted behind screens in the hall, and it is from the Latin for screen, *cancella*, that the chancellor derived his title. Because the bedchamber was the most private part of the household, it was also the most secure, and the king's treasure, in goods and coin, was kept here under the care of the master chamberlain. The treasurer was the chamberlain's deputy, and it was in this room that the modern treasury has its origins. The third department of the household was the hall, regulated jointly by the butler and the steward. Their duty was to provide, respectively, drink and food for the occupants, and they had departments which would later become the buttery and pantry, which exist as rooms at one end of the hall in most medieval houses. The hall itself was the room in which people spent most of the time when they were indoors: the hub of the household. The security of the castle, and of the court, was the responsibility of an officer known as the constable; each royal castle had its resident constable to run it in the king's absence.

The new keep built for William in London preserves in masonry the balance between the elements of the new Norman government. Many of these are reflected, growing fainter and fainter, down the social scale to the lord of a single manor in furthest Lincolnshire, who still needed a clerk, butler and steward, and who sat in his hall with the same authority as the king. Today, among London's ferro-concrete towers stands a building which remains a key to understanding the origins of English society.

2
Tenant and Subtenant

A motorist on the Fosse Way is unlikely to notice the Norman castle at Brinklow, still less to realize that it was the cause of the westward diversion of the straight Roman road, which follows an uncharacteristic kink as it passes through the village. Today the castle is represented only by its earthworks: a motte some 12 metres (40 feet) high, and two baileys below it; the ramparts are still steep, and in wet weather the ditches hold a little water. To the west stands a parish church, with provincial, fifteenth-century nave arcades, and a street which has grown up on the verges of the Fosse where it runs in the shadow of the castle bailey. There is no record of the castle's foundation, though it certainly existed by 1130; obscure, half-forgotten and an inconvenience to the motorist, it nevertheless illustrates the impact which the construction of hundreds of new castles had on the newly occupied country.

In the months and then years after his coronation, William distributed English land to the Normans, Bretons, Flemings and Frenchmen who had fought with him at Hastings, and in towns and villages in every county, the new lords built castles.[1] The terms under which the land was distributed were feudal, and were not previously current in England, though they had formed the basis of social organization in France for some time. The relationship was simple: the king, owner of all land by right of conquest, ceded portions to his tenants-in-chief, in return for a military obligation. Such a parcel of land would be estimated, in relation to its financial value, to be worth so many knight's fees (a knight's fee being a period, often forty days, during which a knight must serve the king), and each year the king could call on the tenant to deliver the service he owed. The tenants-in-chief would apportion lands to lesser men, who would themselves subdivide their holdings and so on, down to the level of an individual knight, holder of perhaps only one or two manors, who would give individual fields to freemen for their own use, in return for their labour on his own land.

The system rested on duties owed by people who knew each other directly, and often felt ties of personal loyalty to one another; service owed by those at the lower end of the scale was balanced by rights of justice and protection. Church lands were held in the same way, for abbots and bishops were secular landlords as well as clerics. Thus the three estates – priest, soldier and worker – were linked like hoops of chain-mail in a structure where each class, at least in principle, depended on the other two: the worker provided the necessities of life, the soldier secured the safety of all to live and work in peace, while the priest prayed for God's mercy on the whole community both before and after death.

Through his distribution of land, William ensured that the

Norman presence was carried to every corner of his Anglo-Saxon kingdom. His own castles secured points of strategic importance and the principal towns; those of his barons and their tenants linked into a *de facto* net of control. The new king granted important groups of estates and manors to his friends and chief lieutenants, although, to prevent any from becoming territorially overstrong, he ensured that they were widely dispersed. For example, the lands given to William de Warenne, who had been a minor Norman baron until his friendship with William elevated him to the first rank of Anglo-Norman society, were scattered through a dozen counties. The new nobles might be rich, but their power was curtailed so that it would not threaten that of the king. The existence in France of subjects, like William himself or the Dukes of Burgundy, who controlled more territory than the royal house, was the direct cause of unceasing inter-baronial fighting under a nominal crown without the power to preserve peace.

Rebellions allowed William to confiscate the lands of the unreliable English nobility and redistribute them, piecemeal over time, among his more loyal companions. The power of the barons was further balanced by the retention of England's already well-developed Anglo-Saxon system of local government through shires. The dispersal of lands encouraged the new landlords to build castles in each of their principal holdings, partly as a home and as a base for themselves, but also partly to defend their new acquisitions: so before long castles were being established across the realm.

Brinklow Castle site plan, with inner and outer baileys. (*After Derek Renn*)

However, an insurrectionist native population was not the only threat: the borders of the kingdom to the north and to the west (and for different reasons to the south) had to be secured and so in these areas trusted men were allowed to hold large areas of land. The Prince-bishop of Durham was a key force in the north, holding, in addition to Durham itself, the Tweedside lands called Norhamshire and the mighty castle which gave them their name. The Earl of Northumberland controlled, from Bamburgh on the east coast, much of the rest of that wild land. In the west, the new earldoms of Chester, Shrewsbury and Hereford were created, each centred on an important town. But Norman mentality saw these earldoms not as mere defensive bulwarks against Scottish and Welsh insurgency, but as advance bases for further conquest in Wales and across the Pennines into Scottish-held Cumbria. The economically poor county of Sussex, and its strategic sea link with Normandy, was divided into five strips, known as rapes, and in each was planted a castle to control the coast:

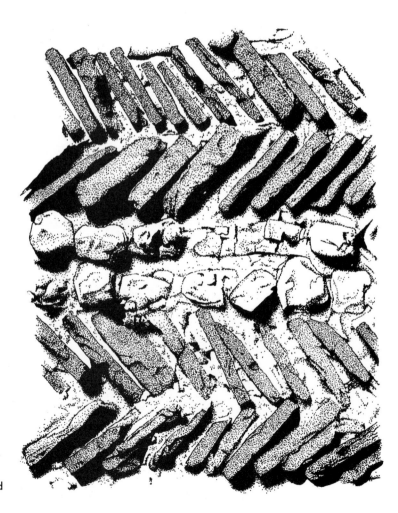

Herringbone masonry from the eleventh-century walls of Colchester Castle keep. It was built on the ruins of a Roman building and flat Roman bricks were re-used for decorative effect.

thus came into being Arundel, Lewes, Bramber, Hastings and, where it had all started, Pevensey.

French knights took possession of towns and villages all over England. They chose a manor as the 'caput', or chief place, of the honour which comprised the scattered lands they possessed; and in that caput, a castle would be erected. These castles were not sited for strategic reasons, but to control land: within the estates they defended and which supported them, a site of tactical advantage was picked, in a centre of population perhaps, or to control a road or river-crossing, or simply to make use of a strong natural feature; it was exceptional for a site to be chosen for its relation to other local castles.

Partly through William's policy of granting lands in dispersed locations, and partly through the twists created by later losses and acquisitions (through marriage, though also through forfeiture), most great lords held estates in many parts of the country. They visited the more important of them regularly, to keep a personal eye on the activities of their deputies, to dispense such justice as fell within their ambit, and simply to live off them; since food was difficult to preserve and expensive to move, the most sensible thing was to take the household to the farms, and not the other way round. Consequently, each important estate had its manor-house or castle, though the latter word was used loosely.[2] The existing duty of work on burghal (or communal) defences was transformed – and never was the Norman genius for adapting what they found useful in a conquered culture more neatly expressed – into a duty of castle-work; the digging of ditches and hewing of logs was done by the Anglo-Saxon peasantry.

No early timber castle has survived, so our understanding of them depends on archaeology and contemporary descriptions. What is certain, however, is that the use of timber should not be thought necessarily to imply a lack of sophistication. Although these castles clearly could be functional, even spartan, they could also offer accommodation which, by the standards of the day, was sumptuous. A famous description of the early twelfth-century castle of Ardres (in Picardy) mentions a great tower of several storeys linked by stairs and housing a hall, great chamber, larders, rooms for bakers and butlers, a dormitory for children and a chapel painted like the tabernacle of Solomon.[3]

The Norman earthwork castle introduced to England in 1066 is defined by historians today according to the form of the castle's strong point (although its builders may not have perceived distinctions between castle types in the same way). The more common form is the well-known motte and bailey where one or more ditched enclosures (baileys) lie beside a large earthen mound (motte) with the profile of a Christmas pudding. In the second type, the place of the motte is taken by a lower and broader ditched enclosure, known as a ringwork. It will be obvious that the boundaries between a small bailey and a large ringwork, or between a low motte and a small ringwork, are difficult to draw. Nor does there seem to have been any obvious reason, other than the choice of the builder, for using the motte-and-bailey plan rather than the ringwork or vice versa, though a recent analysis of surviving earthworks suggests that there are more than three mottes for every ringwork.[4]

The Conquest brought William de Warenne wealth and power and, shortly before his death in 1088, the earldom of Surrey as a reward for his loyalty. A great landowner, he was necessarily a great castle builder, responsible for castles at Conisbrough in Yorkshire, Castle Acre in Norfolk, Reigate in Surrey and Lewes in Sussex.[5] Of this group the first three are ringworks, though of widely different character and strength, while only Lewes follows the motte-and-bailey plan, and even then in a most unusual fashion. Castle Acre and Lewes, the two sites which preserve the earliest remains, are instructive not only in following different plans, but also in defining a range of strength from the powerful fortress which was Lewes to the country house of Castle Acre.

Lewes was already an important town at the time of the Conquest, controlling access to and from the Channel along the River Ouse. Perched on a hill where the river cuts through the South Downs, it remains, despite the insidious suburbanization of the county whose capital it is, one of England's most attractive country towns. The site chosen by de Warenne for his castle was a steep-sided chalk ridge

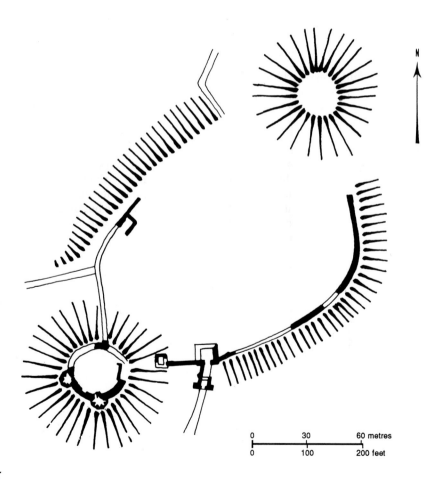

Lewes Castle, site plan. (*After W. H. Godfrey*)

which he took great trouble to improve. On either side of a large oval bailey, he built two huge mottes, a feature which, with the single exception of Lincoln, is unique in Britain and calls for some explanation.

The motte, crowned with its tower, had become more than simply a type of building: it was the very symbol of lordship, the tangible statement of the authority of its owner. It is as hard to see two places of final refuge in one castle as it is to see two lords, although France can show examples of joint-lordship and Lincoln was certainly the subject of some such complex arrangement in the 1140s.[6] Whatever the explanation, and it may have been simply a wish for maximum strength, the two mottes give the castle a unique and impressive profile. De Warenne built with care, for his mottes are not mere mounds of rammed earth, but constructed of squared blocks of chalk. They, and the flat bailey between them, must originally have been defended by strong palisades of timber. Wood, unlike stone, was cheap, readily available and both easy and quick to use: with the pressed labour of local people, a castle might be dug and palisaded in a matter of a few weeks. The palisade could itself be a complex construction: that of the important border castle of Montgomery had a wall-walk behind a crenellated parapet and interval towers.[7]

It was not long, however, before de Warenne began to replace timber defences with stone, making use of the best locally available material – flint. Very early walls, perhaps from about 1080, survive around the perimeter of the southern motte and along the southern side of the bailey, together with the remains of a small square tower in the motte ditch and part of a gatehouse not unlike that at Exeter.

The two elements of the castle served different functions. The motte, behind its palisade, enclosed a level area on which stood a tower which might be residential, but which was, in any case, watchtower and refuge; if the bailey were taken by an enemy, the height and small perimeter of the motte summit made it easily defensible by a few men. The bailey wall sheltered the principal domestic buildings of the castle – the hall, barns and stables, forge, kitchen and brewhouse, and a chapel. This simple structure of earth and wood was a strong fortress in days when men fought with axes, swords and short bows; its wide ditches kept an attacker at a distance, while the banks over which he had to clamber left him vulnerable to arrows.[8] Lewes castle, its bailey encroached upon by more recent buildings, is perhaps difficult to appreciate as an early Norman fortress of earth and timber, but there are many other sites which emphasise different aspects of these early castles.

At Pleshey, in Essex, for instance, is perhaps the most perfect example of a motte-and-bailey castle in the British Isles: a huge mound of rammed earth rises 14 metres (45 feet) from a wet moat, dominating not only a moated bailey but a semi-circular village enclosure. In the south-west, motte-and-bailey castles at Launceston and Totnes reflect the same ambiguous relationship of protector and exploiter of their towns which can be seen at Lewes. Underneath the prickly pinnacles of Arundel and Windsor lie the earthworks of equally early castles, translated into nineteenth-century medieval ideals. Brinklow, on the Fosse, has become a commuter village and its

A small window lighting the basement of Guildford Castle's Norman keep.

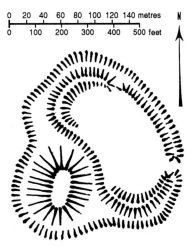

0	20	40	60	80	100	120	140 metres
0		100	200	300	400		500 feet

Pleshey Castle, site plan. (*After Derek Renn*)

earthworks a playground and a convenient place to walk the dog. At Lilbourne, on the border of Northamptonshire and visible from the wasteland of the M1, a once-powerful castle sinks year by year back into the soil, its only companion a neglected church, as time and people have moved on.

Its easily identified character perhaps allows the motte and bailey to overshadow its important relative, the ringwork castle. This was not the case in the eleventh century, for many men built castles of both sorts. De Warenne built ringwork castles at Reigate, probably at Conisbrough, and most impressively at Castle Acre in Norfolk. Today it is the immense earthworks of this castle, gouged out of gentle pastures beside the River Nar, which impress, not the scant remains of masonry. Norfolk, like Sussex, has little building stone, so flint has been widely used and often to splendid effect. Unfortunately, stripped of their dressings, flint ruins resemble nothing so much as the

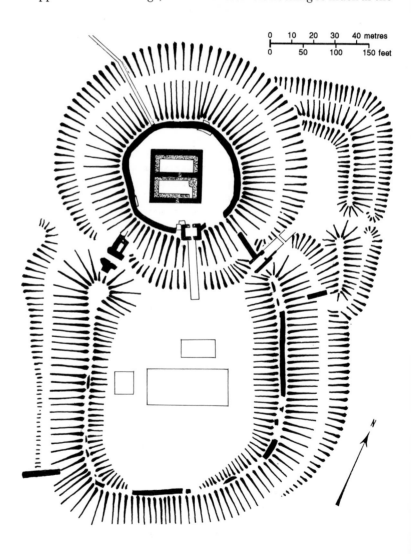

Castle Acre Castle, site plan. The shading indicates the reinforced walls of the keep. (*After English Heritage*)

amorphous piles of sugar-beet which line the county's roadsides in January.

The Norman colonization of England was not just a story of violence and bloodshed; naturally enough, the rebellions and civil strife, the displacement of established leaders (both secular and ecclesiastic), the cruelty which came to be known as the Harrying of the North, all marked the perception of the witnesses and historians of the time, as they do those of today. It is human nature to record terrible events, while a state of peace passes without comment. In many parts of the country, life must have continued much as before for small landowners, farmers and peasants, for craftsmen and merchants, for women and mothers and for children. The social changes instigated by the Normans may have happened overnight in historical terms, but to ordinary people they took effect over a lifetime.

The remains of the castle first built by William de Warenne imply that Norfolk was calm and secure in the 1080s. Acre was laid out as a new town: its grid of streets set out on the north bank of the River Nar, and the ancient path known as Peddar's Way was diverted through it; a navigable river and an important road brought prosperity and, by 1086, its annual value had nearly doubled to £9. The town was protected by a ditch and rampart on three sides; on the fourth lay the fortified home of the de Warenne family. It consisted of a ringwork defended by a low bank – some 3 metres (11 feet) high on the north side and 2 metres (6 feet) on the south – with a square bailey to the south; the ramparts had only a stout fence.[9] In the ringwork was built what has been called a Norman country house: of stone and about 24 metres (80 feet) square, it had two storeys, of two rooms each, and a gabled roof. There was a door into the basement, and an external stair leading up to the first floor where there was a hall and a chamber. The gate through the palisade was later rebuilt in stone, but with an archway whose width suggests an ostentatious rather than a military purpose. The layout of the lower bailey at this time is not known: it may have contained another hall and further domestic accommodation; no doubt it contained a chapel, barns and other such structures.

Acre was a strong house but not, even in terms of the earth and timber structures of the time, a strong castle: the de Warenne family clearly felt sufficiently safe, ten or twenty years after the Conquest, to live in a house secure only against wild animals and brigands. It was certainly a favoured home, for William's wife, Gundrada, decided to have a baby there, dying in childbirth in May 1085. Objects excavated at the castle, including ornaments, games, dice, good-quality pottery and silver coins, suggest a high standard of living. Days would be spent on the business of the estate, but there was also time for hunting and riding, or for walks by the river, or through the orchards and gardens which once lay near every castle; evenings would be a time to enjoy the fruit of the hunt, to play games, to sing and tell stories of love and heroism: perhaps the *Chanson de Roland* itself was once recited at Castle Acre.

If one such lightly defended castle existed in England twenty years after the Conquest, there were certainly others. Probably less than 200 strong castles existed in England by 1100, and many of them

A Norman huntsman with horn and dog, from the scarred twelfth-century doorway of Norwich Castle keep.

were in the hands of the king and a few great nobles; the lesser gentry must have lived in strong houses and fortified manors rather than castles with a genuine military purpose. England could be a dangerous place in the eleventh and twelfth centuries: the credit William I is given for making the roads safe implies that banditry was widespread, while wolves still took pride of place among the non-human predators, and bore a price on their heads until the thirteenth century.

A ditched – or in lowland areas, moated – enclosure, defended by a fence, would keep people, domestic animals and property secure, while posing no threat to the king. Before the civil wars of the twelfth century, most manor-houses must have taken this form. There is an example at Weeting, also in Norfolk, where the hall is stone-built, but old moated sites – some still wet – can be found all over the English landscape: there are more than 500 in Essex alone.[10] Often they were not abandoned but rebuilt in stone and their ditches subsequently filled. Castles strong enough to have a real military value were expensive, and were to become more so as time and technology advanced;

under the strong government of William I and his sons, their numbers were limited, and most men were content with defended houses.

But ringworks were by no means necessarily weaker than motte-and-bailey castles. At Conisbrough, entirely rebuilt in the late twelfth century, de Warenne built a powerful ringwork-and-bailey castle on a steeply scarped hill. A similar plan was followed at the great royal castle of Corfe, in Dorset, where a ringwork perched on a great hill formed the beginning of a castle which eventually spilled down the whole of the southern slope. Among the finest is the perfectly round ringwork castle built in the centre of the old fortified town Sarum (Salisbury). Seeing the awesome bank and ditch today, it is not difficult to appreciate how strong these places could be.

——3——
Nailing Down the Edges

The development in our own day of a sophisticated system for the classification of earthwork castles must not be allowed to obscure the fact that there are many castles which do not conform. Of particular interest, both for the status of their builders and the importance of the remains, are a number of castles built in the English borders: the fortresses which guaranteed the security of the realm and provided opportunities for expansion. In 1071 or thereabouts, Alan the Red, son of the Count of Penthièvre, and leader of the Breton troops at Hastings, founded one of these castles on a bare Yorkshire crag: it was to become known as the fine hill – Richmond.

The county had seen the most dangerous rebellion yet raised against the Norman settlement: Earls Morcar of Northumberland and Edwin of Mercia, the two principal northern landowners, had not fought at Hastings, and by 1068 were ready, with the support of the Danish fleet, to challenge William's government. This rising, like the rest, was crushed, but it was serious and drew savage reprisals from William. The *Anglo-Saxon Chronicle* contains moving evidence of violence which is statistically confirmed by *Domesday*; twenty years later, this survey relentlessly recorded manors and villages simply as 'waste'.[1]

Morcar lived to join Hereward's equally unsuccessful fenland rising of 1071, but Edwin was murdered by his own men and his Yorkshire estates, centred on Gilling West, were granted to Alan the Red. At the same time he was created earl, a title used sparingly by William and always in connection with border territories; attached specifically to duties of national defence, it held a Palatine or semi-Palatine authority.[2] Taking possession as a colonial intruder, Alan wisely sought a more secure base than Gilling. He found it in a previously unsettled outcrop overlooking the River Swale. Much of the castle built by the first Earl of Richmond has survived the passing of the centuries, strong enough from the first to avoid too much alteration by later owners, and remote enough to be neither attacked nor eventually worth dismantling for its site or materials; its tactical rather than strategic situation controlled, apart from its own estates, no route of importance. Nevertheless, in an unstable region, with the Scots not far away on the other side of the Pennines (Cumbria was Scottish until its annexation by William Rufus), Richmond castle had to be strong, and so it was stone built from the beginning.

The castle forms a great triangular enclosure 31 metres (100 feet) above the rapid, shallow River Swale; from the cliff summit, stone walls line the edges of the plateau and converge on a gatehouse (now replaced by the later keep) at the northern apex of the site. There were subsidiary enclosures, at the northern entrance and the south-eastern corner of the main court, defended, like the southern edge, only by palisades. Of the original fortress are the towered walls on the north-east and north-west, the castle hall on the south, and the gateway in the ground floor of the keep. The exceptional nature of this work is apparent from its stone construction, and the regular towers projecting from the curtain-wall at a period when their value appears to have been imperfectly understood and rarely sought.

Towers projecting beyond the outer line of a wall greatly enhanced the strength of a castle by permitting a more effective defence of the wall itself. The base of a castle wall was dead ground, difficult to observe without running the risk of being shot by besieging forces. However, it was possible to observe, from the safety of a tower, the outer face of the wall and to shoot arrows at enemies trying to scale or batter the stones. Given their advantages, it appears puzzling that most early castles were built without regular mural towers. Surviving examples – at Exeter and Lewes, in the re-used Roman walls of Portchester and Pevensey Castles, at Ludlow and, of course, Richmond – prove that towers were known, although a closer look reveals that their possibilities may not have been fully appreciated. For instance, while Exeter has strong, well-positioned towers, neither the small mural tower nor the gate at Lewes projects beyond the castle walls. At Saltwood Castle, in Kent, five towers were added, probably in the twelfth century, to a plain curtain-wall, but the three largest all stand inside the castle *enceinte*. At Launceston, traces of at least two small stone-based towers have been found set not on the rampart but just behind the original timber palisade; similarly placed towers seem also to have existed at the nearby ringwork castle of Restormel. The square towers of Richmond Castle – the best of the period – are equally ambiguous: concentrated on the side of the castle which also had the domestic accommodation, their small windows are not designed for bowmen, while the ground floor of one was occupied by a chapel.

The truth may be, as has been convincingly proposed, that the short bow of the eleventh century, generally unable to pierce chain-mail, was little used in siege warfare.[3] The point at which bows – particularly the crossbows whose iron bolts could pierce armour – came into widespread use is unclear. Although the twelfth and, particularly, the thirteenth centuries saw the development of castle defence largely in relation to the cross- and longbow, eleventh-

Richmond Castle from across the Swale, with the town invisible behind it. The tower keep which dominates the site today was raised about a century after the Conquest.

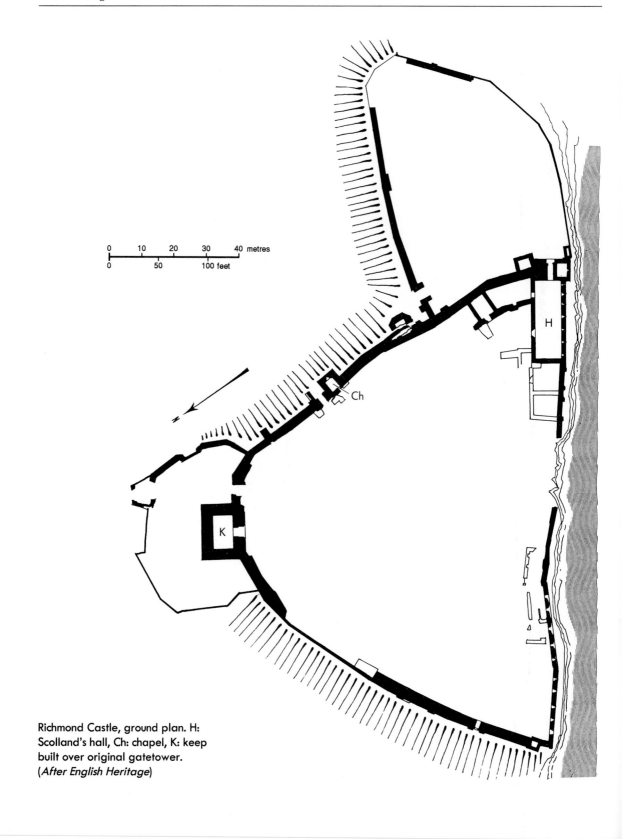

Richmond Castle, ground plan. H:
Scolland's hall, Ch: chapel, K: keep
built over original gatetower.
(*After English Heritage*)

century builders, when they used them at all, seem to have designed mural towers as much for domestic as for military purposes, and then probably not for the use of archers. If a castle was to be defended with sword and axe, with rocks which were cheap and easy to use, and with spears, then wall-towers offered little further advantage to the besieged.

Of the buildings put up by Alan behind his towered walls, only the castle hall has survived; this, with that at Chepstow on the Anglo-Welsh border, is the earliest one to have survived. Like its French precursors, Scolland's Hall was built over a basement and entered through a door at one end of its longer side; there was a chamber at the other end, with its own fireplace, and latrines were provided in the Gold Hole Tower. It was the hall of a great lord: well proportioned and with large windows overlooking the castle court on one side and the valley of the Swale on the other, it was very different to the smoky timber halls to be found in the castles of lesser men. Scolland was the name of Alan's steward and lord of the castle at Killerby. In return for the lands given him by Alan, Scolland would help defend the earl's castle for a certain number of days each year, his defence position, and that of his descendants being the roof of the hall.

The gate from the castle to the outer enclosure, known as the Cockpit, overlooked by one of Richmond's eleventh-century wall towers.

Richmond Castle is unusual in many ways: its early stone construction, its plan and use of mural towers and, not least, its size. Enclosing 1 hectare (2½ acres), its 610-metre (2,000-foot) perimeter had no fewer than four gates and posterns, but neither motte nor keep. The castle had to be held entire or not at all, and to do so would require many men. It must have sheltered a considerable number of Alan's fellow-Bretons in its early years; gradually the knights, like Scolland, established satellite castles on lands nearby, and the ordinary people – craftsmen and farmers – built houses outside the walls, founding the town which has outlived the Norman fortress. In time, the whole area came to be known as Richmondshire, and it, like other border lands, became integrated into the centralized Norman kingdom of England. Between them, lord and tenant, castle and farm, brought about the gradual economic recovery of the area. War, which had spawned the castle, was, after all, only the principal of the scourges it was meant to prevent: famine, its pallbearer, had also to be overcome.

Some of the elements of Richmond can be found in other important

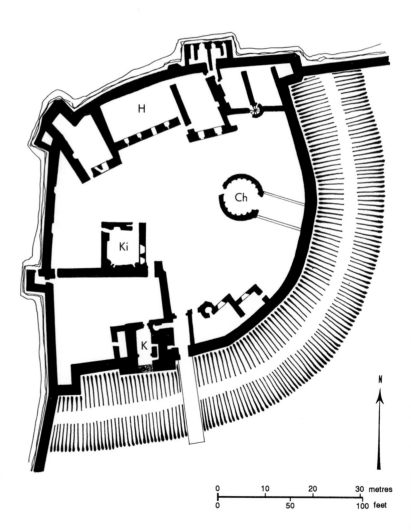

Ludlow Castle, ground plan of the inner ward. The shading indicates the blocking of the original entrance, when the tower was heightened to become a keep. H: hall, Ch: chapel, K: keep built over original gatetower, Ki: Kitchen. (*After Historic Tours*)

border castles, though many, like Hereford, have perished or have been obliterated, like Bamburgh, by the encrustations of time. Ludlow Castle, the finest survivor in the once heavily castled county of Shropshire, has in its early history a number of points in common with Richmond, and probably dates from only twenty years after its northern cousin. Again, a river cliff was chosen for the castle and the town laid out on the sloping ground below. The sandstone from the great ditch which isolates the inner ward was used to build the inner curtain, its four towers and gatehouse.

The quality of this early work, generally inferior to that at Richmond, is obscured by the extensive later buildings. It is clear, however, that only the smallest of the towers had four stone walls, the others being open or timber-framed on their inner faces. More surprising is their positioning, for they all overlook the precipitous fall to the River Teme, the least likely direction of attack, and leave the sweep of the curtain overlooking the flat outer bailey entirely unflanked. And here the two-storey gatehouse (subsequently heightened and blocked to make it a keep) projects inwards from the curtain, like that at Lewes. It is not easy to explain such planning if the purpose of the towers was to enable archers better to defend the walls. If, however, towers were principally residential in purpose, it would be sensible to place them on the more inaccessible side of the castle.

By 1086, when the Conqueror ordered the survey of Britain which has come to be known as *Domesday*, the castle was spread throughout the kingdom. There were probably not more than a couple of hundred strong fortresses at the time, but well dispersed and held by men whose common interest in conquest made them wary of disloyalty. Varied in strength, in plan, in building materials, between them they enabled the mounted Norman knights to create a new order in Britain. A comparative peace had been created and it was possible to travel the highway – even, as the *Anglo-Saxon Chronicle* puts it, with a bosom full of gold – in safety.[4] A new, vigorous Church had been established; great cathedrals, abbeys and parish churches were being built in the spiritual image of the military world; William himself had founded a monastery on the very site where God had permitted him to defeat Harold. Then, abruptly in September 1087, William died from wounds sustained during an insignificant siege on the borders of Normandy.

—4—
Learning the Hard Way

At William's death, the victors of Hastings fell out over the division of the spoils. The old king allowed preference for his second son to get the better of his judgement and he determined that the crown of England should go to William Rufus. Robert, the eldest, became Duke of Normandy, while Henry, the youngest son, had to make do with 5,000 pounds of silver. The separation of England from Normandy was a grave mistake, for most important barons held land on both sides of the Channel; now they owed feudal service to Rufus for lands in England and to Robert for those in Normandy. Divided loyalties were ever a fruitful source of trouble during the Middle Ages; war was inevitable, and it came.

The dying William, making his peace with God, had ordered the release from prison of a number of his political opponents, including his half-brother Odo, held since 1082 for conspiracy. Odo, Bishop of Bayeux in Normandy, was also Earl of Kent, and lord of the strategic castle of Rochester. A dangerous man, he quickly became central to a revolt of the Anglo-Norman barons against William II, the aim of which was the installation of Robert on the English throne. Fighting occurred in several parts of England during 1088, but the real threat was in Kent and Sussex where Odo and other rebels held lands. Rufus besieged and took the great motte-and-bailey castle at Tonbridge, and followed his success with the capture, after six gruelling weeks, of the castle of Pevensey, and Bishop Odo with it.[1] By then the only important rebel stronghold was Rochester, held by Robert de Bellême with troops sent from Normandy. Odo was brought there so that he might persuade his allies to surrender, but in the event he was freed by them and brought within the walls.

The castle at Rochester, whose value lay in its control of the Medway bridge used by the road from Dover and Canterbury to London, was one of those established soon after the Conquest. The castle overlooked the river, the road from the coast and the bridge itself. As at London or Lincoln, the existing Roman wall formed two sides of an enclosure completed with ditches and timber palisades. Before 1089, and probably to repair damage caused during the fighting, Gundulf, Bishop of Rochester and designer of the White Tower of London, built a new stone wall for William Rufus. Stretches of Gundulf's curtain can be seen at Rochester today, together with the twelfth-century keep, but little remains of the castle besieged in May 1088. The royal forces invested both castle and town but did not immediately attempt to take them.

Rufus's options at this stage were neither extensive nor particularly sophisticated. His soldiers could attempt to climb the castle walls with ladders, an operation which was certain only to be bloody. More time-consuming, but perhaps more effective, would be attacks on the fabric of the castle itself: ditches could be filled with earth and other available rubbish so that men could approach the walls with battering rams and axes. They could get some protection from the hail of missiles flung at them by using *pentises* (timber shields on stands), but the attack would still be perilous. Those stalwarts of later medieval sieges, the mangonel and *petraria*, do not seem to have been widely used in the eleventh century, while the trebuchet, the best catapult of all, was not developed until the beginning of the twelfth.

Only where the walls, or better still the gate, was made of wood did the besieging forces have any real advantage, for then they could use fire. Straw and brushwood would be piled against the gate and set alight, while the defenders attempted to drop stones on their enemies and water on to the fire. The Bayeux Tapestry shows two dismounted knights setting fire to the castle of Dinan with torches and the consequent surrender of its garrison. The only defence against fire was to try to cover wood with wet hides, and this technique was used by both sides, for the men under the *pentise* were themselves in danger from fire. In the final analysis, the human cost of any such assault could be great and so, where speed was not critical, a blockade would often be imposed in an attempt to starve the castle into surrender. In such an event, to protect themselves from an unexpected mounted sortie by those within the castle, the besiegers often raised a simple earthwork castle for themselves. In 1088, Rufus, unable to take Rochester by force, ordered the construction of two such siege-castles and waited until heat, flies and disease forced the rebels to surrender.

Following the capitulation of the castle and the city, Rufus was obliged – as was usually the case during the early Middle Ages – to deal leniently with the rebels, for the relationship between king and barons was delicate. Castles were confiscated and fines imposed, but only Odo was banished from England. He returned to Normandy and eventually died on the journey out with the first crusaders. The fate of the rebellion had been decided through siege warfare, through the possession and loss of castles, not through pitched battles like Hastings. Already the country was like a chess-board, where the castles were squares which opponents sought to occupy; since horsemen controlled the land some 16 kilometres (10 miles) around, holding a castle meant holding territory. Each was simultaneously an aggressive base from which raids could be launched, and a defensive stronghold capable of containing an attack. To take Kent from rebel control, the king had had to take the rebel castles. The ultimate danger in this castle warfare, of being trapped in a castle without allies outside to help, was what had happened to Odo and his friends.

The fall of Rochester ended opposition to William Rufus by those who would have preferred to see Robert King of England, but the struggle between the brothers continued in Normandy. Then, in 1100, Rufus was killed, perhaps murdered, in a hunting incident in the New Forest. His brother Henry, who was present, rode to Winchester to secure the treasury (and the crown), leaving some peasants to return the body for burial in the cathedral. A man of few attractive qualities, Rufus's only lasting contribution to English history was the successful annexation of Cumbria from the Scots in 1092, and the construction of a castle in Carlisle to prevent its reversal.

His death made way for a new player in the power struggle for the Conqueror's inheritance, but it did not immediately affect the outcome. A lasting peace was not found until – such are the ironies of history – the fortieth anniversary of William's landing in England: on 28 September 1106, Normandy fell to the English forces of Henry I at the Battle of Tinchebrai. Henry made himself Duke of Normandy as well as King of England, and so brought peace to both sides of the sea. Thereafter, his reign was militarily uneventful, if not actually peaceful, for though there were always enemies on the Continent, he was largely successful in discomfiting them by diplomacy rather than force of arms. In England, things were quieter, and Henry's efforts were directed at consolidating royal control over Cumbria and keeping Welsh raiders and his own barons in order.

The development of the castle in England at this time is obscure for several reasons. There appear to have been relatively few new castles begun under Henry I, except in the unsettled borders of England and in Normandy, which occupied much of his attention.[2] Since contemporary witnesses tend to record new castles rather than improvements to existing ones, and in the absence of records of royal expenditure (which do not begin in earnest until 1155), documentary evidence is often unhelpful. Furthermore, much of the work undertaken in the early twelfth century has been swept away, either in later reconstruction or during the demolition of castles like Cambridge, Gloucester and Bristol in the seventeenth century. Thus, in those cases where masonry appearing to belong to Henry's reign does

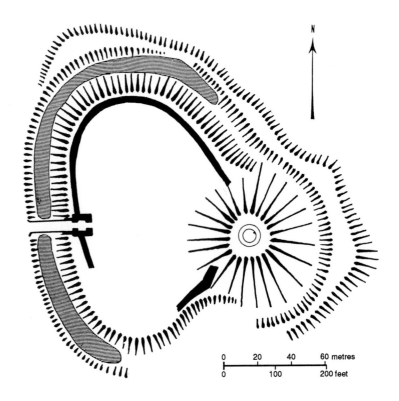

Tickhill Castle, ground plan. (*After Ella Armitage*)

0 20 40 60 metres
0   100   200 feet

Part of the decoration applied to the outer face of Tickhill Castle's early Norman gatehouse.

survive, as at Corfe, it is rarely possible to date it confidently.

That said, it can be inferred from the evidence that there was a constant programme of rebuilding and improvement in both royal and baronial castles. The opportunity afforded by peace was taken by many to replace wooden defences with stone, for the hard lessons learned in England and Normandy can have left no one unconvinced of the value of fireproof castles. There were stone walls at Lincoln by 1115, built on a timber framework to help spread the weight, as well as to tie the masonry together during the slow setting-time of Norman lime mortar. Henry I was probably responsible for the massive keeps at Corfe, Norwich and Canterbury. The first, jutting out of its hill like a great broken tooth, transformed both the appearance and the strength of the ringwork castle to which it was added; something of its original beauty can still be discerned in the gleam of its white limestone walls. It was in this castle that Henry kept his brother Robert prisoner after his defeat in 1106.[3] Corfe originally had three storeys with battlemented walls carried above the line of the pitched roof. Norwich and Canterbury were also very large towers, though the former, of only two storeys, appears prosaically squat next to the tall elegance of Corfe. Though of considerable interest, neither keep has survived in good condition: Norwich, refaced without and gutted within, now serves as part of the county museum; while Canterbury, having declined from prison to coke store, is now a roofless shell. To this list of Henry's keeps must be added that of Gloucester Castle, surviving as no more than a crude fourteenth-century drawing, and perhaps others which have vanished without trace.

But more widespread than these master-works must have been the replacement in stone of the timber defences of castles like Tickhill, on the very southern edge of Yorkshire. The castle's ramparts are so huge as to completely obscure the bailey, while a motte like a slag-heap was made by raising a natural hillock to a height of 23 metres (75 feet). Beside it, and easily controlled from the motte, lies a kidney-shaped bailey of about 1 hectare (2 acres). The whole castle

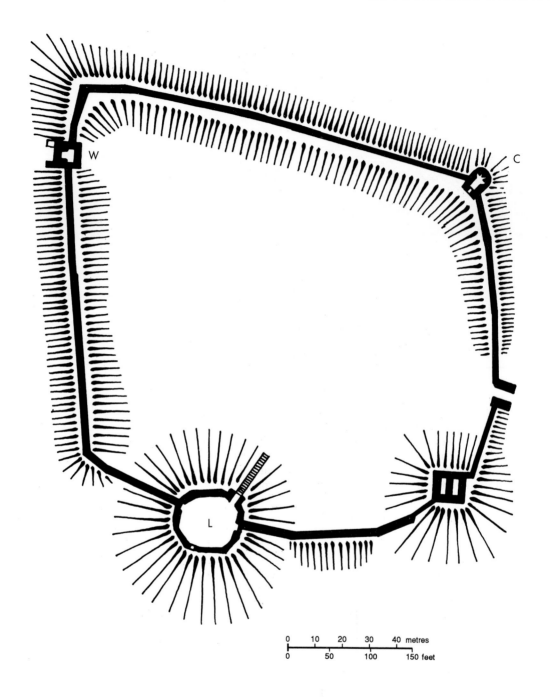

Lincoln Castle, ground plan. W:
West Gate, L: Lucy Tower, C: Cobb
Hall. (*After FLARE*)

Lincoln Castle's west gate, now walled up, but with the remains of the original barbican still visible, as well as the blocked doorway which once gave access to it.

was surrounded by a wet moat – in poor shape, but still holding water – some 9 metres (30 feet) wide, but if there was once a ditch isolating the motte from the bailey, it has been filled in. Though the summit of the motte has lost its keep, there remains much of the bailey wall and a stone gatehouse of the early twelfth century. The gate was, for obvious reasons, the most vulnerable part of any castle and likely to face the brunt of any attack. The potential use of fire made timber gates particularly insecure and so the entry to the castle was often the first part to be built or rebuilt in stone.[4] The gate at Tickhill is probably the work of Henry I who, in 1100, confiscated the castle from the same Robert de Bellême besieged by Rufus in Rochester.

The curtain is built in the usual Norman fashion, with ashlar enclosing a rubble core, its outer face strengthened (and embellished) with shallow buttresses and a stepped batter. The gate itself is entire to the level of its missing battlements, though without floors or roof, and consists of a rectangular tower with a room above the gate-passage closed at either end by doors. The room above has been altered and now has a fifteenth-century fireplace and a Tudor window; access to it was gained from buildings abutting it within the castle, not from the gate-passage itself. This strong tower, protected by a removable bridge over the moat, not only made the castle entrance difficult to force, but stood as a strong point within the bailey. Its military purpose did not, however, prevent its builder from considering its visual impact, for above the outer arch there survives some naïve decoration in the form of stone lozenges and figures. These have no purpose but to impress: one of the most important elements of castle design is the architectural symbolism of grandeur, since to build lavishly, and apparently strongly, was to demonstrate wealth, authority and power.

Tickhill Castle has one of a number of contemporary gate towers; less well-preserved examples can be seen at Castle Rising and Castle Acre in Norfolk, Egremont in Cumberland and Thurnham (Godard's Castle) in Kent. The northern entrance at Richmond was defended by the same type of gatehouse, and its internal archway still forms the ground-floor entrance of the later keep. Subsequent building, however, often meant the destruction of these early towers, which is what happened at Lincoln, where the east gate of the castle was rebuilt in the thirteenth century; the west gate, fortunately, was not.

The stone wall of Lincoln Castle, which survives entire if renovated, was probably built following a fire in 1113, but stone had been used in the construction of the west gate from the beginning.[5] This entrance to the castle from beyond the city walls gradually declined in importance as the castle's role changed, until it was finally sealed in the early fifteenth century. Its decline preserved it both from the improvements made to its partner on the east side, and from Victorian restoration, and it is today one of the finest examples of an early castle gate in Britain. It has been the subject of excavations in recent years which have shown that it had a predecessor of wood and stone, built at the time of the foundation of the castle itself. That was replaced around 1100 by the present two-storied tower, with a vaulted passage and a room on the first floor; the chamber had small round-headed windows, and a doorway giving access to a wooden gallery above the doors, from which they might be better protected.

There was also a small barbican in the form of two walls jutting forward into the ditch and joined at the end by an arch enclosing an outer gate. The wall-walk of this extension was reached from the main gate through the timber hoarding. The barbican helped prevent a surprise seizure of the inner gate, but a more important function was to channel an attacking force between high walls where it would be unable either to manoeuvre or to protect itself from missiles flung from above. Although gatehouses subsequently grew in the sophistication of their defences, the west gate at Lincoln is perhaps the earliest example of a barbican: the great gate at Warwick, built in the 1380s, was conceptually no advance on this. The Norman abhorrence of flat wall-surfaces did not extend to this gatetower. The plain walls would have satisfied even the most rigorous modern champion of the unity of structure and form: no embellishment is offered, only mass. Perhaps the unnamed builder believed its severe austerity said everything he wished to say about himself.

—5—
The Church Militant

In 1127 Rochester Castle was granted by Henry I to William de Corbeil, Archbishop of Canterbury, and the knights of the castle guard now found themselves under the command of the country's premier churchman. The lords of the Church played a very real military role in the difficult century which followed the Conquest. They held huge swathes of land, and gained more as questionably penitent donors sought to ease their way into heaven with gifts. Irrespective of whether their lord was a secular baron or a prince of the Church, these lands had to supply knights: this was, after all, the age of the crusade. In any case, a number of bishops, martially trained younger sons of the nobility, were more used to the weight of a sword than a crosier. To fulfill their military duties, a number of bishops made castles of their palaces and fortresses of their manors, although there was controversy within the Church as to the theological justification for doing so. Experienced in the planning and design of stone churches and well-resourced by their flocks, they were able to build to an altogether higher standard than most barons. So when King Henry, on giving Rochester to the archbishop, added his permission to strengthen it with an *'egregiam turrim'*, he was taken at his word.

The great tower erected by the archbishop represents perhaps the most enduring symbol of the medieval castle. Today, glimpsed from a car on the Medway Bridge, Rochester's keep still stands aloof from the cluttered maritime landscape; even the cathedral seems huddled in its shadow. To say that it dominates the city is right, for donjon, the common medieval word for keep, has its root in *dominium*, the Latin for lordship. The stone keep, a permanent translation of the motte and its tower, was the physical expression of feudal lordship, the symbol of the authority king and Church vested in its owner; it crowned the landscape like gold crowned the king's head.

The intangible language of symbolism was applied to a structure which already sought to meet two conflicting material purposes: the military dictated compression, tiny openings and many barriers; while the domestic sought space, light and ease of access. The varying emphasis between these contradictory impulses contribute to the medieval castle's lasting interest, for at its best, the castle flowers in the dynamic tension of opposing forces. It does not draw upon intellectual and emotional responses to offer the pure architectural experience of a great Gothic church, but unites fallible human desires for security, comfort and symbolism in the context of a religious system which accepts, if not that might is right, then at least that authority is God-given and its holder the chosen agent of God on earth.

William de Corbeil, God's chosen agent in Canterbury, built at Rochester a tower which balances perfectly the opposing forces of

Windows from Hedingham Castle keep.

security, comfort and symbolism, and built it so well that it has outlived its creator by 700 years. The keep stands four-square in its bailey, its white rubble walls climbing 35 metres (113 feet) sheer to the corner turrets, pierced lower down only by slits, and higher up by gaping dark holes which once were elegant windows. On the north face is a rectangular projection, a forebuilding which protects the entrance, with the remains of the stairs ascending to it still visible. Within the 21-metre (70-foot) square tower were three floors and a basement, each containing two main rooms and a number of alcoves serving variously as sleeping rooms or latrines. The two rooms were created by a cross-wall which rose the entire height of the keep, adding to its strength and enabling the floors to be spanned by timber

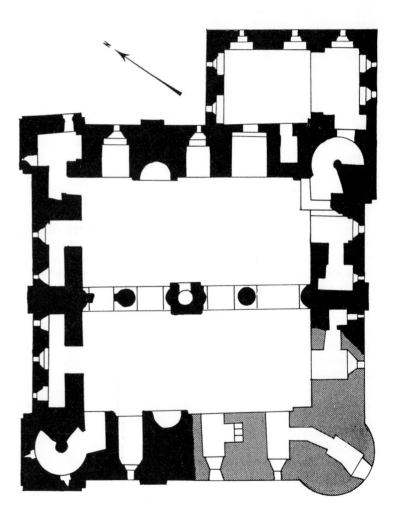

Rochester Castle keep, plan of the hall. The corner rebuilt after the siege of 1215 is shaded. (*After English Heritage*)

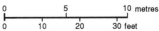

joists. All the floors and roofs have gone, but there is still access to most parts of the building.

The entrance floor, over the basement, probably served as a guard-room and servants' hall, for it is lit only by tiny loops.[1] From here spiral stairs, in opposite corners of the keep, ascend to the second floor. This was the hall and rose, like the equivalent level in the White Tower, through two storeys, with a gallery running where the next floor would be. The purpose of such a gallery was partly to admit more light (it is only in the gallery that large windows appear) and partly to allow onlookers to watch great feasts, or the settlement of judicial questions and petitions; it also maintained the proportions of the space. Here the cross-wall opens into an arcade of narrow bays whose arches are lavishly decorated with roll-mouldings and zigzag motifs.

A fireplace in the hall of Rochester keep.

The third and top floor – one more than the White Tower – is, like the ones below, provided with fireplaces and latrines, and the surviv-ing decoration is as fine as that of the hall beneath. It probably served in its northern half as a private chamber, while a part-destroyed arch in the east wall of the southern chamber suggests the existence of a chapel there. Since one existed in the top room of the forebuilding, at the level of the hall, this was probably the archbishop's private chapel. Battlements and turrets rise undamaged above the lost double-pitched roof, protecting it from missiles. Holes for timber hoarding can still be seen: these temporary walkways, projecting beyond the wall, were erected in time of war to enable the defenders to cover the dead ground at its foot without having to lean over the battlements.[2]

The Archbishop of Canterbury was by no means the only ecclesias-tic to be building castles during the twelfth century. In the north, Rannulf, Bishop of Durham, not only rebuilt in stone the castle in that city, but undertook the construction of an imposing castle on the southern bank of the Tweed at Norham; its much-disputed ruins stand today, shrouded in trees, sadly peaceful. The jurisdiction of Alexander, Bishop of Lincoln, extended over a diocese which ran from the Humber to the Thames, and which he intended both to control and develop. His three principal foundations, at Newark-on-Trent, Sleaford and Banbury, were all associated with the establish-ment of successful market towns. Banbury Castle, in Oxfordshire, has disappeared almost without trace beneath the brittle devices of the Castle Shopping Centre; while Sleaford, in Lincolnshire, is little more than humps in a field. But at Newark, much of the castle survives, including the splendid three-storey gatehouse, a less intimidating cousin of the gates at Tickhill and Lincoln. The quality of the masonry is excellent throughout and reveals the touch of a man who had cathedral masons at his command.

Another such man was Henry of Blois, Bishop of Winchester and nephew of Henry I, who undertook in the years after 1138 the con-struction of no less than six castles and palaces: Wolvesey (Winchester), Bishop's Waltham and Merdon, all in Hampshire, Farnham in Surrey, Downton in Wiltshire, and Taunton in Somerset. More of this sequence survives for, though Downton has gone and Merdon nearly so, there are the foundations of large square keeps to

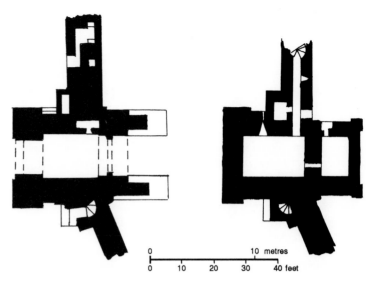

Newark-on-Trent; the ground (right) and first floors (far right) of the Norman gatehouse. (*After Derek Renn*)

be discerned through later work at Taunton and Farnham, and complex ruins, perhaps influenced by monastic planning, at the castle-palaces of Wolvesey and Waltham. The inspiration of these last two may owe something to the great building works of Henry's neighbour, Roger, Bishop of Salisbury.

Roger of Salisbury began life in France as a nobody and finished it one of the most powerful, and richest, men in England. He achieved this by his quick mind, administrative abilities and loyalty to Henry I who, apparently impressed by the speed at which Roger said mass, recognized a kindred spirit and took him into royal service. He made him chancellor, then justiciar and Bishop of Salisbury, an elevation which the king had no reason ever to regret. Roger, who lived openly with his mistress Matilda, founded an ecclesiastical dynasty (Alexander of Lincoln was a nephew, as was Nigel, Bishop of Ely), prospered and built castles.[3] From Devizes and Malmesbury, next to nothing has reached us; but at Old Sarum itself, the derelict site of the original Salisbury, there are substantial ruins.

Best of all is the castle Roger built at Sherborne in Dorset, where he was, in addition to his other offices, abbot of the monastery. The plan is uniquely regular and suggests a very different cast of mind to that of most barons; it may be in Roger's obscure background, as well as his Church experience, that his underivative approach should be sought. His castle has two principle elements: an octagonal curtain-wall (of four long and four short sides) armed with at least five towers, and a compact courtyard house in the centre. Though much ruined during the Civil War, enough survives to show what once was there and to inspire regret at its passing. The bailey wall enclosed an area about 137 by 100 metres (450 by 330 feet) and had towers at four corners, two of which contained gateways. The south-west gatehouse stands almost complete, a tall tower faced in ashlar, slightly altered by Sir Walter Raleigh during his later tenure. A spiral staircase gave access to the upper floors, from which doorways led on to the wall-walk. The rubble curtain-wall is perfectly straight, a rare thing at the

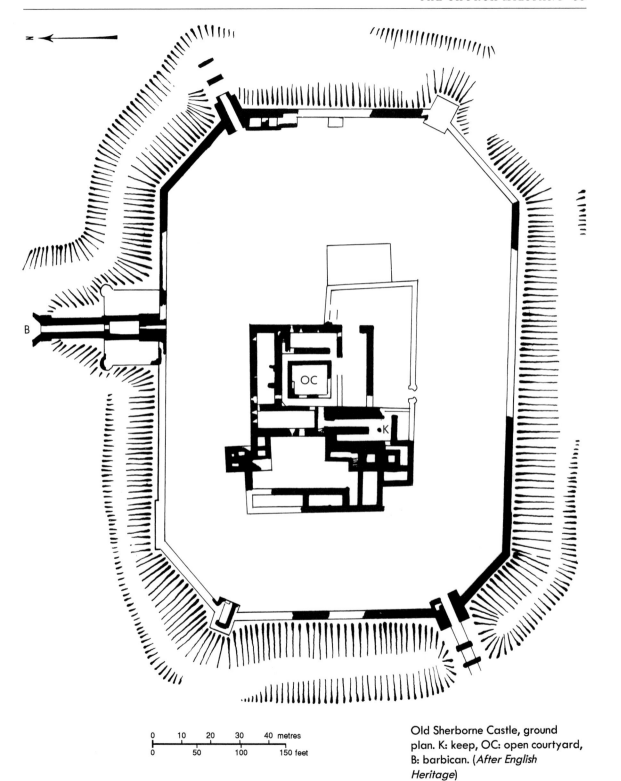

Old Sherborne Castle, ground plan. K: keep, OC: open courtyard, B: barbican. (*After English Heritage*)

Sherborne Old Castle, seen
through the surviving gate.

time, allowing full view of the outer face from the towers. A fifth tower (subsequently enlarged to the scale, if not the function of a keep, and now much ruined) stood in the middle of the long north curtain and protected a postern gate.

The main building within the walls had four ranges round a small court, and would be square, were it not for the large keep which protrudes at the south-west corner. The principal apartments were all on the first floor, above vaulted basements used for domestic functions. On the south was the hall and on the north a chapel whose early-Norman windows can still be seen; of the east range nothing is known, but it is suggested that the west formed a gallery between the chapel and the solar which was probably in the keep.[4] The central court was much like a cloister, with four paved and covered walks round an open space. This building was enlarged long after Bishop Roger's death, but the castle remained substantially unchanged until the sixteenth century, when Leland, the great antiquary, was able to observe that

there be few pieces of work in England of the antiquitie of this that standeth so whole and well couched. One Bishop Langeton made of late tyme a new piece of work and lodgings of stone at the west end of the haul: other memorable work was none set up since the first building.[5]

A corner of the hall gallery at Hedingham Castle keep, in Essex.

A castle must have been extraordinarily well designed and built to have continued in use for 400 years without being substantially improved.

The courtyard plan of Sherborne was used by Roger at Old Sarum and may have influenced the work at Wolvesey and Bishop's Waltham. Unfortunately, these castle-palaces, both individually and as a group, have until recently been too little studied and they certainly have much more to reveal about the lives and ideas of their builders. And yet those men had the resources, the education and the ambition to produce work which could rival the king's. William de Corbeil's keep at Rochester, Alexander's gatehouse at Newark, the work of Ranulph at Durham, Henry's at Wolvesey and Farnham, and Roger's at Sherborne and Old Sarum: these were among the finest castle-works in twelfth-century England, and represent the apogee of the military power of the Church. The collapse of political order on the death of Henry I had many consequences, not least of which was the loss of most of these castles by their builders.

——6——
A Sword into the Kingdom

England in 1120 must have seemed as stable as any part of Europe. Late that autumn the court was returning from Normandy; the king's 17-year-old son and heir, William, embarked with many other nobles in a ship that was among the finest of its time: but like the *Mary Rose*, the *White Ship* was to be remembered only with sadness. The passengers were drunk, and pressed the equally sodden crew to overtake the rest of the fleet; in the attempt the craft struck rocks and sank, taking with it the equilibrium which Henry had been building for twenty years. The king's only other legitimate child was his daughter, Matilda. Rightly fearing baronial unwillingness to recognize a female sovereign, Henry married again, but no son was born. An oath of allegiance to Matilda was extracted from the English barons, but it was conditional on their right to be consulted about any foreign marriage the young woman might contract. When she secretly married Geoffrey of Anjou, many seized the excuse to release themselves from that oath.

Henry I died, anxious for the future, on 1 December 1135, and was buried in his abbey at Reading. Almost instantly Stephen of Blois, Henry's nephew, raised at the late king's court and knighted by his own hand, crossed the Channel and seized the throne. He was welcomed by Londoners as king, and with the help of his brother, Henry, Bishop of Winchester, he seized the city's castle and the royal treasury within it. He was crowned before Christmas, and early in 1136 his position gained papal legitimacy. But Matilda's followers, too strong to accept the situation, would have none of it and took to arms; England was subjected to nineteen years of civil war.

The period is known as Anarchy because, although neither Stephen nor Matilda had enough support to govern, each had enough to prevent the other from doing so. As the rivals and their adherents struggled, lords great and small exploited the vacuum to increase their power and wealth at the expense of their neighbours and their neighbours' tenants. They slipped on the cloak of allegiance to one side or the other to mask actions which were wholly self-interested. In such times it was the poor, the defenceless and the innocent who suffered. Henry, Abbot of Waverley, had in his youth taken an active part in these wars, and recalled their savagery in his later, better years:

In the time of King Stephen, men took advantage of a providential period of peace, affronting God who had given it with their growing lawlessness, whereupon there was sent, as you know, a sword into the kingdom of England, which banished peace from the land, severed alliances, created conspiracies, and eventually wreaked general havoc. Like beasts of the forest leaving their lairs at nightfall, the men of war sallied out of their hiding holes, and dispersed to rob and pillage throughout the land, and the thoughts of many hearts were revealed. The enemies of peace prospered in their ways and wickedness believed it had seized the opportune moment, and was active all night long in works of darkness.[1]

When men of war roamed the country unchecked, seizing land and castles where they could, pillaging where they could not, the stout fence around the house at Castle Acre was no longer secure. The second Earl of Surrey died in 1138, to be succeeded by his son; under one, or perhaps both, of these men improvements were made to the fortifications of Acre.[2] It was decided to turn the house into a keep and in order to do this, its thin walls were strengthened internally with new masonry. At the same time, the ringwork in which it stood was heightened until it became like a vast motte, and the lower part of the building buried in it; the new rampart was capped with a wall of chalk rubble faced with flint. Had this been completed, a strong castle would have been created, but the plan was abandoned and the north side of the mound was again raised, and a new wall, reinforced with shallow buttresses, was built on top of the first. The unfinished keep was half-demolished, and what had been its cross-wall was strengthened to serve as the outer wall of a smaller structure. The intention must have been to raise the new keep to something like 18 or 20 metres (60 or 70 feet) high, if it were overtop the new higher curtain-wall. Whether the new keep was ever completed is not known.

Explanation of these alterations and changes of plan must be sought in the ebb and flow of local campaigns whose story is now lost, but the basic need for the fortification lay in the sudden violence into which the kingdom was plunged by the disputed succession. With no central hand keeping a check on the construction of castles, men found themselves with both the motive and the opportunity to fortify their homes.

It may be that the majority of earthwork sites to be seen today were established during these years when people needed protection

Castle Acre, the upper ward seen from the bailey.

and there was no one to prevent them resorting to castle building to get it. Most are unexcavated and find no mention in contemporary chronicles; they were occupied only briefly or, like Stephen's own castle at Burwell in Cambridgeshire, were destroyed before their completion. Many will have been rudimentary earth-and-timber forts, but there is no doubt that considerable stone building, like the work at Castle Acre, was also going on; it was slower, but since no one knew how long the fighting might go on, the greater strength of a masonry castle was worth working towards.[3]

These illegal castles gave their owners a new power which many found tempting, and there was a dreadful rise in brigandry and petty feuding. In a famous passage, the *Anglo-Saxon Chronicle* laments the building of castles throughout the land, and their occupation by 'devils and wicked men' who tortured those whom they believed to be wealthy, and extorted protection money from villagers.

From the moment of his accession, Stephen sought to establish his royal authority in England and Normandy, with some initial success. However, his brutal treatment of the elderly Roger of Salisbury and his family, accused by envious barons of being on the point of changing sides, marked a turning-point in his fortunes and, indeed, in those of the powerful bishops. At Oxford, in the summer of 1139, Stephen seized Roger, his son the chancellor and his nephew the Bishop of Lincoln, and demanded the surrender of all their castles.[4] Nigel of Ely escaped the trap and fled to the castle of Devizes in Wiltshire, then in the custody of Roger's mistress Matilda, and fortified it against Stephen. This act of open defiance convinced the king that the rumours against the bishops' loyalty were well founded and he marched on Devizes.

According to a contemporary, the bishop's castle was built with such wonderful skill as to be impregnable, and perhaps this forced Stephen to use ruthless means to secure its surrender. Having lodged Bishop Roger in a cowshed, he announced to Matilda that he proposed not only to starve her partner, but to hang their son before the castle gate if she did not open it forthwith; not surprisingly she submitted. The bishops, stripped of their castles, were suffered to return to their sees as purely spiritual princes and, although the see of Lincoln eventually regained its castles, the bishops were never again to be the military force they were in the early twelfth century. Stephen acquired a chain of important castles in the south-west and the Midlands, but his support in the Church was weakened by this episode, which many, including his brother the Bishop of Winchester, saw as an attack on the privileges of the clergy. At the height of the controversy, towards the end of September, the Empress Matilda, rival claimant to the throne of England, landed at the castle of Arundel in Sussex.

Arundel was one of the castles established shortly after the Conquest to guard the south coast. Perched on a hill above the Arun and commanding a distant view of the sea, it has a large rectangular bailey on either side of the central motte. It had been given by Henry I to Alice de Louvain, his second wife, who held it still. Three years after his death, Alice married a minor East Anglian nobleman, William de Albini, an alliance which was to trigger a castle-building

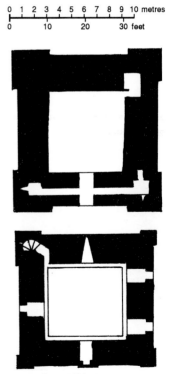

Two simple twelfth-century tower keeps: Sutton Valence and West Malling, both in Kent. (*After Derek Renn*)

programme of exceptional splendour. His marriage transformed de Albini's social standing for, as husband to the late king's widow, he found himself uncle to King Stephen, and stepfather to Matilda, as well as Earl of Sussex. Small wonder that this meteoric rise should be seen with a jaundiced eye by some of his contemporaries, who thought him 'intolerably puffed up' and complained that he held no man but the king himself to be his equal.[5]

As the principal home and power-base of the new couple, Arundel Castle was probably the object of de Albini's first attentions. Today it is the late-nineteenth century which Arundel evokes, for most of the castle was rebuilt in a display of self-importance by the fifteenth Duke of Norfolk. At its heart, however, and almost untouched by friend or enemy since it was put up by Wiliam de Albini, stands one of the most perfect shell keeps in Britain.[6]

The term 'shell keep' was coined towards the end of the last cen-

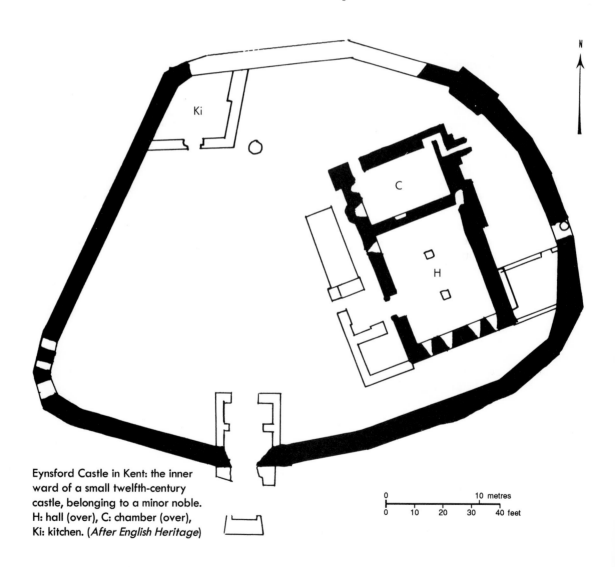

Eynsford Castle in Kent: the inner ward of a small twelfth-century castle, belonging to a minor noble. H: hall (over), C: chamber (over), Ki: kitchen. (*After English Heritage*)

tury to describe the circular stone towers which were built on mottes throughout the Norman period. They represent the translation into stone of the palisade round the motte summit to form a secure space for living accommodation. Timber-framed buildings were erected against the inner face of the new wall, leaving a small central court-yard for the admission of light and air. Although generally a combina-tion of stone and wood, the shell keep was conceptually a single building, as may be appreciated at Tamworth Castle, where the keep walls shelter a warren of post-medieval rooms.

The motte itself was as much part of the shell keep as the super-structure for, with the exception of the ringwork castle of Restormel, such keeps were built exclusively on mounds: indeed it is the motte which produced the shell keep. When reconstruction of a castle in stone was planned, the shell keep offered a solution to the difficulties created by existing mottes. In most cases, Norman builders seem not to have trusted the ability of artificial mottes to take the weight of any but the smallest stone keeps. The towers at Rochester, Hedingham and Corfe were all added to ringwork castles, while at Canterbury the keep was built on an altogether different site to the old motte, which was then abandoned. The massive keep at Kenilworth, distinctive in a number of respects, simply enveloped the motte in stone, while at Guildford, in Surrey, and Clun, in Shropshire, the keeps were built on the motte-slope in the search for good foundations.

A motte could not be abandoned in favour of a new keep in the same castle – its control of the bailey was too dangerous – and yet to dig it away would be expensive and wasteful. The best answer, cheap and technically simple, was the shell keep. High on its motte, a two-storey building could easily dominate the castle and its walls; isolated from battering rams and miners by that huge mound of earth, it need only be 2 to 3 metres (6 to 10 feet) thick rather than the 3 to 4 metres (12 to 14 feet) deemed necessary at Rochester or Kenilworth. It had the advantages of the round keeps then making their first appearance in France, for its curving wall would offer no right angles to the pick and would tend to deflect missiles, but its greater area certainly offered more comfortable accommodation than most of those towers.

With these advantages, shell keeps were added to castles all over England during the twelfth and thirteenth centuries, but their thin walls have suffered greatly since. At Pickering in Yorkshire, Clare and Eye in Suffolk, at Tonbridge and Warwick, there is little to see but small panels of walls and foundations. At Lewes there is more – part of the wall and two turrets by which the keep was strengthened in the thirteenth century – and at Lincoln the keep stands to half its height. At Berkeley, in Gloucestershire, and Farnham, in Surrey, late twelfth-century shell keeps actually enclose the moderate mounds on which they stand, their stone walls brought down to ground level. The keep of Totnes in Devon still crowns the old borough with its red circlet of stone, and not far away at Restormel, there survives a huge shell keep added to a ringwork with the stone walls of its internal buildings still visible; at Windsor and Tamworth, timber buildings survive.

Arundel, with its impressive white ashlar walls, is perhaps the finest of all. It stands on a tall grassy motte, joined by steep walls to the rest of the castle. One of these shelters a stair from the gatehouse – the other substantial medieval survivor – up the slope to the keep. A late thirteenth-century tower now defends the entrance, but the original door can still be seen, blocked and part-hidden, to one side. Inside the keep, fireplaces and corbels reveal the former existence, at least in part, of two storeys of buildings.

From the wall-walk the whole castle, Arundel town and coast beyond can be surveyed. Today, for all its pretentious surroundings, the keep can still evoke the pride of the house of de Albini.

Restormel Castle, in Cornwall. The internal buildings date from the fourteenth century but must replace earlier structures. H: hall (over), Ch: chapel (over). (*After English Heritage*)

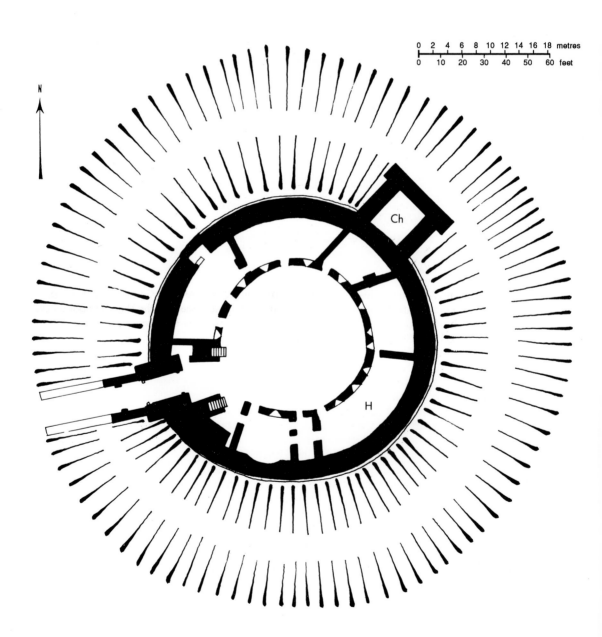

Arundel was one of only three castles where de Albini's building works were designed to demonstrate his new social status. Since his father still occupied the family castle at Buckenham in Norfolk, William de Albini decided to build a new fortress at Rising. For years Rising had remained an inconsequential village, its value no more than the revenues of the nearby port of Lynn. Now it entered the front rank of English life as work on its castle, founded to mark a political rather than a territorial conquest, began to be undertaken. This new fortress informed Norfolk that de Albini had arrived and provided him not only with a home fit for a queen, but the military strength to back his position.

The castle is a ringwork with a small bailey on either side; de Albini's stone keep is obscured by gargantuan earthworks, but they were originally lower and the tower was clearly visible in the middle. Apart from a rectangular gatehouse of familiar design, but notable for having had an early portcullis, the defences of ringwork and baileys have gone; in the twelfth century they may only have been wooden.[7] Within the irregular oval defined by the ringwork, a number of buildings were raised, of which only the foundations of their fourteenth-century successors are visible. They were always subordinate to the palatial stone keep, which was a strong point and the principal accommodation in the castle, and which survives almost entire.

Arundel Castle; the shell keep, showing the Norman door blocked by the later tower.

The principal entrance door of Castle Rising keep stands at the top of a noble flight of steps contained in the forebuilding.

The keep has only two floors and rises, without its turrets, to a height of just 15 metres (50 feet), or half that of Rochester. It is built of local stone, brownish in colour, and laid uncut in courses, but the dressings are of Barnack limestone, ferried across the fens from near Peterborough. This fine ashlar was used for the pilaster buttresses and corner turrets of the keep, and the forebuilding.

The aesthetic impact of the latter has been marred by the top storey and roof which have been added to it, for this was once an elegant façade designed to be the first thing seen by a visitor. The composition rose in three broad steps from left to right; marked by ashlar buttresses, they have a decorative scheme of blind arches below moulded roundels, of a standard and style comparable with the contemporary gate of Bury St Edmunds Abbey or Norwich Castle keep.

Cracked and broken though its details are, the work remains true in a way that the walls of Norwich Castle, refaced in the 1830s, do not: it continues to impress us with the de Albini style. All his efforts were concentrated here – the other walls are starkly plain – for the approach was everything: the entrance to the keep, the stairs up to the first floor and the lobby, the grand doorway of the hall itself, all were designed to sustain the impression first made by the exterior of the forebuilding. Security was not neglected of course, for the stair to the hall is divided into two flights by an arch in which stood a two-leaved door, covered from above by a meurtrière.

The keep was divided by a cross-wall into two principal rooms, hall and chamber, and a number of smaller ones. Because the kitchen was at the far end of the hall from the entrance, de Albini could not preside at its upper end: instead he sat in the middle of the long wall, his dignity emphasized by a recess behind him and a large two-light window in the wall opposite. The standard of living of the de Albinis was high: a dog-leg passage to the latrines, kitchen and service room (buttery and pantry combined) ensured that food would be served hot. Both these rooms stand on a stone vaulted floor (the rest were wooden and have gone) to safeguard against fire. The hall had no fireplace, though there is one in the chamber next door; presumably it was heated by braziers, in spite of the wooden floor.

Castle Rising, plan of the principal floor of the keep. H: hall, C: chamber, Ch: chapel, Ki: kitchen, S: service room, L: latrines, F: forebuilding. (*After English Heritage*)

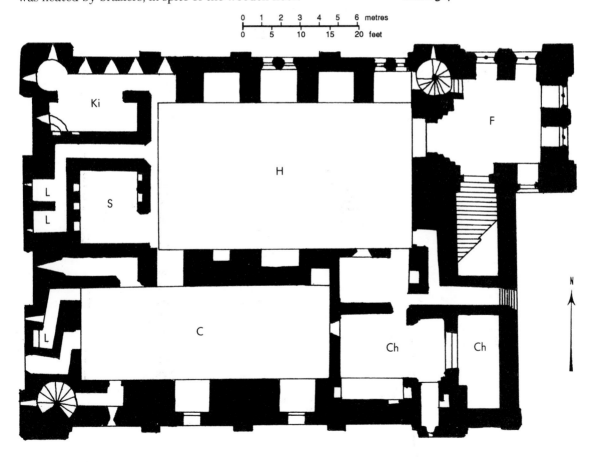

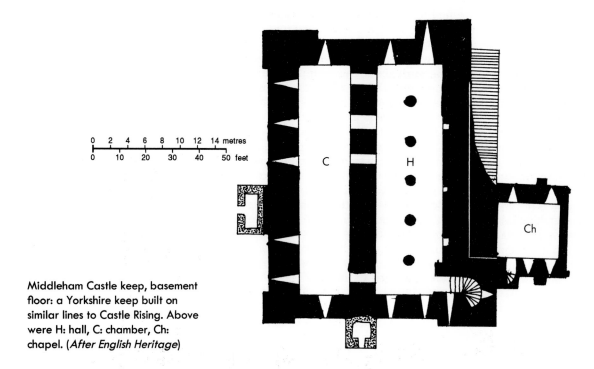

Middleham Castle keep, basement floor: a Yorkshire keep built on similar lines to Castle Rising. Above were H: hall, C: chamber, Ch: chapel. (*After English Heritage*)

The rest of the building is divided between chamber and chapel. The former was large and comfortable, with its own wall fireplace and two separate latrines: since only one of these possesses the unusual feature of a urinal, they may have been designed for use by different sexes. From the chamber a small chapel, with rib-vaulted chancel and wall-arcading in the nave, could be reached.

The walls of Castle Rising can hardly have been very high when de Albini's father died in 1139, and to his existing estates were added the honour and castle of Buckenham. The old, undoubtedly timber castle did not satisfy the earl's exacting standards, so he promptly began work on a new one about 3 kilometres (2 miles) away. Again he built a huge ringwork, perfectly circular and protected by a deep wet moat. A bailey lay to the east; beyond, the streets and building plots of a new town (a quiet village today) were set out. New Buckenham Castle is an eerie place, its banks rising steeply from dark water, their tops hidden by a protective ring of trees; rusting iron gates bar the bridge and crows caw angrily. Again there are fragments of a stone gatehouse and beyond it, within the ringwork, the ruins of a keep; unlike its cousin at Castle Rising, this keep, whose lower 7 metres (25 feet) still stand, is circular. It is not a shell keep on a motte, but the base of a true tower in the manner of Rising, Canterbury or Norwich. Unfortunately, given that it is probably the earliest round keep to have been built in Britain its condition is poor and the only significant feature is a great cross-wall similar to those found in large rectangular keeps of the period, and not at all characteristic of surviving circular towers in Britain or France.

These three keeps – the shell keep at Arundel, the great rectangular building at Castle Rising, and the round tower at New Buckenham – prove that, to William de Albini at least, one form was not necessarily superior to the others. Round keeps were not thought simply to be better than rectangular ones: what really mattered was to marry the demands of the site with the available resources into a framework which suited the ideas, both military and social, of the builder.

The wars triggered by the landing of Matilda at Arundel are too complex to follow here. Fought largely in the Midlands and the south-west – where Matilda's brother, Robert of Gloucester, drew his strength – they raged inconclusively for years, first the king gaining the upper hand, then Matilda and her party taking control. Stephen rushed round England like a man trying to put out a bush fire with a bucket of water; every local problem quelled, every county in which peace was restored, was followed by the disintegration of order somewhere behind his back: each castle taken was balanced by another lost as some previously loyal baron chose that moment to change sides. By the end, Stephen was a more experienced besieger than builder of castles. The struggle for control of Lincoln provides a perfect example of the role which castles played in the fighting, and underlines the personal ambitions which made it drag on for so long.

So impressive is the three-towered silhouette of Lincoln Cathedral, the spiritual overseer of the city's inhabitants, that it is easy to overlook the rather squat profile of their temporal defender, the castle with which it shares the hill. Although the distant view of a city like Rochester or Durham seems to emphasize the dual nature of authority, Church and State, in the medieval period, in both cases it is an inaccurate reflection, for their castles were ecclesiastical and served

New Buckenham Castle, site plan.
(*After Derek Renn*)

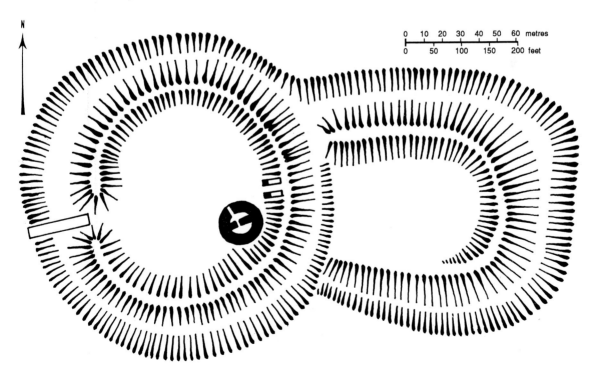

N

| 0 | 10 | 20 | 30 | 40 | 50 | 60 metres |
| 0 | 50 | | 100 | | 150 | 200 feet |

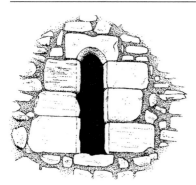

A simple window lighting the basement of the keep at Castle Rising.

the military needs of the Church. At Lincoln, though the struggle for visual dominance has been won by the cathedral, the partnership existed and still does. *'Regnum et sacerdotium'* divide the hilltop as they have since 1067, leaving only half the area of the Roman town for houses; today the church fulfills its original function, though under an altered creed, and the authority of the State is still exercised in the Crown Court which stands in the castle bailey.

The greatest puzzle of Lincoln Castle, the existence of two mottes, has to some extent been resolved by recent excavations which showed that the easternmost of the two, which now carries the so-called Observatory Tower, was not put up until the middle of the twelfth century: the period of the Anarchy. So the castle built by William I in 1068 had only the large motte on the south curtain with a shell keep, known as the Lucy Tower.[8] No firm date has been assigned to this tower, although it is likely that a stone keep was raised in 1115, at the same time as the curtain-wall and west gate.

The keep is not round like Arundel's, but composed of a series of straight sides, the angles strengthened with pilaster buttresses. There were rectangular turrets where the bailey wall meets the keep itself: the western one containing latrines; the eastern, rooms of unknown purpose. A flight of steps climbs straight up the side of the motte to a large arched doorway. A second door leads from the keep to the ground outside the castle, combining the functions of sally-port and escape route. There are no loops in the wall, so the windows of the rooms within the tower must have opened on to a small courtyard; the internal structure would have been timber framed, its wall-spaces filled with wattle and daub – a sort of woven oat mat plastered with a mixture of clay, dung and straw.

In 1140 the castle, which had been peripheral to the fighting between Stephen and Matilda, was brought to the forefront of the conflict by Rannulf, Earl of Chester. He was one among many who had no scruples in switching allegiance, or promising to do so, whenever it suited him. As Earl of Chester, he already controlled a large part of the Welsh March with a semi-independent authority; he had also inherited large Lincolnshire estates and held directly, or through his family, much more.[9] His ambition was to control everything between Chester and Lincoln – between Wales and the North Sea – a territorial holding which divided England and would make him the greatest power-broker in the land. The possession of Lincoln Castle, the strongest in the county, and the town it controlled, fourth or fifth in the realm, was crucial to that ambition. In addition, since his mother Lucy had been wife to a former constable of the castle (indeed the Lucy Tower is named after her), he may have felt a personal attachment to it.

In 1140 he threw in his lot with Matilda, but instead of assisting her campaign, he took the opportunity to sieze Lincoln from Stephen's constable. At Christmas that year, he and his half-brother William, the Earl of Lincoln, apparently sent their wives on a social call to the castle. Like most royal castles not actually in danger, it was held by a constable with a few men-at-arms; indeed the soldiers are said to have been 'engaged in sports' at the time of the visit.[10] Rannulf arrived at the keep a little later, unarmed but with three other knights and, while the women chatted to the wife of the constable, the newcomers seized weapons that were lying about and ejected the rightful occupants; thereupon William rode in with a company of knights, and the surprised constable was left with no alternative but to vacate the castle.

Rannulf spent a pleasant Christmas that year, for when Stephen reached Lincoln, he tried to buy the earl's allegiance by confirming him in his possession of Lincoln and adding further lands and castles to it. In return for his support, Rannulf was to hold the castle of Lincoln (and to fortify his own separate tower within in it), until the king surrendered various other lands and castles to him; thereafter, he was to retain possession of the constableship of the castle and of a tower, which must, by implication, have been the Lucy Tower. The discovery of mid-twelfth century pottery in the composition of the eastern motte suggests that it was raised by Rannulf as a result of this pact.[11]

That the king could thus concede rights of ownership within a royal castle implies that twelfth-century nobles saw castles as comprising distinct elements. In fact, reference is commonly made to the 'castle and tower' in documents of the period; while in France the terms '*donjon, château, basse-cour*' correspond to the keep, bailey and outer bailey. It would appear then that the word castle could, according to context, mean the whole structure or just the bailey, and that it was possible for different people to have rights in a single structure. The

The interior of Lincoln Castle's shell keep (the Lucy Tower) in the snow. It was once twice its present height, and contained timber-framed buildings instead of the sad graves dug there during the castle's life as a Victorian prison.

existence of two mottes at Lewes may be due to a similar arrangement under William I.

However, if these arrangements seemed politic to a king who was already militarily over-stretched, it brought him no advantage, for a few weeks later the complaints of the oppressed citizens of Lincoln forced Stephen to return in the full panoply of war. Rannulf slipped through the king's fingers, leaving his wife and Earl William to defend the castle.

In the *Gesta Stephani* there are several extraordinarily vivid descriptions of the sieges of King Stephen and the tactics he employed. He seems generally to have built himself a siege-castle from which to direct operations before launching his assault with a hail of missiles from catapults, archers and javelin-throwers. Then soldiers would seek to scale the walls and engage in hand-to-hand combat 'with nothing but the palisade to keep the two sides apart'.[12] But at Lincoln he had time to do little more than blockade the castle before the massed forces of Rannulf and Robert of Gloucester appeared on the marshy ground to the south-west of the city. Such a trap was the greatest danger faced by a castle's besiegers, for if those within could hold out until their allies could relieve them, the attacker would be caught between two forces. On this occasion it was fatal: the battle was bloody, with many of Stephen's men killed or drowned in their flight. The king himself was felled by a blow from a stone and taken prisoner. Rannulf kept Lincoln.

The details of the struggle for Lincoln underline how important a single castle could be. Stephen was freed a few months later, following the capture of Robert of Gloucester, and the futile war continued. Lincoln Castle, for a few weeks the hinge on which everything turned, returned to obscurity. Stephen briefly attacked the castle in 1144, when he used the west end of the cathedral as a siege-castle, but that assault failed. Lincoln was only recovered two years later by imprisoning Rannulf until he surrendered all the lands and castles he had wrested from royal control. The castle was never again in the hands of the Earl of Chester.

——7——
Four-square Order

In 1153 a negotiated settlement brought the civil war to a close; under its terms Stephen was to reign until his death, following which the crown would pass to Henry of Anjou, Matilda's son. In the event, Stephen died only eighteen months later, and Henry II came to the throne in 1154, only 21-years old, but already experienced in the political and military battlegrounds of England and northern France. That experience would come in useful, for, though his accession was undisputed, he inherited a land riven by civil war. Royal authority had all but disintegrated as men like Rannulf of Chester exploited the king's good nature and military weakness to increase their power; in particular, Stephen's inability to restrain illicit castle building meant that the kingdom was littered with fortresses.

Most were of earth and timber and exist today as shadows on the landscape; but in an age of lances and arrows, these molehills could be mountains to those who fought over them. It was not so much the degree of their strength, however, which posed a threat to Henry, as their very number: in 1154 private castles outnumbered the king's by nearly five to one. Henry's first task was to curb the power of his leading subjects by confiscating as many of these adulterine castles as he could. After the experience of localized feudalism, there was a general readiness to accept Henry's centralist policies and many barons submitted to the new king, surrendering unlawfully held castles which were then destroyed, taken over by the crown, or sometimes even returned to their owners on payment of a heavy fine – an ingenious device which brought the State revenue while reducing the financial strength of the opposition: it underlined the king's rights over the castle but left the cost of its maintenance to the tenant.

William of Aumale, created Earl of Yorkshire by King Stephen, had grown enormously powerful in that county during the Anarchy, and had marked his new status by the construction, around 1140, of a castle at Scarborough. Some royal pressure was necessary before this over-mighty baron would surrender his castles, but William's submission to Henry II at York was, in the end, achieved peacefully. In 1155 the castle passed to royal hands, and the royal accounts began to record expenditure on it almost immediately.

The site was a large flat headland protected on three sides by vertiginous cliffs and the sea, and accessible only along a thin ridge of ground. According to William of Newburgh, the earl's castle consisted of a wall above a ditch separating peninsula from mainland, and a tower defending the entrance. That tower was probably in poor condition when Henry ordered its replacement with a new stone keep: over £650 was spent on the castle between 1157 and 1169 under the supervision of a certain David Lardener.

The principal cost was the beautiful keep whose ruin can still be

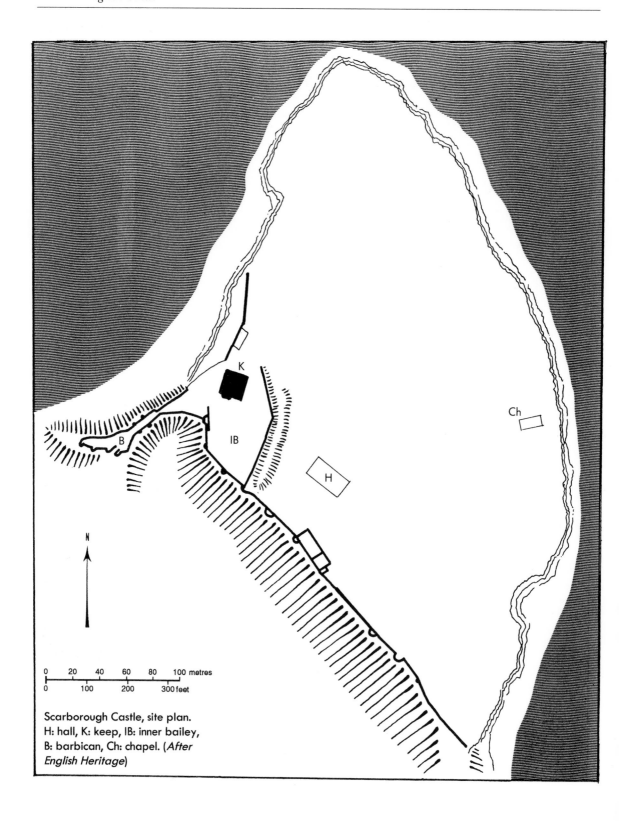

Scarborough Castle, site plan.
H: hall, K: keep, IB: inner bailey,
B: barbican, Ch: chapel. (*After
English Heritage*)

A window from Scarborough keep.

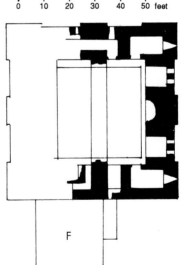

Scarborough Castle keep, hall floor; F: forebuilding. (*After Derek Renn*)

seen on the bleak heights above the seaside resort; smashed by one generation, restored by another, the tower retains, in spite of it all, a certain impressiveness. Some 17 metres (57 feet) square externally, it once stood about 31 metres (100 feet) tall, with walls 4 metres (12 feet) thick: only slightly smaller than Rochester. It has shallow buttresses rising from a battered base, and once contained four floors: the first of which, above the basement, was once spanned by a great arch supporting a dividing wall on the floor above. There were fire-places and latrines and fine two-light windows looking east over the sea. The spiral stair was in the middle of the west wall; to allow for it, and because it faced the direction of attack, that wall was 1 metre (3 feet) thicker than the others. Sadly, that strength was not proof against the power of Parliamentary cannon during the long siege of 1645.

At the foot of this new keep, a small inner bailey was laid out; the motte-and-bailey plan had become the keep and bailey. But the keep was not conceived as the last line of defence, though it always could be that: here it was actually the first, for it was placed so as to be able to overlook the causeway into the castle. Anyone crossing the ditch from the mainland was obliged to pass under the keep before entering the bailey. The tower was an offensive, as well as a defensive, structure, and from its battlements archers commanded the bailey, the ground outside the castle and the approach; rocks and stones thrown down would rebound from the sloping base against an enemy below.

Twelfth-century keeps are sometimes seen as passive defences relying on sheer mass to protect those inside. However, crucial to an assessment of their varying roles is their position in a castle: if Scarborough's was to have been a bolt-hole, it would have been built by the cliff edge, not the entrance. The strong gatehouses erected in the reign of Edward I are not such an advance on earlier castle design as they might appear, for they follow the same thinking as Scarborough's keep in concentrating the castle's strength, and best accommodation, at the entrance – the weakest point. Apparent development is no more than the rearticulation by a later generation of an established idea.[1] In the twelfth century, such forward defence was not unusual; two among the many new keeps built during the reign of Henry II can serve to make the point – Peveril and Richmond.

Peveril is a remote Pennine fortress, whose principal military role was the protection of the local lead mines. The triangular site has cliffs on the west and east, and a very steep slope to the north, at the foot of which grew Castleton: visitors still ascend this slope and use the postern created for the medieval inhabitants. The path from the village is, however, too precipitous for war-horses and their riders: the main entrance was at the south-western tip of the site, over a rocky ditch, from an outer bailey on the adjoining hill, and the footings of the drawbridge can be seen in the ditch today.

Over this lost entrance stands a keep built for Henry II in the years after 1174. Reflecting the minor importance of the castle itself, the keep is small, only 12 metres (40 feet) square and about 18 metres (60 feet) tall. It had a basement and a room above with a latrine but no fireplace. Windows in the northern sides of the keep overlook the bailey and the entrance passage, but the only opening to the field is a loop above the roof-line: it must have been a cold watch, huddled on the roof and peering through the slit to keep an eye on movements on the other side of the ditch. But the keep, whose doorway was accessible only by a ladder, was never meant to be comfortable (the castle hall stood in the bailey for everyday use), for it served a military function: like Scarborough's, it was a concentration of strength at the weakest point.

Peveril Castle seen from Castleton, the village which grew up at its feet; Henry II's keep stands behind the eleventh-century bailey wall. The original outer bailey was on the adjacent hill, to the extreme right of the picture.

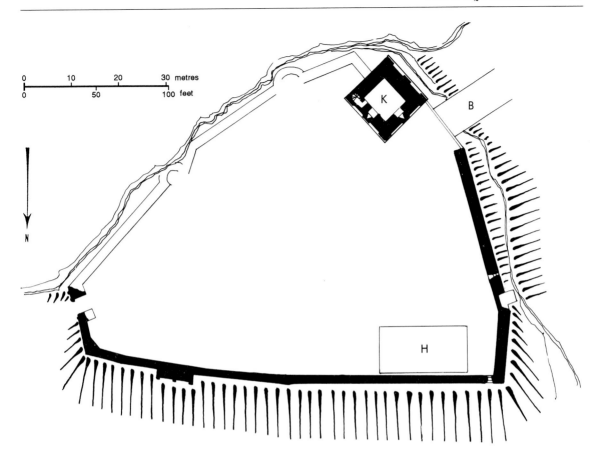

The similarities in the plans of Peveril and Richmond Castles are obvious, and are not the only points they have in common: both were eleventh-century foundations in previously unsettled wilderness, and both gave rise to new towns; they were stone built from the first, but did not have keeps until about a century after, when towers were raised in similar positions. At Richmond, the gatehouse at the northern end of the castle was walled-up and used as the base of a tall, three-storeyed keep, whose battlements are visible from most parts of the town. The work was probably begun by the fifth Earl of Richmond, and finished by Henry II after his death in 1171.[2] Some 31 metres (100 feet) high, the keep is rectangular in plan and has a single large room on each floor; straight flights of stairs ascend in the thickness of the southern wall from first to second floor, and from there to the wall-walk. When the gateway was blocked, a new gate was made in the curtain just to the east of the keep, so that it fulfills the same active role as the others described above, though here the design originated from the Earl of Richmond, not Henry II.

Although the virtually complete destruction of its bailey makes it difficult to be sure exactly how the great tower of Newcastle-upon-

Peveril Castle, the inner ward. H: site of hall, K: keep, B: lost bridge to outer bailey. (*After English Heritage*)

Peveril Castle seen from the village gate. The keep which guarded the principal entrance is the only surviving building.

Opposite Newcastle-upon-Tyne, section through the keep; shading represents the modern alterations. (*After Brian Jobling and Margaret Finch*)

Tyne related to the outer defences, it remains one of the latest and finest of the rectangular keeps built by Henry II. It is almost perfect, apart from nineteenth-century battlements and some unsympathetic patching of its gritty sandstone walls. The castle, originally a Norman foundation of about 1080, had fallen into Scots hands and was recovered following an agreement made at Peveril Castle in 1157 between Henry II and Malcolm of Scotland. Ten years later, Henry undertook its reconstruction in stone, spending £1,144 on the keep, wall and gate, to the design of a master mason, or 'ingeniator', named Maurice. He was also responsible for the similar, though larger, keep raised at Dover in the final years of Henry's reign.

The tower at Newcastle was of similar size to Scarborough's – 17 by 19 metres (57 by 62 feet) in plan and about 31 metres (100 feet) high – but it was much more complex in its internal arrangements. There were two floors above a vaulted basement, each of which had, in addition to a principal room, a number of small rooms contrived in the thickness of the walls. The entrance was on the top floor which, as at London, was twice the height of those below, and it was reached by a steep and well-defended stair in the forebuilding on the east side of the keep. From the well which rose to this level, fresh water could be hauled up and distributed through pipes to other parts of the keep. In addition to the usual provision of latrines and other small rooms,

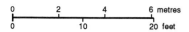

both the principal floor and the one below were furnished with comfortable private chambers or bedrooms, each with an elegant fireplace. The finest and most moving room in the keep is the rib-vaulted chapel which occupies an unusual position in the basement of the forebuilding.

The aggressive siting of keeps is but one among many fresh ideas tried in England during the second half of the twelfth century. Advances were made both in the planning of castles and in the design of their architectural elements. Many have survived and the royal accounts preserved from the reign of Henry II greatly assist in the interpretation of the remains.

But perhaps the most important change was simply the amount of money which the Angevin kings, Henry II and his sons, Richard and John, were prepared to spend on castles. After 1154, 8 to 10 per cent of the Crown's annual income was devoted to castle-works, and this level of expenditure remained constant, at least until the 1350s, though the nature of the work it paid for changed significantly. Most of the money was not spent on new castles (the Crown found it sufficiently difficult to maintain its existing fortresses without adding to the number), but on the maintenance and improvement of old ones. The expenditure of such a high proportion of the revenue on building works was necessary because, as well as being the king's houses, castles formed the tangible embodiment of the State throughout the realm – the bones of the kingdom. Through them peace was kept, justice administered, and revenues collected; the king's officer in each county, the sheriff, resided in the castle and used the power and authority it conferred to govern on behalf of his lord and master.

The increase in expenditure on castle-works had a secondary welcome result: it forced most of the smaller knights and landlords to drop out of the arms race. Strong castles now cost far more to build than most men could afford; the days of the Anarchy, when a motte-and-bailey stronghold had a real military value, were gone and since few could afford the aggressive stone castles of the time, most had to be content with fortified houses. From the reign of Henry II onwards, the story of the castle becomes more and more that of the fortresses of the king and the great barons.

—8—
A Delight in Innovation

Orford is a quiet village on the Suffolk coast. The River Alde slides past the end of Quay Street, but the spit of marshland which made a safe anchorage in the twelfth century has grown southwards and destroyed it. A walk along the flat strip of Orford Ness is not easily forgotten, but the memory is of birds and grass, not ships: the rich medieval port has gone. It has left behind a church and a castle to recall the years when the King of England focused his attention on Orford.

When Henry II came to the throne there was no royal castle in Suffolk, and few in all East Anglia. He waited three years before trying to alter the balance of power in the region; then, in 1157, he struck at his most powerful opponent, Hugh Bigod, the Earl of Norfolk. Having already taken the castles of Norwich, Acre and Eye from the late King Stephen's son, William of Blois, he confiscated the four major Bigod strongholds – Thetford, Framlingham, Walton and Bungay.[1]

In 1165 the last two were given back in return for a payment of £1,000, and that year, or the next, Henry began construction of a new castle at Orford. On completion in 1173, this work had cost about £1,500, so Hugh Bigod's money largely defrayed the cost of a castle designed to limit his power. Unlike Scarborough or Peveril, Orford was built in a single campaign on a site unencumbered by earlier buildings. The plan adopted – a keep surrounded by a curtain-wall – was superficially conventional; in fact, both the polygonal keep and the large towers which studded the wall were quite new. The towers, and their importance to the development of the English castle, will be discussed in the next chapter; it is only necessary to say here that they no longer exist.

The keep, which does survive entire, is the first of many experiments in design conducted during the late-twelfth and early-thirteenth centuries and indeed, in the case of Knaresborough Castle, on into the fourteenth. Orford's is circular inside but has fifteen or sixteen unequal sides on the exterior, to which are added three rectangular turrets and a forebuilding: it conforms to no type and can only be described as polygonal.

It has been suggested that it, and other related keeps like Conisbrough (Yorkshire) or Chilham (Kent), form some sort of transitional stage between the rectangular keeps of the twelfth century and the circular ones built in Britain during the thirteenth, but the idea does not bear examination. As has been noted, William de Albini built a round keep at New Buckenham in the 1140s – that is, two decades before the keep at Orford which is meant to be a move towards that shape.[2] More important, however, is the evidence from Normandy: when Henry II began the castle at Orford, he had himself built or repaired both simple octagonal keeps (Gisors) and cylindrical ones (Neaufles and Château-sur-Epte) in his lands on the Continent. Therefore, we must accept that Orford was intended to be what it is – indeed, it is far too clever to be otherwise. These keeps are experiments, products of the imaginative minds which were at the same moment developing English Gothic architecture. To see them as half-way houses to something better is to undervalue their achievement and their originality.

At Orford, that originality is expressed in the way in which the principal rooms are supplemented by a large number of subsidiary chambers. Although a good deal smaller, Orford offers a higher degree of comfort and privacy than most earlier rectangular keeps. The entrance is on the first floor, reached through a forebuilding (beneath is a room which was probably a prison cell).[3] The first floor contains a

Henry II's keep at Orford in Suffolk.

tall circular apartment with a fireplace and two-light windows set in large recesses; from it, doorways lead to a kitchen, latrines and bed-chambers, as well as to the broad spiral stair which runs from basement to roof-top. The smaller rooms, and the stair, are contrived in the turrets flanking the body of the keep; because the main apartments are so tall, two turret rooms were superimposed in the height of each floor. The top floor of the keep was the main apartment, but was different from the entrance floor only in having a tall conical roof.

Orford seems never to have been a royal home, like Nottingham, London or Windsor, and its later history was the same as many Crown castles which were not regularly visited by the king: its maintenance was assured, somewhat grudgingly, and the castle itself was handed over to a succession of constables who were, as often as not, also sheriffs of the county. It was taken, undamaged, in the Magna Carta war but afterwards was put on a war-footing only twice before being permanently alienated by the Crown in 1336.

Such an insignificant history should not, of course, be taken as evidence that the castle was unimportant. It symbolized the royal presence in that part of the kingdom and guaranteed the peace. Indeed, it had barely been completed when Hugh Bigod, the very man it was designed to contain, joined the rebellion of King Henry's son in 1173. Orford was hurriedly provisioned and its defences improved: a ditch was dug and a palisade set above it. Houses belonging to a townsman were appropriated – he was compensated when peace was restored – by the constable, probably to be re-erected in the bailey for the use of the knights and men-at-arms posted to the castle. There must have been many of them, because in 1173 nearly £160 was spent on their wages: a common soldier would only get a penny a day in the twelfth century, though archers and crossbowmen might get two or three times that amount. Apparently the preparations were effective, because there is no record of the castle being attacked during the rebellion. For his part in the revolt, Hugh Bigod

The English royal castle at Gisors, in Normandy, not only preserves an excellent shell keep, but also an octagonal keep thought to have been built by Henry I and heightened by Henry II.

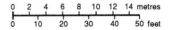

Orford Castle, the hall of the keep. (*After English Heritage*)

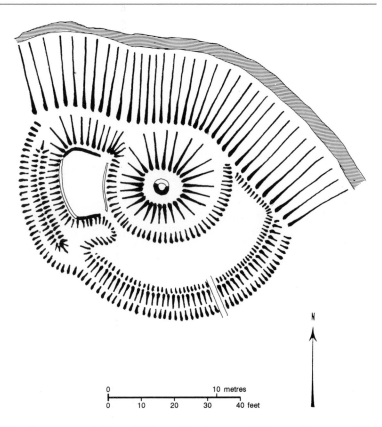

Neaufles, site plan showing Henry
II's round keep.

0   10 metres

0   10   20   30   40 feet

N

lost Bungay and Framlingham for the second time; they were dis-
mantled on royal orders, and were not rebuilt until after Henry's
death.

The problems of castle design must have been a common topic of
conversation at the court of Henry II, for during his thirty-five year
reign, new ideas were being tried throughout the country, both by
royal masons and by those of the great barons. The king is said to
have taken particular delight in the keep at Orford, and his works at
Newcastle, Dover, Windsor and elsewhere show both the importance
attached to the royal castles and the inventiveness of their designers.
On the motte at Tickhill, Henry raised an eleven-sided tower whose
slight corners were strengthened with shallow buttresses; it has been
destroyed to the foundations, but must have been a glorious sight in
1180. At the same time, and not more than a day's ride from Tickhill,
Henry's own half-brother, Hamelin Plantagenet, was building a
beautiful polygonal keep which survives almost entire.

Conisbrough Castle had come to Hamelin through his marriage to
Isabel, widow of William of Blois, and heiress to the huge de Warenne
estates. After an attempt – blocked by Thomas Becket – to push his
younger brother William into her wealthy arms, Henry arranged her
marriage to Hamelin in 1163.[4] As a result he became the fifth Earl of
Surrey and lord of the de Warenne castles of Reigate, Lewes,
Conisbrough, Sandal and Castle Acre. (Like all their contemporaries,
Hamelin and Isabel divided their time between the court and their

various estates, but they seem to have been the first of the de Warennes to make much use of Conisbrough; indeed, the standard of living at Castle Acre declined significantly under Hamelin and Isabel, which may point to a gradual abandonment of Acre as a regular home in favour of Conisbrough.)[5] The ruins of Conisbrough Castle, surrounded now by a pit town, date principally from the tenure of Hamelin and his son, and represent a castle which was not only militarily powerful, like Orford, but also a home.

The outer ward has all but gone now and only its banks can be traced, but of the inner ward, built on a powerfully scarped hill, much survives. This oval enclosure, about 76 by 46 metres (250 by 150 feet), contained all the principal buildings of the castle, including the keep, and was defended by a thick wall of roughly coursed limestone with a number of semicircular bastions. But the wall was built after the tower (it is not keyed in, as the illustration on page 85 shows), so the tower probably stood as the only stone building in a wooden castle; indeed, there is a self-containment about the keep which implies that it was meant to stand alone.

It is built of the local creamy-white limestone, but its walls are of ashlar not rubble. It rises, quite round, from a sloping plinth, its curved flank interrupted by six semi-hexagonal buttresses which project boldy and rise above the level of the wall-walk to form turrets. Surely medieval architecture never evoked, consciously or not, the feudal Crown with more confidence than here. The tower has lost its battlements and appears a little more squat than it did; otherwise its proportions are excellent. Aesthetic quality in architecture is not the product of chance: a close look at the base of the tower reveals how, in the sides of the buttresses, every second course of masonry has been cut back. The effect is to bring these planes vertically to the ground; the reason can only have been a wish to avoid an impression of undue weightiness at the foot of the tower – a purely aesthetic judgement.

But architecture is a balance between aesthetics and necessity, and the Conisbrough keep was designed as a strong, as well as a beautiful,

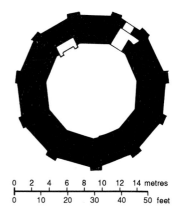

Tickhill Castle, plan of the keep. (*After English Heritage*)

Conisbrough Castle on its hill, with the remains of bailey walls and the buttressed keep.

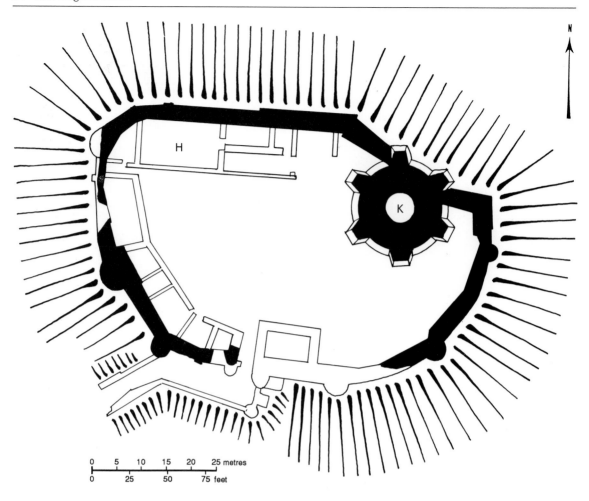

0 5 10 15 20 25 metres
0   25   50   75 feet

Conisbrough Castle, site plan. H: hall, K: keep. (*After English Heritage*)

home. Though its floors have fallen – except the vault over the base-ment – it is still possible to explore the whole tower. Since daylight floods in where there was once a roof, it is difficult to appreciate how dark these rooms once were – the basement and first floor have no windows at all while the two upper floors have but one each. Except the last, where a tiny chapel is contrived in the thickness of a buttress, each floor has a single circular room: the massive walls accommodate no convenient chambers (except tiny latrines), and only the broad staircase rises through them. Above the entrance floor – quite bare, and presumably a guardroom – there is a hall and above that a chamber; each has a window with stone seats in it, a stone basin to which water was piped from a cistern on the roof, and a fireplace.

The quality of the design and masoncraft still to be seen in the two top floors at Conisbrough is wonderful, and nowhere more so than in the oratory on the top floor. This little room is rib-vaulted and embel-lished with characteristic Norman motifs – zigzags, roll-mouldings, and carved capitals including the latest waterleaf. So often, it is in the chapels of the early castles that the Norman spirit – or, at least, its best side – lingers, at places like London, Newcastle, Dover or Ludlow, of course, but also in many little-known chapels like this one or the one on the ground floor of the Robin Hood Tower at Richmond.

Since the bailey accommodated the castle hall, chamber, kitchen and chapel, one is forced to question the extent of the peacetime use made of the keep at Conisbrough and other castles during the thirteenth and fourteenth centuries. The evidence of construction can be summarized briefly: the last great rectangular keep was built before 1189 by Henry II at Dover, but small rectangular towers were built after that, for instance at Horston in Derbyshire, Gidleigh in Devon,

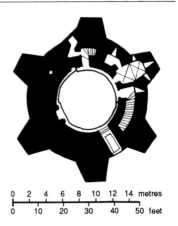

Conisbrough keep, plan of the chamber and the small chapel built into one buttress. (*After English Heritage*)

The battered base of Conisbrough keep, showing how every other course on the buttress has been cut back to achieve a more elegant profile. The inferior quality of the later wall (on the right of the illustration) is also clear.

The hall window in Conisbrough keep.

and Edlingham in Northumberland.[6] Polygonal and round keeps were built during the thirteenth century, notably a group of the latter in Wales and the Marches, among which may be listed Longtown, Skenfrith, Caldicot, Penrice, Pembroke and, a little later, Flint; similar round donjons were built around 1240 at the Tower of London and Barnard Castle in Durham, and round keeps dating from between 1230 and 1270 exist at Dirleton, Kildrummy and Bothwell in Scotland. Polygonal keeps were built in the same century at Odiham, Sandal and York, and in the following centuries at Knaresborough, Pontefract, Roxburgh, Southampton, Raglan in Gwent, and Warkworth in Northumberland.

This partial list suggests a tailing-off in the construction of keeps, and a movement away from a rectangular plan, though if fewer keeps were built it must have been largely because most important castles already had them. But evidence of building is not evidence of use; how much, and in what way, were the many existing keeps used? Records of Crown expenditure suggest that where a castle was kept in repair, its keep was kept in repair, and it is likely that its military function – as a strong point defensible by a small number of men – was never discredited as long as the medieval castle continued to be both home and fortress. Indeed, even in thirteenth-century castles built without keeps, the gatehouse was often designed to fulfill that role, as it had done as early as 1135 at Newark. However, the nature and extent of the everyday use of these buildings – which were, after all, dark, inconvenient and cramped – in the thirteenth and fourteenth centuries is unclear.

The communal, almost tribal, way of life of William I and his knights was changing throughout this period, and by the thirteenth century noble society had become very sophisticated. The beautiful domestic buildings demanded by that society could shelter safely beside a stone keep; as the defences of the bailey perimeter improved, elegant unfortified halls, like those which survive at Oakham and Winchester, became *de rigueur* in the higher circles. The accommodation of the Orford keep was certainly designed for everyday use, but if

The round keep added to Barnard Castle, in County Durham, in the mid-thirteenth century.

A stair window in Conisbrough Castle.

the same was true of Conisbrough, its role must have changed after the reconstruction of the hall and chamber in the bailey: its uncompromising strength did not offer much comfort.

The function of a keep must have varied from castle to castle after 1200, depending, as always in the medieval castle, on the conflicting demands of security and comfort. The troubles in Wales and Scotland, and in the English counties they bordered, must have lent a continuing importance to the great tower and kept it in daily use; while in the more settled counties, it may have been abandoned rather earlier as regular accommodation by the lord of the castle. Later in the medieval period, most keeps degenerated from royal or baronial home to arsenal and storehouse, prison, and lodging for the constable and castle servants. But the idea of the keep was to be tenacious, and if fewer and fewer were built after the reign of Henry II, they continued to dominate the existing castles, and to be one of the principal symbols of secular authority.

—9—
Walls of Death

Although the keep was paramount to the extent that it could be the only stone part of a castle, as at Bowes in North Yorkshire, the protection of the bailey also occupied the thoughts of Henry II and his circle. Plain walls, even of stone, were hard to defend from attack by troops increasingly supported by crossbowmen.

The development of the crossbow, a powerful weapon, well capable of piercing armour, is obscure, although its use clearly became widespread during the twelfth century.[1] The crossbow upset feudal order because it permitted the puniest peasant to assassinate the noblest lord, so incurring the wrath of the Church, which sought in 1139 to ban it. The ban was ineffective and by the time of Henry II, experienced crossbowmen, many returning from a crusade, were readily available for hire. As attackers, their iron bolts made the conventional defence of castle parapets almost impossible, for they could shoot down any man who allowed himself to be seen, while still out of range of spears and rocks. However, as defenders, crossbowmen could help to keep an enemy well away from the wall – if it was designed for such defence.

Towers, provided with loopholes for shooting, permitted an archer to rake the foot of the wall and the ditch beyond from the relative safety of his stone shield. These towers were much more aggressive than their domesticated cousins at Richmond and Ludlow, for though they could be adapted for daily living, their primary function was to guarantee the security of the walls. The earliest was probably the wall around the keep of Orford Castle, the last section of which collapsed in 1841, leaving a seventeenth-century drawing as the only evidence of its appearance. This shows the keep encircled by a battlemented wall with a ruined gateway and at least four towers. The towers are rectangular and have, to judge from the late-medieval windows shown, two or three storeys of accommodation; they divide the curtain-wall into short stretches, and stand considerably higher. The towered walls of the upper, private ward at Windsor Castle are still essentially the work of Henry II, but later generations have so changed them that they are no more instructive than the drawing of Orford. But both these fortifications were, in every substantial point, imitated by Henry's masons a little later at Dover where, though reduced in height, the towers survive in excellent condition.

The site of Dover Castle, on a cliff-top overlooking the harbour, was first occupied in the Iron Age when the original ditches were cut and a hill-fort established. Subsequently occupied by the Romans, it had become an Anglo-Saxon burh by the time William I built a castle there after the Battle of Hastings. That fortress was maintained by his successors, but in 1168 Henry II began a reconstruction so complete that no trace of the earlier castle can be seen, and so vast that

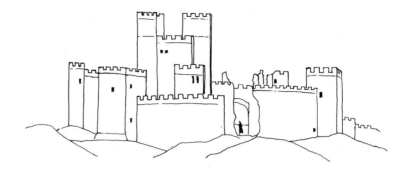

Orford Castle about 1600, after
John Norden.

when completed by his grandson, it eventually took over the whole
area of the hill-fort. The gargantuan scale was appropriate to a castle
which was, as a great knight put it a few years later, the key of
England. The enormous amount of money invested in the castle – up
to £7,000 – bought Henry security, status and comfort, and built the
bones of one of the greatest castles of Europe. The order in which the
work took place is still not certain, but the inner ward and keep
probably went up in the decade after 1180, following the construction
of a stretch of the outer curtain left unfinished by Henry. The inner
ward shows the same plan as Orford, though on a much greater scale:
a huge cubic keep, 29 metres (95 feet) high, is closely encircled by a
thick curtain with fourteen rectangular towers perched over a deep
ditch, now partly filled.

But it is the towered curtain-wall which made Dover such a strong
fortress, for it divided the perimeter into a series of short straight
walls, clearly visible and easily defended from the towers. The top
level, much to the castle's diminishment, was chopped away by the
Victorian engineers who adapted the castle for artillery defence, but
the remainder is largely intact, including the paired arrow-slits which
overlook not only the slope of the ditch, but also the outer face of the
walls themselves. Any assailant who got to the foot of the wall – and
none ever did – would have been a target in a shooting gallery.

The arrangements of the entrances to the inner ward are equally
impressive. For the first time in the English castle, the gateway itself
lies between two towers built close together. By this means, the gate-
passage could be defended from guard-rooms on each side, a real
improvement on the design of Lincoln or Tickhill, where the passage
was built through a single tower; the twin-towered gates at Dover
were to prove so effective that the idea was imitated widely in the
subsequent years.[2] A further improvement may be seen in the design
of the barbicans which had grown, from the basic structure in front of
Lincoln's west gate, into elaborate defences which channelled a
potential enemy into a narrow space overlooked not only by the
gatehouse, but also by the inner bailey wall and towers.

The final innovation to be seen in Henry's work at Dover was the
outer curtain, which he built on the north-eastern side of the castle,
from Pentchester's Tower almost to the Fitzwilliam Gate.[3] The idea
of encircling one strong wall with a second one was quite new in
relation to the English, and indeed the European, castle, though
there are important precedents in the classical world: Constantinople

and Nicea were walled in just this way during the early fifth century. The provision of two walls, and two lines of defence, enabled archers on the higher inner wall to support troops on the outer wall below. The system, now termed 'concentric' since one ring of walls encircles another, was to become important during the thirteenth century. Although the two lines of walls at Dover make the castle the first example of its kind in western Europe, it is possible that the construction of an outer wall was suggested by the existing ditches and ramparts, rather than by an awareness of classical precedents. Certainly the space between the walls (which ranges from 37 to 55 metres/120 to 180 feet) is five or six times that found in the true concentric castles of the next century.

But the double wall was not the most immediately influential element of Dover's defences: it was the towered curtains designed for defence by crossbow which found imitators. The walls of Framlingham Castle in Suffolk, the most outstanding example of this flattery by imitation, have been little touched since they were built

Dover Castle, inner ward. H: site of hall, B: barbican, K: keep. (*After English Heritage*)

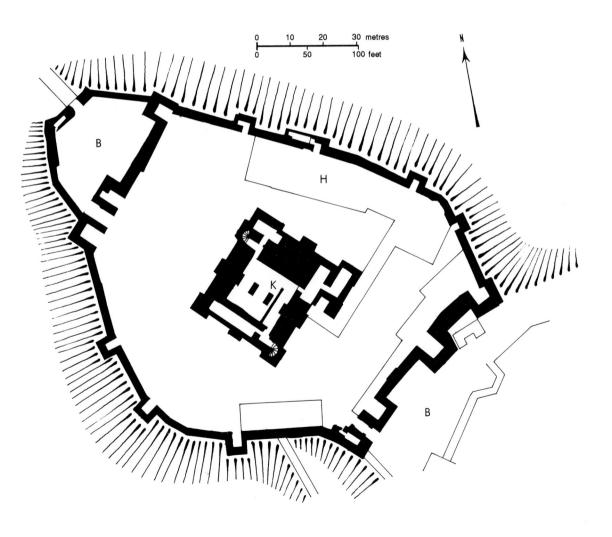

The towering walls of Dover Castle's inner ward, now shorn of their battlements, but retaining the original arrow-slits guarding each face.

during the reign of Richard I. Glimpsed across the mere on a misty November morning, or glinting in early spring sunshine, they have more appeal than the hard grey walls of Dover which, for all their importance, have been over-scraped by military engineers. Framlingham, still the crown of its little market town, has the patina of age and an atmosphere, if not entirely medieval, at least Tudor.

The first castle had been confiscated twice from its owners, the Bigod family, by Henry II and was not finally recovered by them, in a ruinous condition, until some time in the 1180s. Roger Bigod, second Earl of Norfolk, completely rebuilt it in close imitation of the nearby royal fortress of Orford but with the significant omission of any keep. Thirteen towers enclose a large bailey of irregular shape which once sheltered hall, chapel, and all the various buildings of the typical twelfth-century manor; an extension to the west enclosing a lower court has now mostly gone. The walls are studded with arrow slits at three levels: at the tops of the towers, in the battlements on the wall-walk and in the lower part of the wall. There can be scarcely a patch of ground beyond them which is not covered by these loops. In the end, however, the best-designed castle depended upon sufficient men to defend it. During the Magna Carta war, and within a few years of its construction, Framlingham was seized by royal forces after a two-day siege: the thirty-one men within were not enough to withstand their attackers, though seven of them were crossbowmen.

Henry II died in 1189, aged only 56, the achievements of the king temporarily overshadowed by the miseries of the man. Betrayed by his wife, his sons in rebellion against him, he must have felt little satisfaction in his life's work at the end. But he had brought England from anarchy to stable prosperity and time would reveal him to be one of the more successful of English monarchs.

Of his successor, his son Richard, the same can scarcely be said: Richard the Lion Heart, his image drawn in the garish colours and sentimental line of the worst Victorian stained glass, is a powerful creation, but unlike the man himself. In many ways the most French of England's kings, he spent less than six months of his ten-year reign in England, visiting his realm like an heir visits the bank manager; England seems to have meant little to a man whose interests were in the crusades and whose affections lay in France. To the story of castle building in England, he is all but irrelevant, his great Normandy fortress of Château Gaillard having no marked influence on design in Britain, and falling permanently to the French within ten years of its completion.

After his coronation, he granted too much land and too many castles to his brother John, and divided his authority between the Bishops of Ely and Durham, appointing them joint justiciars, or regents. Having sown the seeds of a power struggle, Richard left England for the Holy Land; he returned only once, in 1194, to reassert his authority, and to collect more money. Thereafter, until his death and the accession of King John, the country was governed by others in his absence.

Framlingham Castle; the Tudor chimneys have been omitted in this view, in order to restore the castle to something like its original appearance.

In the first years of Richard's reign, the Bishop of Ely, William Longchamp, undertook some overdue work on the royal castle of London.[4] In 1190 the castle stood much as William Rufus had left it when he had completed his father's great keep and surrounded it with a stone wall; the White Tower was still the principal building, the bailey between it and the river containing only a kitchen, bakehouse and gaol. In the era of Windsor and Dover, the Tower was *déclassé*. The work of 1190 sought to rectify the position with a telling emphasis, sustained in subsequent reconstructions, on the defence of the castle from the city, rather than the open country to the east.

Longchamp spent £2,880 on extending the area of the castle, new walls and towers, and improving the accommodation. The northern ditch was brought west to the site of the present Beauchamp Tower

Framlingham Castle, ground plan.
(*After English Heritage*)

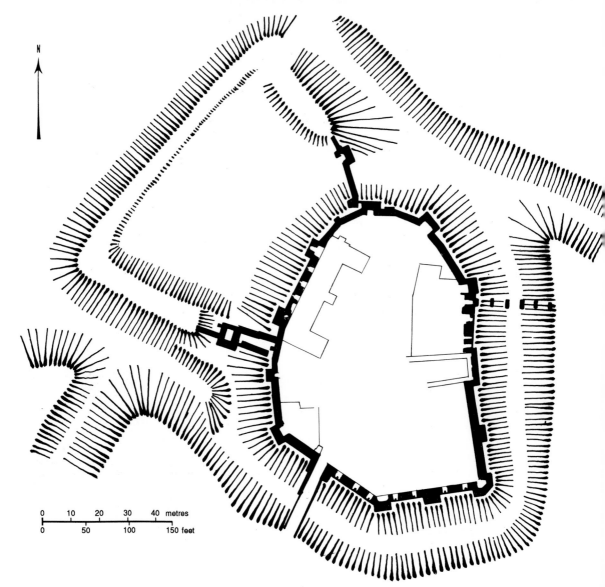

N

| 0 | 10 | 20 | 30 | 40 metres |
| 0 | 50 | 100 | 150 feet |

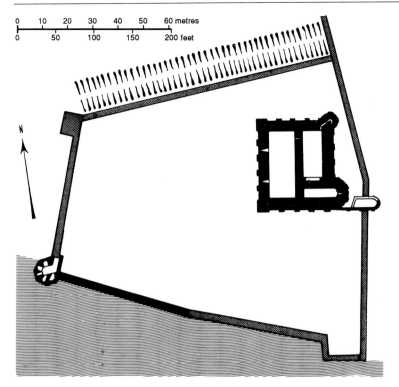

London Castle after the construction of the Bell Tower, showing the conjectural line of north and west curtain. (*After English Heritage*)

(where a new gate was probably made) and then south to the Thames, but attempts to flood it from the river were unsuccessful. The bailey south of the keep became the heart of the castle and the site of the palace buildings which gradually replaced the White Tower in domestic use: they may have been begun by Longchamp but the whole complex has vanished almost without trace. Of this work, the most important survival is the octagonal Bell Tower which defended the south-western corner of the new castle.

The towers of Framlingham Castle and Dover's inner ward follow a simple square or rectangular plan, and mostly have open backs. Such simple ideas were soon revised by designers and masons who applied their minds to stronger and more effective towers. Already in Dover's outer wall a different kind of structure had been built: the Avranches Tower which guarded a re-entrant angle forced by the earthworks of the original hill-fort. The boldly projecting tower transformed a weak point in the defences into a very strong one: each face of this semi-octagonal tower had no less than six arrow loops below the battlements, with shooting positions on two floors. The mural tower was rapidly becoming an aggressive structure of considerable sophistication.

The Bell Tower served a similar function to Dover's Avranches Tower. As built, it rose sheer from the river, so its octagonal plan was chosen not for its strength against the miner, but for good visibility. The lower floor, which stands above some 6 metres (15 feet) of solid masonry, was designed like a twelfth-century pillbox, stone-vaulted

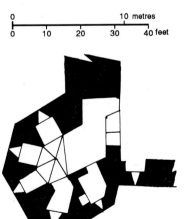

Bell Tower, London Castle, ground-floor plan. (*After English Heritage*)

Arrow-loop from the Bell Tower, London Castle.

and with arrow-loops in every face but one (the side of the tower which faced away from the city was used to accommodate the archers' latrine). There was no access from here to the room above, which was, and still is, residential. The quality of the work is high throughout: even in the wholly functional ground floor, the ribs of the vault spring from corbels carved into leaves, and their junction is masked by a small foliated boss. Today's visitor can only see the outside of the tower, its dangerous slits high above ground level now that the Thames has been pushed south, and it is not easy to imagine it rising from the water at the corner of a twelfth-century castle.

The importance of the Bell and Avranches Towers lies not so much in their non-rectangular plans as in their independence from the walls on which they stand: each is conceived as a building rather than as a mere projection of the wall. It is a strong point capable of separate defence. Other strong towers were added to vulnerable corners of castle perimeters in the two or three decades following the accession of Richard I: for instance, at Lincoln a D-shaped tower was added about 1220 to the north-eastern corner of the bailey; Cobb Hall, as it is known, preserves two of its three original storeys, and both were given over to the needs of crossbowmen. The arrow-loops are positioned so that those in the lower room cover the ground not clearly visible from above; there were also sally ports from which

Cobb Hall, an early thirteenth-century tower at Lincoln Castle. Despite the loss of its upper storey (the battlements are nineteenth-century replacements), it can be seen to be entirely military in purpose, the staggered arrow slits covering every patch of ground beyond the walls. A walled-up sally port can also be seen.

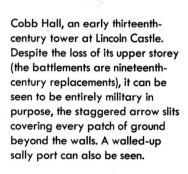

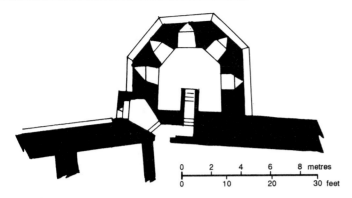

Warkworth Castle: the well-preserved thirteenth-century Grey Mare's Tail Tower. (*After English Heritage*)

soldiers could emerge to engage with an enemy at close quarters. Other less well-preserved examples can be seen at Warkworth, in Northumberland (the semi-octagonal Carrickfergus Tower), and at Kenilworth (Lunn's Tower); both are thought to date from the beginning of the thirteenth century. In a very few years, the methods employed to defend the castle bailey had improved beyond measure; if the keep continued to dominate most castles physically and symbolically, thought and money would henceforward largely be expended on bailey walls and gates and the buildings they protected.

—10—
The Castle at War

John, Henry II's youngest and favourite son, succeeded his childless brother, Richard when the latter was killed by a crossbow bolt in 1199. With the possible exception of Richard III, no other English king has a more controversial reputation than John: genial, lascivious, possessed of the common touch, cruel, paranoid, intelligent, passionate and energetic – such was the contradictory nature of this man who had far more impact on England than ever his brother did. The first turning-point was the loss of Normandy to the French in 1204. England, abruptly separated from continental Europe for the first time since 1066, became the centre of its monarch's dominion: John could not be an absentee like Richard. After 1204 his relationship with the barony, with the clergy, and indeed with the people of England, deteriorated steadily.

A crisis was reached in the early summer of 1215, when all parties, under the guiding wisdom of Stephen Langton, Archbishop of Canterbury, negotiated an agreement designed to regulate the relationship between king and subject.[1] Magna Carta was sealed by John at Runnymede on 19 June and all parties swore to abide by it; the choice of an open meadow rather than a castle for this rendezvous fairly reflects the degree of mistrust which existed between the factions.

That the peace agreed that day should break down within a matter of weeks suggests that, sophisticated though the charter was, the young barons who forced it on the king put more faith in the force of arms than of law; perhaps they had always intended the actual deposition of the king. At any rate, by the early autumn, the country was at war. The struggle for control of the kingdom was waged almost entirely in the eastern and central counties and lasted, on and off, for two years. The part played by castles is revealing and sometimes – in terms of which castles were taken and which were not – surprising. The two which did most to ensure ultimate royalist success, Lincoln and Dover, were at opposite poles of twelfth-century castle design, yet they resisted equally well.

The first action of the war, King John's attempt, during October and November 1215, to recapture the castle of Rochester, is well documented, and vividly conveys the violence of a full-scale siege. Although he still had the support of many powerful barons, when hostilities broke out John sought the assistance of continental mercenaries; he planned to assemble his army at the castle of Dover, where he had recently spent much money completing his father's outer wall. The rebels, for their part, sought to bar John's route to their headquarters in London.

They rode out to Rochester, where the great castle guarded the principal crossing of the Medway and the road from the coast. John had already demanded possession of the archbishop's castle and was enraged to learn that its constable had opened the gates and invited the rebels inside.

Without waiting for his reinforcements, the king marched on the city, leaving his enemies only three days to provision a castle which they had found almost bare. Unless they were relieved, the knights – numbering between 95 and 140 – and other soldiers would soon be short of food.[2] John's first action was to ensure that there would be no relief: he sent troops south to cross the river nearer its source and attack the city from the London side of the Medway. On the second attempt, they took the bridge and broke it down, thus isolating Rochester from London. The royal army pushed their enemies back within the castle and occupied the city, using the cathedral as a makeshift fortress.

But John was temperamentally unsuited to waiting for hunger to deliver the castle, so it is no surprise to find that he assaulted it at once with stone-throwing engines.[3] The five catapults seem to have made little impact on the walls, so John passed to slower but perhaps more effective means: he set miners to work against the south-eastern

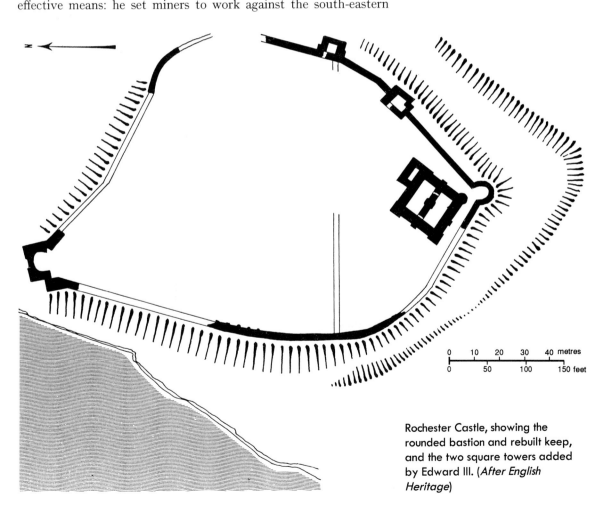

Rochester Castle, showing the rounded bastion and rebuilt keep, and the two square towers added by Edward III. (*After English Heritage*)

corner of the bailey. The mine, whose first recorded use in England was during William I's siege of Exeter in 1068, presented the greatest threat to the besieged. It involved tunnelling under the walls and excavating a large area which was progressively shored up with timber; when complete, it would be filled with brushwood and set alight so that, as the wooden props burned through, the weight of the walls above caused them to collapse into the hole. The only security against the mine was to build on to solid rock or, better still, to surround the castle with a moat whose water would flood his tunnels long before they reached the walls. In desperate circumstances – as at St Andrews Castle in 1546, or Pontefract in 1645 – a counter-mine might be dug out from the castle in an attempt to get at the enemy sappers. King John's miners soon brought down Gundulf's old wall; the royal troops fought their way through the breach, but many of the rebels sought refuge in the great keep.

It is not difficult to imagine the fury with which John ordered the mining of the keep itself. Never before had such resources, and especially such ferocious determination, been brought to bear against the masonry of an English castle. Never before had a castle been defended so desperately by men who knew that, according to the contemporary rules of war, should the castle be taken by assault rather than surrendered, their lives were forfeit. John requested his justiciar, Hubert de Burgh, to send forty fat pigs 'of the sort least

Rochester Castle from the south-east, showing the round tower added to the bailey wall, and the rounded turret with which the keep was repaired after King John brought down the corner with mines in 1215.

good for eating' to light the mine under the keep; it must have been impatience which prompted John to make use of such a simple substance, for in the siege of La Roche-aux-Moines the previous summer, he had experimented with mixtures of sulphur, tallow, gum, pitch and quicksilver. Simple perhaps, but the pig fat worked very well and the south-eastern corner of the keep fractured and collapsed into the mine. Even then the rebels did not give up, but barricaded themselves behind the cross-wall; they were forced by hunger and sickness to capitulate a few days after.

The psychological impact of the fall of Rochester Castle, powerful and well defended as it had been, seems to have been great; indeed a chronicler wrote shortly afterwards that there were few who now put their trust in castles.[4] The power and authority of a king who could hammer down the strongest castle was enormously enhanced, exactly as Prince Louis' failure to take Dover the following year was to undermine his reputation. But to say that few depended on castles was a considerable exaggeration, for they remained the basis of power; about 150 were still held for the king, and the rebels, without John's siege-train, stood little chance of taking them. Instead, they provided bases from which the successful royal forces could assault the lands and castles held against them.

Between December 1215 and March 1216, the king trooped from Winchester to Berwick and back, subduing towns and castles, granting pardons, and restoring individuals and communities to his favour in return for sums ranging from 10 marks to £1,000.[5] By March only London held out, and John was in Hertford preparing to move against it. The rebels had previously offered the English Crown to Prince Louis, son of the French king, but he had been slow to come to their aid. Now, in their darkest hour, he did come, landing at Thanet on 21 May 1216 and joining them in the capital.

Except for short periods of tension, and the end of John's reign was one of these, most English castles had relatively peaceful existences; four or five centuries of occupation may record only one or two short sieges, and often none.[6] Castle Rising is a case in point: the only evidence of a threat to the castle is in the order made by King John from Hertford to fortify it against an attack which, as far as is known, never came; its later history was untroubled. The concept of deterrence is not a recent invention: the castle was one of the rocks on which medieval society was built and when that society was stable, it helped preserve the peace; but when it was not, the castle became the means by which war was fought.

Since the Norman invasion, warfare had turned on the mounted knight and the castle in which he lived. The castle was the means both of protecting the knight's dependants and property, and of providing a base from which to police the lands around it. A troop of armed horsemen could expect to cover about 32 kilometres (20 miles) in a day, so its effective range, if it was to be safe home by nightfall, was between 8 and 16 kilometres (5 and 10 miles). A castle without knights was of no value, so major fortresses were garrisoned throughout the year: forty knights had a duty to defend the royal castle at Norwich in groups of ten for three months each, while Richmond was supposed to be held by thirty knights at a time.[7] However, a minor castle was not maintained so expensively and, for most of the time, would be home only to a constable and few servants and men-at-arms. War did not come without warning, so castles could generally adopt a more domestic appearance, the comfort and daily needs of their inhabitants coming before defence. Land outside the walls was given over to gardens and orchards, and the activities of the farm and estates took up people's time. During the day, the drawbridge would be down, and the gate open, and anyone with business inside would expect to be questioned by a porter, not a soldier.

However, when trouble was abroad, orders were given to prepare for it. Instructions went out to each constable to put his castle on a war-footing. Knights, archers and men-at-arms arrived and had to be found quarters. Cellars were stocked with dried and preserved food, corn, wine and so on, and livestock and their fodder might be brought within the walls. Weapons had to be obtained, either by bringing them from another castle, or by manufacturing them on the spot; during John's wars the constable of Knaresborough Castle spent £100 on its defence, a good part of which must have paid for the 109,000 crossbow quarrels made there at the time. If the smiths were busy making and mending weapons, the carpenters were at work erecting timber hoarding over gateways and on towers; their duties would also involve the construction of the catapults which might be set up on platforms in the bailey. (Nottingham Castle was, from the time of King John, a major royal arsenal and centre for the construction of catapults). Large crossbows, or ballistae, could be positioned on towers whose masonry might be damaged by the recoil from the heavier mangonels. Ditches were cleaned, and if the ramparts between them supported *herrisons* (fences of pointed stakes named after the French word for hedgehog), these were made good where necessary. Thus, in a relatively short time, a castle's aspect could become far more hostile, by a simple shift of emphasis from the domestic to the military.

By the time of King John, the basis for the conduct of warfare had begun to change from a feudal to a financial one; although many of those who held castles for the king in 1216 were feudal tenants, many were paid soldiers, proven military commanders like Fawkes de Bréauté, who eventually held the constableship of the royal castles in the counties of Buckingham, Hertford, Northampton, Bedford and Cambridge. The desire of Richard I and John himself to be able to field larger armies when and where they wanted, had made them more and more amenable to the commutation of feudal service for cash. At the same time, many knights were becoming more interested in improving their estates than in the fortunes of war; after the final loss of Normandy in 1204, it became harder than ever to persuade men with no financial interest there to fight in France. A lump sum which released a knight from his obligation of service was increasingly attractive to both parties. Although the core of the armies fighting in England in 1216 were linked by feudal and personal loyalties, their ranks – particularly in the case of the royal forces – were swollen with professional crossbowmen and engineers, younger sons, landless knights and a good few errant assassins.

The change in the composition of the forces did not yet affect the

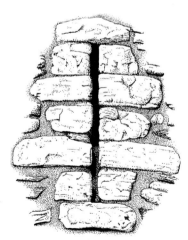

An arrow-slit from early-thirteenth-century work at Dover Castle.

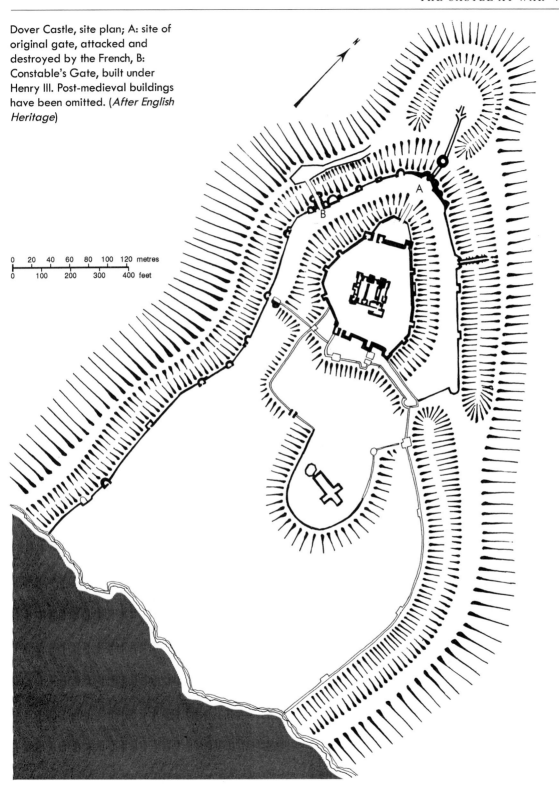

Dover Castle, site plan; A: site of original gate, attacked and destroyed by the French, B: Constable's Gate, built under Henry III. Post-medieval buildings have been omitted. (*After English Heritage*)

way war was waged: it remained, as it had since the emergence of the knight and castle, a question of taking and holding castles. It was dangerous simply to avoid a castle, since its troops might emerge and attack at any moment, but to besiege each one could be disastrously time-consuming. King John's new castle at Odiham in Hampshire tied up the French Army for two weeks in June 1216 and yet, when it was finally surrendered, the besiegers were galled to discover that they had been opposed by only three knights and ten sergeants.[8] It was possible to leave a section of the army to blockade a dangerous castle and move on, but it could be unwise to split one's forces. In practice, however, other factors came into play, and the full-blown siege undergone by Rochester was exceptional. The spirit, loyalty and political position of the constable were enormously important, and never more so than in a civil conflict. Although the French were stoutly resisted at Odiham, in succeeding days the castles of Reigate, Guildford and Farnham were surrendered to them without opposition.[9]

When Prince Louis finally came to the aid of King John's enemies, he brought a full siege-train with him (including the new trebuchet, a catapult far more effective than existing ones), and it was soon put to use. The combined forces of the rebels and the prince began to retake the eastern counties. The heroic resistance of Odiham has been mentioned already, but short and violent sieges were more common, and a number of castles, like Hedingham and Colchester in Essex, changed hands more than once during 1216 and 1217. Others fell as their constables or owners, sure that King John's cause was lost, switched sides. Within three months, the only important castles held for John in the south-east and East Anglia were Windsor, Lincoln and Dover. On the walls of these three fortresses hung the crown of England, but Louis's powerful engines could not batter an entry.

Windsor, under the mercenary leadership of Engelard de Cigogné, underwent a heavy siege and was not taken. The French prince's inability to take Lincoln (defended by the widow of its constable) and Dover not only prevented him from moving against the royalist counties in the west, but also sapped the strength, time and morale of his forces. Crucially, it did nothing for Louis' reputation as a potential king and war-lord. The defences of Dover had been improved by John and now the castle, full of troops commanded by Hubert de Burgh (John's justiciar and a great soldier), was far too dangerous for Louis to leave untaken. Not only did it contain a small army, but the example given by its resistance encouraged the men of Kent and Sussex to harass the French on both land and sea; Louis' communications with France were not secure while Dover stood against him.

The siege began late in June 1216, when a huge French army invested the castle. Behind the ramparts lay two lines of stone walls defended by towers and, overlooking everything, the massive keep. The new trebuchets were set to work at once, lobbing great rocks at the walls, but the English made repeated sorties and killed the French engineers; so effective were these forays that the catapults had to be moved back to a point where they were all but ineffective. Louis directed his assault on the north gate of the outer wall, preparing a belfry and battering rams for the purpose, but opposition was too fierce, and his soldiers were unable to carry the gate. Once again, the attackers turned to the mine, and French sappers drove a tunnel towards the castle. When the mine was fired, it brought down one side of the gatehouse, but the breach was ferociously defended and the French soldiers could not get through; they were repulsed and the gap filled with timber and stones. So, like a terrible arm-wrestling match, the struggle continued without resolution: weeks and months passed and summer turned to autumn. His inability to take Dover, even after four months of constant siege, demoralized his army and damaged Louis' reputation; it became a matter of honour, as if everything depended on this grand form of single combat. By October, a weary stalemate existed when the situation changed abruptly.

John died of dysentery in Newark Castle on 18 October 1216, while a storm raged over the town, and even as messengers brought more letters from rebels wishing to make their peace. On hearing the news, Prince Louis made a truce with the exhausted garrison of Dover and marched north, believing the throne to be his. He had some successes, notably in taking the castle of Orford, but his star was waning. Under the regent, William Marshal, the cause of John's son, the 9-year-old King Henry III, was succeeding and many barons were changing sides for the last time. The castle of Lincoln, still held for John by Nichola de la Haye, was finally relieved by the royalist troops in May 1217, and a large force of English and French knights was routed; the defeat was followed by yet more defections from their party. The French were pushed back to the south-east, and finally Louis returned to the castle which had opposed him so determinedly; he met with no better fortune than during his first attempt. The reinforcements, which alone could have saved him, were destroyed in August by the English Fleet, and the French prince, the last foreign invader of England, was forced to come to terms. By September 1217, two years after the beginning of the barons' war, England was once more at peace.

The fighting had hinged entirely on the possession of castles. In taking Rochester, John had brought about the demoralization of his enemies, who no longer trusted in their castles to withstand him; only the French invasion had prevented him from pressing home the advantage and regaining control of the realm. In turn, that invasion

Dover Castle, general view.

had ultimately failed because the invaders had been unable to take the castles of Lincoln, Windsor and, particularly, Dover.

In considering the fortunes of the various castles between 1215 and 1217, it becomes clear that architecture, and the techniques of fortification, are only a part of the story. Certainly, the advanced design of Dover helped secure it from assault, but much of its strength lay in its size, its hilltop site and in the courage of its defenders. The new castle of Orford was taken with little trouble by the French, while Framlingham fell quickly to the royal forces. At the same time the decidedly old-fashioned castle of Lincoln was held throughout the wars, though the very town at its feet was in French hands. Real security was only to be obtained through treating feudal dependants justly, and paying wages promptly. Unless relationships with those into whose trust castles were given were kept in as good repair as the buildings themselves, all the ingenuity in the world would be of no use. Finally, there was the unquantifiable element of belief – in the will to overcome, and in the justice of the cause. In a society which believed that God would give victory to the man in the right, the success or failure of a siege as critical as those of Rochester or Dover had an importance which reached far beyond the purely military. All in all, the royalist party must have felt a good deal of confidence in young King Henry's castles in 1217: the bones of the kingdom had held it together in the time of its greatest need.

—11—
Castles Without Keeps

King John had been, like his brother and his father, a great builder of castles. Apart from his new foundations at Odiham in Hampshire, Hanley in Worcestershire and at Sauvey in Leicestershire, there were important works at Dover, Corfe, Knaresborough, Horston in Derbyshire, Kenilworth, Nottingham and Scarborough.[1] Among other royal castles to benefit from his attention were those of Hertford, Tickhill, Cambridge, Guildford, Peveril, Wallingford and Windsor. Although relatively little of this work can still be seen, it appears to have developed rather than altered the ideas of Henry II. At Dover, for instance, John followed his father's plans by completing the outer wall, but he gave his towers newly fashionable rounded faces. The curved wall, with no vulnerable right angles and on which missiles tended to strike glancing blows, had clear advantages. Consequently, D-shaped and, to a lesser extent, round towers had something of a vogue during the thirteenth century and are particularly characteristic of the period. The rectangular tower, however, always easier to build and furnish, was not abandoned; indeed it had an Indian summer during the fourteenth century and was used at a number of important castles, including Pontefract, Rochester, London and Pickering, as well as in such hybrid structures as Bolton: the coincidence of this revival with the decline in the castle's military importance cannot be fortuitous.

But in the decades after 1200, it was the rounded tower which castle builders preferred. Helmsley Castle, in North Yorkshire, was built between about 1200 and 1227, and is a curious example of the developments in planning which were happening at the time. It was a rectangular enclosure with round, or partly round, towers at three of the four corners; on the north was a twin-towered gatehouse, and astride the long east curtain stood an unusual keep, rounded to the field, but square within the castle. The whole castle was greatly strengthened by an outer bank which, though it only carried a timber palisade, echoes the concentric planning first attempted at Dover, and fully developed at London some fifty or sixty years later. The use of such forms was undoubtedly advanced. However, a square keep-like tower was built in a re-entrant angle on the west curtain, and a simple rectangular gatehouse – on the model of Tickhill – guarded the entrance to the castle from the south.

To find such old-fashioned and, in the case of the west tower, clumsy arrangements alongside the more sophisticated ones described above, suggests that Robert de Roos, the castle's builder, was either unsure of the use, or unconvinced by the superiority, of the currently fashionable ideas. The whole design of Helmsley, strong as it is, suggests indecision: ideas pull in opposite directions. The keep, which defends the curtain, seems to aspire to become a wall-tower,

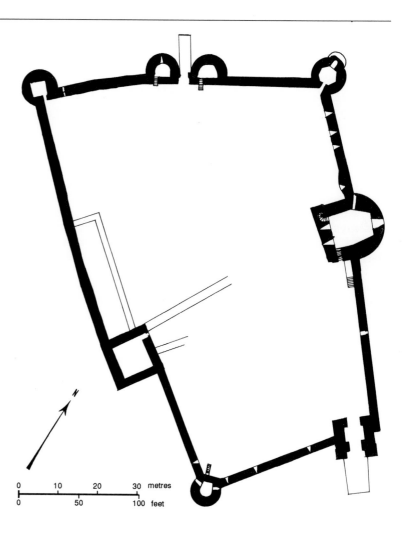

Helmsley Castle, ground plan of the castle built in the early thirteenth century. (*After English Heritage*)

0   10   20   30 metres
0   50   100 feet

but across the courtyard the west tower (at the upper end of the hall and clearly private accommodation for the lord) wants to be a keep.[2]

In the 1220s, as work at Helmsley came to an end, a chain of three castles was built across the north Midlands, each different, yet revealing none of the indecision apparent at Helmsley. The builder was Rannulf, Earl of Chester and of Lincoln, and a loyal supporter of King John. Returning from a crusade in 1220, and presumably in pursuit of his grandfather's ambition of linking Chester with Lincoln, Rannulf began the construction of castles at Beeston in Cheshire, Chartley in Staffordshire, and Bolingbroke in Lincolnshire.[3] Of the three, Chartley is the least adventurous, probably because it was a reconstruction of an existing motte-and-bailey castle, so the plan was predetermined. It stands on a thin ridge, not high but, in the rolling mid-Staffordshire countryside, commanding very wide views. The motte, which supports the remains of a circular tower keep, lies at the western end of the ridge, and below it is a rectangular bailey, abandoned and much overgrown. It originally had six D-shaped towers, though only the three on the south stand to any height; they are, like all of Rannulf's work, of well-dressed stone, and have cross-shaped arrow loops. The outer bailey, a little further along the ridge, probably never had stone defences.

Beeston Castle was begun in 1225, on a high outcrop which commanded the south-eastern approach to Chester. Most of the hill was taken into a vast outer ward enclosed by a stone curtain; a large twin-towered gatehouse defended the entrance and close-set D-shaped towers dominated the wall itself. Seven of these towers survive in part; they had two storeys and were left open-backed so that a tower overrun by an enemy would afford him no protection from crossbowmen in the bailey. The towers were originally taller than the wall, which could be raked by crossbows' bolts from their summits; by dividing it into short stretches they also helped ensure that an enemy who gained the wall-walk was trapped between two bastions. The northern tip of the crag formed the inner ward, isolated from the rest of the castle by a deep rock-cut ditch which provided the building stone. To the north and west, precipitous falls made a plain wall sufficient defence, but above the new ditch a thick stone curtain was built and studded with five D-shaped towers. Two were built as one unit to form a gatehouse with a passage between them and a single large room above. No keep was built. This citadel was so inaccessible that it is impossible to see how it could be taken by direct assault: it

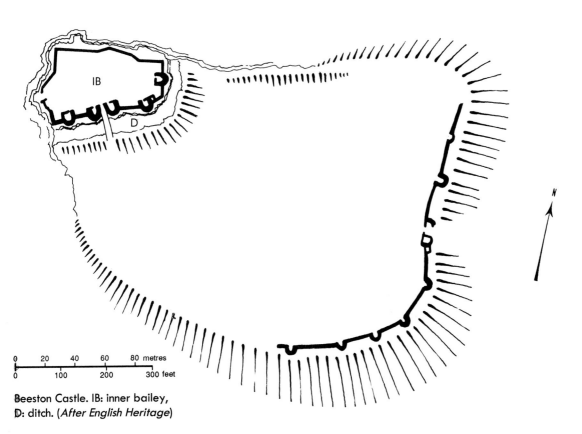

Beeston Castle. IB: inner bailey, D: ditch. (*After English Heritage*)

was as near to being impregnable as it is possible to get. Sadly, the castle was unfinished at Rannulf's death, and the domestic buildings were never built by its subsequent royal owners, for whom Beeston was a useful military tool, but never a home.

The third castle, Bolingbroke, is so ruinous that there was no visible masonry at all when excavation of its grassy mounds began in 1965; in the event the whole ground floor was recovered and proved to be of great interest. The castle lies in a hollow at the southern end of the Lincolnshire wolds, in what is today a small village, but was then a market town close to the port of Boston. William de Roumare, brother-in-law of the old earl and his accomplice in the seizure of Lincoln, had built an earth and wood castle about a hundred years before, but Rannulf abandoned that hilltop site and started again in the valley. A glance at the plan explains why, for it is regular and compact, unsuited to a hillside: the castle formed a hexagon with massive towers at five corners and a twin-towered gatehouse at the

Beeston Castle: the gateway to the inner ward above its rock-cut ditch.

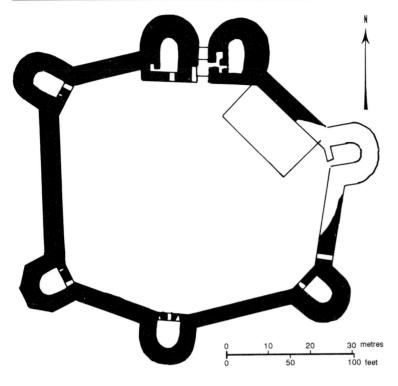

Bolingbroke Castle, ground plan.
(*After J. Forde-Johnson*)

sixth.[4] The second, and perhaps more important, reason for the move
was the broad moat – about 31 metres (100 feet) across – which once
surrounded the castle; the essential pragmatism of the castle builder,
which made him choose a rocky crag at Beeston, led Rannulf to prefer
water in the soft Lincolnshire soil. On completion, the castle presented a tight group of towers linked by straight lengths of curtain-wall,
above which they rose. Timber-framed buildings which, with the
rooms in the towers, formed the accommodation, were built against
the inner face of the walls; windows gave on to the central courtyard
rather than the outside world.

Rannulf died in 1232, and his heir in 1237; the line was extinguished and the castle passed into other hands, becoming a royal
possession in 1399. It remained important throughout the Middle
Ages, replacing Lincoln as the principal Crown fortress in the county.
Leland, who saw it in the 1540s, called it 'meetly well maintained',
and the antiquary Gervase Holles, describing it in the seventeenth
century, had nothing but praise for its strength and 'uniforme'
aspect.[5] Although, like most castles at the time, its rooms and lodgings were decayed, and some roofs had fallen, Holles felt that, once
repaired, it could 'receyve a very great prince with all his trayne'. Its
life was terminated by Parliament in 1648 when, as a result of its
having been held for King Charles, an order was made to slight the
castle.

That it could be described as 'uniforme' 400 years after its construction implies not only that it was built so, but also that its later
owners found little cause to alter the castle: there was indeed no

A cross-shaped loop from Chartley Castle, with a 'fish-tail' base permitting better coverage of the ground at the foot of the tower.

reason why they should, since it was built to a plan which would become more and more popular during the following centuries. Only two or three decades after a first castle with towered walls and no keep had been built at Framlingham, Rannulf had developed the idea to a point where it would not be substantially improved upon by later designers. Framlingham was a wall thrown round a group of buildings, a ringwork with a stone palisade instead of a timber one, but Bolingbroke was a single building, towers, walls and apartments forming a unit.

The new castles built in England during the thirteenth and fourteenth centuries – though it is an ever-decreasing number – seem almost exclusively to follow the concept which first emerges in Lincolnshire during the 1220s. The great Welsh castles of Edward I, although certainly more sophisticated in their details, are similar to Bolingbroke in seeking to combine towered curtain with accommodation to make one strong building; later castles like Bodiam, in Sussex, or Sheriff Hutton and Bolton, in Yorkshire, find new idioms to articulate the same idea.

The origin of Rannulf's ideas is obviously important and, since he began work on his return from the Middle East, it is natural to look for sources there – particularly since the experience of crusading warfare is often said to have transformed the English castle. However,

The low ruins of Bolingbroke Castle, seen from the now-dry moat.

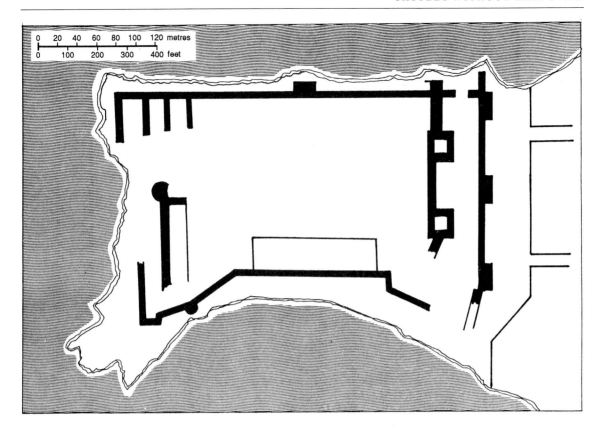

the case for the influence of the military architecture of Palestine on
that of England remains unproven: not enough is known, and too
many background differences exist to make comparison easy. The
mountainous topography of the Middle East, for example, lent itself
naturally to the construction of crag-top fortresses, while the shortage of trees made the use of stone vaults – which are uncommon in
English castles – an appropriate way of roofing towers. The political
and military context was equally different, with many castles serving
a purely military purpose, unencumbered by the social and administrative duties of an English castle. The perpetual shortage of man-
power influenced design as did the great military orders – the
Templars, Hospitallers and others – whose communal religious life
created an architecture all of its own.

The great fortresses of the period – Saone, Margat, Safita, Krak des
Chevaliers – impressive as they are, remain the products of local con-
ditions and local culture: they are neither more nor less like those of
England, than are those of France, Germany, Italy or Spain.

Chastel Pélerin for instance, begun in 1218 on a previously unfortified site, is contemporary to Beeston and Bolingbroke, but has little
in common with them. The site was a peninsula on the Mediterranean
coast, south of present-day Haifa, a landing-place for the Christian
pilgrims who provided the labour and the name. The castle belonged
to the Knights Templar and presumably represents their ideas of

Chastel Pélerin, sketch ground plan.
(*After T. E. Lawrence*)

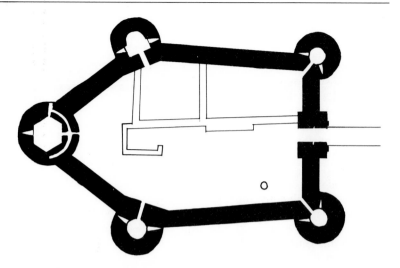

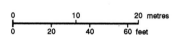

Montlhéry Castle, ground plan.
(*After Viollet-le-Duc*)

effective fortification, so it is noteworthy to find that rectangular rather than round towers were used. The whole strength of the castle lay in two massive lines of walls and a ditch barring access to the peninsula, and the castle itself, from the mainland. The low outer wall had three towers, and was dominated by a higher wall behind it on which stood two further towers of keep-like dimensions. T E Lawrence described the design as unintelligent, and claimed that its strength was brute strength; none the less, the castle was never taken, unlike the far more sophisticated Krak des Chevaliers, a concentric Hospitaller stronghold which fell after a five-week siege in the spring of 1271.[6] But in any case Rannulf, who fought in Egypt not Palestine, did not see these famous castles at first hand, and if he heard about them, he clearly did not imitate them.[7]

The experiences of the crusaders probably influenced the English castle principally through the filter of French architecture. Indeed, when seeking a source for Rannulf's ideas, France is much more rewarding than the Middle East. In 1204, when Normandy was finally lost to Philip Augustus, Rannulf held extensive lands in the duchy as well as being married, for a time, to Constance of Brittany, so he must have known the country and its castles well.[8] As early as 1162, a keepless castle had been built at La Robertière, in Eure et Loire, where the Count of Dreux enclosed a quadrangle with a stone wall reinforced with irregularly placed square and round towers. During the first three decades of the thirteenth century, the concept was developed and used widely; among many examples may be mentioned some built both by the counts of Dreux and by King Philip of France, a castle builder as energetic as Henry II of England.

At Montlhéry, in Essonne, south-west of Paris, Philip built a castle with a tall round keep dominating a rectangular bailey, walled and strengthened with four circular towers; and the resemblance of this plan to that of Chartley is striking. At Yèvre le Châtel, in Loiret, stand the ruins of a small keepless castle, probably also built by King Philip; the castle is lozenge-shaped with a tower at each corner, and a hall along one side of the enclosure.

Perhaps the closest to Bolingbroke is the Dreux castle of Fère-en-Tardenois, in Aisne: this was raised in 1206 on a scarped hill to the west of Reims, and is a rough oval defended by seven round towers, separated by short straight walls, and a gatehouse. The accommodation inside was rebuilt during the sixteenth century, and subsequently ruined, so little can be said about its disposition in 1206, except that it abutted the curtain. Finally, between 1228 and 1234, a castle was raised at Boulogne which follows the same keepless plan; again it forms an oval with seven round or D-shaped towers in addition to a massive twin-towered gatehouse.[9]

It is improbable that Beeston, Chartley and Bolingbroke were directly modelled on any of these examples, but they show how much thought was being given to this sort of castle in thirteenth-century France. It is more likely that Rannulf, with his important interests in France, should be influenced by what he saw and heard about there than by his time in Egypt. But his was an expanding world where people travelled much, where cultures met in conflict and in peace, where the arts of warfare and architecture were pursued with equal vigour: centuries later it is rarely possible to draw precisely the routes along which ideas travel.

The castle of Bolingbroke, like those at Fère and Boulogne, was a major advance on current thinking, and one which was not substantially improved upon by later designers. That is not to say that there

A latrine drain which once emptied into Bolingbroke Castle moat.

was no further development in the English castle: each generation altered, embellished and rethought the architectural idiom until the mid-fifteenth century. But in most cases the central idea was the strong building where living quarters and defensive structures formed a single unit. There is more difference between Bolingbroke and Lincoln, than there is between it and Harlech or Bodiam.

—12—
Shimmering Halls

The medieval castle was a weapon, a means of territorial control and administration, and those purposes profoundly affected its design and use. But it was also a home, the place in which a knight, his family, dependants and servants lived, and the domestic needs of everyday life exerted an influence equally important. Nor should those varying purposes be seen to be *necessarily* contradictory, though they often were, for conspicuous consumption as a means of demonstrating wealth and, by implication, power is an idea almost as old as power itself. To live splendidly, as a medieval king or baron, was not only pleasant in itself, but sustained belief in a man's authority. The castles of the thirteenth century grew more splendid not only in their military aspects but also in their domestic accommodation. Medieval images of castles as shimmering white palaces, tall pinnacles reaching towards heaven, symbols of pure majesty in a rural landscape, are indeed images, but they present, none the less, a mixture of reality and aspiration: they reveal how their owners wanted to see their castles and perhaps how others actually did. In *Sir Gawain and the Green Knight*, a fourteenth-century poet attempts to create the same picture in words:

> The comeliest castle that ever a knight owned,
> It was pitched on a plain, with a park all round,
> Impregnably palisaded with pointed stakes,
> And containing many trees in its two-mile circumference.
>
> The knight, still on his steed, stayed on the bank
> Of the deep double ditch that drove round the place.
> The wall went into the water wonderfully deep,
> And then to a huge height upwards it reared
> In hard hewn stone, up to the cornice;
> Built under the battlements in the best style, courses jutted
> And turrets protruded between, constructed
> With loopholes in plenty with locking shutters.
> No better barbican had ever been beheld by that knight.
> And inside he could see a splendid high hall
> With towers and turrets on top, all tipped with crenellations,
> And pretty pinnacles placed along its length,
> With carved copes, cunningly worked.
> Many chalk-white chimneys the chevalier saw
> On the tops of towers twinkling whitely.[1]

In this cynical age such images can appear wholly false when contrasted with a picture of the Middle Ages as a world of mud and slaughter, plague and superstition, where brevity was the only

A dog-tooth ornament from the windows of Oakham Castle Hall.

redeeming feature of a nasty and brutish life. Although the incomparable brilliance of its ecclesiastical architecture goes some way towards its rehabilitation, the castle remains largely a symbol of barbarism. This is, of course, but half the truth. It is the nature of massive towers and deep ditches to survive the passage of time when the flimsier walls of bedrooms and halls, to say nothing of their furniture, curtains and paintings, are destroyed like matchwood in the gale of history. Survivals of these domestic parts of English castles are rare and scattered – a hall here, a chapel there, a kitchen somewhere else – but they do exist and provide an essential counterpoint to the crossbow loops and barbicans of the castle at war.

Perhaps the earliest complete example is the castle hall at Oakham, once the county town of Rutland, now subsumed into Leicestershire. First built before 1086, the castle had a low motte in the corner of a square bailey, and was surrounded by a moat. The mound was later buried in the castle rampart, perhaps during the thirteenth century when a stone curtain-wall with at least two round towers was built. In this enclosure stands the hall built for Walkelin de Ferrers, the castle's owner, built between 1180 and 1190. As Earl of Derby, Ferrers also held castles at Duffield in Derbyshire, represented only by the neglected foundations of a huge keep, and Tutbury in Staffordshire, where later ruins still jut from an enormous hill. Oakham was not in this class, its purpose as the centre of a large agricultural estate and forest being more economic than military. That nature is emphasized in the survival of the hall which, as a magistrates' court, continues to serve one of its original functions.

It is a spacious and elegant room, built by masons who had been working on the Gothic rebuilding of Canterbury Cathedral. The hall measures 20 by 13 metres (66 by 44 feet) internally and has two aisles; the arcades, of four bays, have wide round arches and slim circular piers with crocket capitals exactly like those at Canterbury. The capitals themselves, the dog-tooth ornament round the windows and arches, and the figure sculpture on the spandrels, are carved with such freshness and cleanness of line that it is easy to forget the work is 700 years old.

The hall was always the most important room in the castle and the centre of activity. At one end sat the lord of the manor, at the other were doors to the courtyard and to service rooms and a kitchen, often screened by a wooden partition. Buttery and pantry stood on either side of a passage leading to the kitchen which might, given the dangers of fire, be a free-standing building; above the service rooms, or raised over a storeroom at the other end of the hall, was a private bedchamber. A chapel for the castle's inhabitants stood in the bailey, and one or more private chapels might also be provided for the lord and his family. Rooms and lodgings for chaplains, constables and other socially elevated members of the community were also provided in the inner bailey of most castles: at Pickering, the foundations of a large house occupied by the constable can still be seen.

The farm buildings – essential to a self-sufficient agrarian community – were generally contained in an outer ward and included a dairy, bakery and brewhouse, barns and stables, a forge and a mill (Leeds Castle had a water-mill, but horse-mills, like those at Bolton or

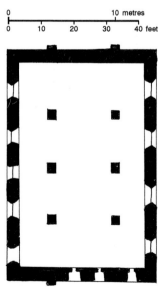

0 _____ 10 metres
0   10   20   30   40 feet

Oakham Castle hall, ground plan.
(*After Derek Renn*)

The arcades of Oakham Castle hall are supported by pillars with exquisite crocketted capitals.

Middleham, were more common). In a minor castle like Oakham, it is likely that pigs, poultry and other domestic animals would have found a home here. Finally, beyond the walls lay pleasure gardens (useful for herbs), orchards, fishponds, and the fields of the demesne – the castle's own land on which every tenant had a duty to work.

The appearance and plan of these domestic buildings varied greatly, but was largely without overall symmetry. Designers were capable of great ingenuity when required to compress living-rooms into a single unit, as the keep of Orford testifies, but where there was space, buildings were arranged primarily for convenience. This made changes and additions easy, and created pleasant courtyards and open spaces. In the early wooden castles, the buildings were simply enclosed by the palisade but, as stone replaced timber, it became common to abut the buildings on to the inside face of the wall, as was done at Conisbrough and Bolingbroke.

In a number of lesser castles, however, and Oakham was one of these, the stone curtain continued to enclose a free-standing collection of buildings in the fashion of an ordinary manor-house. Although the greater protection afforded by towered walls made it possible to build more pleasant, unfortified domestic suites in the bailey, the cost of modernizing an old castle was enormous. The Earl of Derby, a wealthy man and holder of strong castles at Tutbury and Duffield, could afford to carry out work largely domestic in nature at his castle at Oakham. Without the benefit of towered walls Oakham Castle became, in reality, a fortified manor-house, whose value was economic and whose duties were administrative and judicial instead of military: it was kept in good repair during the next century and more because it was the centre of a manor whose value steadily increased. Few of the hundreds of castles built in England between 1066 and 1154 were important enough to maintain at the apex of current design; the rest either became fortified manors, like Oakham, or, like Thetford, were abandoned altogether. During the next three centuries, castles in England would find it increasingly difficult to justify the cost of their maintenance in the face of other demands on their owners' purses.

But no dislocation of the roles of home and fortress was yet apparent in the principal castles of the king and the major barons. In the mainstream of the English castle's development, as against the back-waters and quiet pools, the combination of functions was energetically pursued, as the reconstruction of the Tower of London by Henry III demonstrates. The young king's regents may have been prompted to improve the tower's defences because of the role London had played in the struggle against King John.

The work, which was begun in 1220, transformed the area south of the White Tower, which already served as an inner ward, into a much stronger unit. A round tower, the Lanthorn, was built on the south-eastern corner of the castle, where the east wall met the river.[2] The river wall was rebuilt, and a very large drum tower – the Wakefield – built astride it, next to a water gate, known today as the Bloody Tower. The west side of the inner ward was closed by the main guard wall and the twin-towered Coldharbour Gate was inserted between it and the keep. The new inner bailey was a rectangular area between the Conqueror's keep and the river, well protected by a tower at each corner. Within it, the hall, chambers, kitchen and so on, of a principal royal palace were disposed. This first building campaign introduced, in the Wakefield Tower, a new round donjon of the sort then being built in France.

In the early years of the thirteenth century, during and after the battle for Normandy, the French king Philip Augustus had added round keeps to his own, and to newly won, castles. The first of these may have been the tower added to Gisors (surrendered to Philip by Prince John in 1193, while his brother Richard lay in an Austrian prison); it was built astride the curtain and replaced the existing keep, isolated on a central motte, as the castle's strong point. It stands whole today, its three floors vaulted to protect against fire, and well provided with arrow loops. Raised about 1196, it was widely imitated in the following half-century, both by its builder and by others.

Most English barons who campaigned in France during these years must have learnt from what they saw: Hubert de Burgh, for instance, builder of a round keep at Skenfrith in Monmouthshire, was actually held prisoner by Philip after 1204. The circular keep, placed so as to help defend the castle perimeter, became positively fashionable, and about a dozen were built in Wales in the early thirteenth century, including fine examples at Tretower and Bronllys in Powys. By then, most English castles had keeps of one sort or another, and the only examples of the new style found in England itself are at Barnard Castle, on the Tees, and London.

The Wakefield Tower, like the Bell Tower, had a ground floor devoted to defence and an upper floor which formed a private residential apartment, in this case designed for the king's own use. The king's hall and chamber lay along the inner face of the river wall, so the Wakefield Tower provided a sort of inner sanctum to which Henry could withdraw. This large octagonal room gives a fair indication of the architectural grace of which the thirteenth century was becoming capable.[3] It had windows overlooking the river and

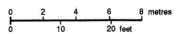

Gisors, section of the donjon. (*After A. de Caumont*)

opposite them was a recess which framed the king's chair of state. Next to this is a large hooded fireplace, while on the other side, once hidden behind a screen, was an oratory.

The small size of this room when compared with the halls of the period, and its relationship to the more public rooms in the courtyard below, underline the social changes which had taken place since the Conqueror's time. Then, the entire household could be catered for in the White Tower and most of the royal business was conducted publicly in the hall; now, the new tower was but one element of a complex of domestic accommodation. The genuinely communal life of the Norman hall was too crude, too unsophisticated for the court of Henry III, although its simplicity still had a sentimental appeal. It is probably not coincidental that baronial complaints about the king's favourites began to make themselves heard during Henry's reign: if smaller rooms in greater numbers increased the king's privacy, they also fuelled suspicion. Who knew what the king's advisers and friends were whispering to him in private? Here are the first signs of the hall's relegation from its central place in the household to the mere repository of coats and umbrellas it generally is today.

Paradoxically, as the hall loses its real importance, so it becomes more and more grandiose. Henry III's hall at London has long been destroyed, but its contemporary can be seen at Winchester – indeed it is the only substantial survivor of one of the country's greatest royal castles. It covers more than twice the area of the hall at Oakham, but of more importance from an aesthetic point of view, it is far loftier. It is divided into nave and aisles by two grand arcades, the pillars of which are of dark Purbeck marble, and it is lit by tall traceried windows. Its beauty characterizes the architecture of Henry III, and suggests something of the treasures which have been lost elsewhere. The chamber in the Wakefield Tower, for example, is all that is left of a huge programme of work on the castle's domestic accommodation.

There is no trace today of the five shiploads of Purbeck marble bought in 1239–40, nor of the quantities of carved woodwork and wainscotting accounted for. The very walls of the king's chamber have gone, still more its glazed windows and their shutters painted with the royal arms; likewise the queen's chamber, panelled and painted with roses, along with its privy (for which it had been necessary to build a new turret). The two small bells and the stained-glass windows depicting the Virgin and Child, the Trinity and St John have been lost from the chapel in the White Tower. That building itself no longer gleams with Henry's whitewash, while even the lead drainpipes he provided, so that rainwater would not stain the walls, have long since been melted down.[4] The Tower of London was favoured, but by no means unique: everywhere he went, Henry issued the most detailed writs ordering the improvement of his castles and houses. Over £10,000 was spent at Windsor for instance, largely on domestic work which included a whole new set of royal apartments in the lower ward. At Winchester, the chambers, including that of Henry's mistress Rosamund, were rebuilt, wainscoted and decorated, and a map of the world painted in the hall.

Henry's attention to detail went beyond the buildings: at Bristol Castle, the clothes issued to staff (four janitors, a cook, two carters,

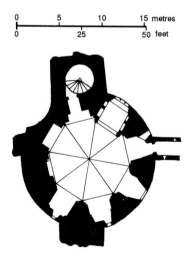

0   5   10   15 metres
0   25   50 feet

Wakefield Tower, plan of the principal floor. (*After English Heritage*)

Mid-thirteenth-century monument to a knight at St Thibault (Côte-d'Or).

seven watchmen, a clerk, a spenser (steward) and a recluse) were carefully specified and in a number of cases had linings of lambskin. The enormous variety of meats, poultry, fish and fruit enjoyed by the royal court is hard to imagine today, but the exotic provisions ordered for Christmas 1236 at Marlborough Castle, including dates, figs, pressed grapes and ginger, indicate both a highly sophisticated taste and the wealth to satisfy it.[5]

But for all the luxury of his life-style, Henry III remained a medieval king whose position and power depended on the strength of his castles. Following his coronation, at the age of 9, and the gradual re-establishment of peace, the king's ministers gave their attention to the defences of the king's castles. Men like Peter des Roches, Bishop of Winchester, William Marshal and the justiciar, Hubert de Burgh

A stair built into the thickness of the keep wall at Barnard Castle.

were anxious to secure the kingdom for their young lord; they knew, and none better than Hubert de Burgh who had held Dover, how great was the need to make good the damage caused in the fighting of 1215–17, and to take back into royal control the many castles which John had entrusted to mercenary castellans. Once recovered, the castles had to be repaired and, where possible, strengthened.

Dover, so important in the recent wars, was one of the first to receive attention: the breached north gate was blocked with the existing coagulation of towers, and a new gate and barbican, of sophisticated but curious design, was contrived on the west side. The smashed wall of Rochester Castle was made good, shortly after 1221, by the insertion of the strong tower which stands there today; but repairs to the keep progressed more slowly, and were completed only in 1232. Lincoln, so long and so bravely defended, was not neglected: between 1217 and 1234 about £580 was spent on the keep and the east gate, which was rebuilt and strengthened by the addition of a barbican. By 1230 work had begun at Windsor Castle on the curtain and the three enormous towers which close the west end of the lower ward and face the town; though restored in the last century, they still impress, and were powerful additions to the castle's defences.

The military works undertaken by his ministers in Henry's early years were continued throughout his uneasy reign. The king was personally unwise and politically insensitive; dissent which had grown under his father's rule was not stilled by such a man. The civil

London Castle: the improvements of Henry III. IB: inner bailey, WT: Wakefield Tower, G: site of probable gateway. (*After English Heritage*)

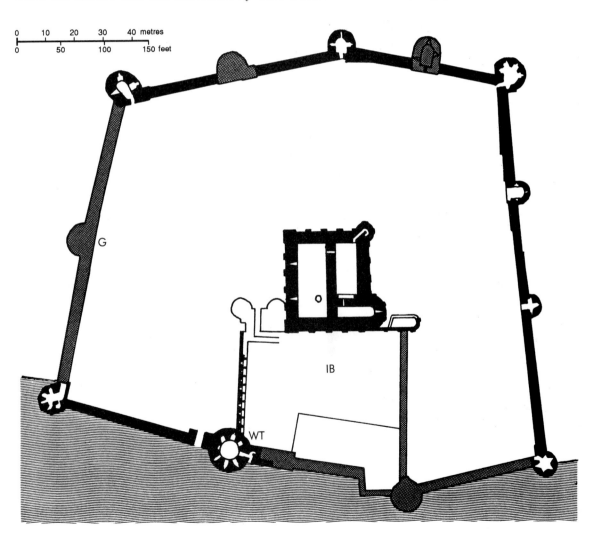

A double-cross arrow-slit, Barnwell
Castle, Northamptonshire.

tensions which finally erupted into open conflict in 1264 were ever-present and Henry, much as he might have wished to spend on the domestic parts of his castles, was never able to neglect their military condition. The reconstruction of Westminster Abbey captured his heart and £50,000 of his money, but he also had to spend £2,500 on the castle at York, following a visit in 1244. He further improved the well-tried defences of Dover, and spent some £8,500 on the walls, towers, keep and gatehouse of Winchester Castle.

At Newcastle-upon-Tyne, a large new gate, perhaps inspired by that at Dover, was built out into the ditch at a cost of over £500. In order to restrain the piratical activities of its lord, a new castle with a rectangular keep was raised on the island of Lundy in the Bristol Channel. The middle bailey at Nottingham was walled and given 'a good stone gateway with twin towers where the gate now is, a chamber above it with a leaden roof and a fireplace, and two round towers with loopholes at the angles of the bailey, open towards the castle'.[6] The barbican was added to Scarborough Castle, walls and towers to the outer bailey at Corfe, and lesser works undertaken at castles such as Northampton, Carlisle and Oxford.

In 1239, immediately after a political crisis which had forced him to take temporary refuge within the Tower, Henry began a complete transformation of that castle, wrapping his gilded palace within a powerful circuit of walls. The first result was another enlargement of the area occupied by the fortress: the east wall was demolished, the ditch filled and work began on a new curtain some 46 metres (150 feet) further out. More land was also taken on the north side and at least £166 was paid as compensation to people who suffered losses as a result.

Henry's intention was to surround the inner ward on its three landward sides with a new towered wall similar to that being completed at Dover. The river side of the castle was left untouched, except for an eastward extension to the new corner of the site, where the Salt Tower was built. The north-east corner was defended by the circular Martin Tower, and the wall running south to the river by the Broad Arrow and Constable Towers, both D-shaped. Three similar towers studded the north curtain and the large, almost ovoid, Devereux Tower stood at its west end. All this work survives, though in some parts rebuilt or masked, like so much of the castle, by nineteenth-century buildings.[7] It is entirely of its time: thick straight walls divided into short lengths by well-designed towers, rounded to the field and studded with arrow-loops for an aggressive defence. But, as was becoming common, the towers also provided bedrooms which improved the standard of accommodation offered to valued household officials and loyal friends; each tower is a perfect balance of military and domestic function.

The west curtain and the main gate, which stood on the site of the present Beauchamp Tower, caused problems. Work must have proceeded apace, and the gate been nearing completion, for it collapsed in the spring of 1240, to be followed exactly a year later by a section of the wall beside it; the citizens looked on with glee and put it down to the intervention of St Thomas Becket, for whom, perhaps because he had opposed the Crown, they seem to have felt a special affection. How and when the damage was made good is not known, for the west curtain was swept away thirty years later by Edward I. The last substantial work ordered by Henry was the creation of a broad moat, filled by the Thames, all the way round the castle.

Henry was right to mistrust the citizens of London, for in the crisis of 1258 to 1265, they sided with Simon de Montfort and his friends in their attempt to restrain the power of the Crown. There is some irony in the fact that, despite all Henry's work, London served once more as a base for the rebels, and the great metropolitan castle was out of his reach. When the conflict came to a head, outside Lewes on 14 May 1264, de Montfort had the armed bands of London on his left flank.

—13—
The Classic Moment

The thirteenth century – almost entirely the time of Henry III and his son Edward – was characterized by expansion of all sorts: economic, cultural, intellectual and territorial. Perhaps because the English Crown's continental interests were now limited to Gascony, its military power was turned on those parts of the British Isles which had not yet accepted its sovereignty. Wales, Scotland and Ireland all received the attentions of their stronger neighbour and so, during the reigns of Henry and Edward, the most innovative examples of the English castle are to be found outside England itself. New foundations of the period are virtually absent south of the Tees and east of the Severn, while the often-important works of renewal undertaken at the older castles have vanished in the wholesale destruction of fortresses like Nottingham, Cambridge, Winchester and Bristol. Nevertheless, both Henry and his son devoted, like their royal predecessors, at least a tenth of their annual income – sometimes considerably more – to building works.

In this context, it would appear absurd to suggest that, within England itself, the castle's *tactical* importance was already declining in the 1260s, but the fact remains that the civil war of those years, unlike the struggles of King John's reign, was not fought over castles. The alliance of barons and Londoners, led by Simon de Montfort, defeated the royal forces in open battle at Lewes; a day's fighting left the earl triumphant, holding King Henry and Prince Edward prisoner. A year later, the situation was reversed in an equally brief, and just as violent, encounter at Evesham, where de Montfort himself was killed.

The only siege forms an interesting postscript to the war itself: the leaderless remnants of the opposition were trapped in Kenilworth Castle where, protected on all sides by water, they withstood the concerted assaults of the king's troops for six months. They eventually surrendered, in December 1266, when provisions had been exhausted. The siege demonstrated that no castle, however strong, could hold out indefinitely in territory held by, and loyal to, the forces besieging it.[1] An open battle to secure mastery, followed by a steady suffocation of any hostile castles, was beginning to appear an effective strategy of war.

Although the capitulation of Kenilworth marked the resumption of power by the Crown, royal authority had been seriously damaged by Henry's conduct, and was not easily regained; its re-establishment became one of Edward's fundamental goals in the coming years. The ageing king's reign meandered on until his death in 1272, but his son was already in charge, guided by a subtle and intelligent papal legate. So well was the work of reparation done, that in 1270 the prince was able to go on a crusade with taxes voted by Parliament; so stable was that work that he could take two years to return to England after his father's death. King Edward I was crowned in his late father's abbey church in August 1274. He was 35 years old.

The new king soon turned his thoughts to a final transformation of the Tower of London; work began in 1275 and was largely completed by 1285 (though minor operations continued for a dozen more years). In that decade, Edward spent twice as much on the castle as his father had in the previous fifty, making it probably the first concentrically fortified castle in England. The principle of concentric fortification made an early appearance as part of Henry II's work at Dover, and reached a spectacular maturity in the refortification of the French city of Carcassonne between 1220 and 1250. During the second half of the thirteenth century, it seems to have exercised a considerable fascination on English castle builders, though such fortifications were beyond the means of all save the king and his wealthiest barons; Edward himself found it particularly compelling.

As it occurs in England – or rather in English castles built in Wales

Kenilworth Castle, the water defences. (*After English Heritage*)

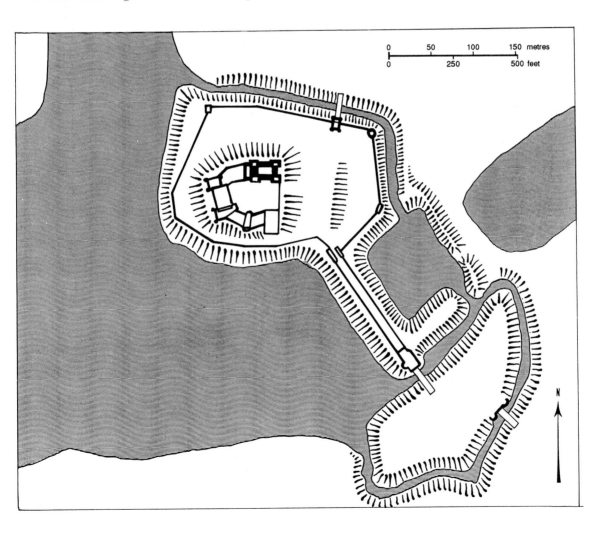

– the system involved the construction of a tall curtain defended by strong rounded towers, then an open space varying in width from about 9 to 27 metres (30 to 90 feet), and then a second curtain whose towers, if they existed at all, were open-backed; beyond the second wall was a ditch, or preferably, a moat. Compared with the single-wall defences current in English castles of the time, the double walls of the concentric castle offered several advantages. First, they made the task of the enemy sapper far more difficult: not only did he have to mine two walls, but the inner one was strengthened by the plinth of earth which separated it from the outer. Secondly, archers could defend the two walls at the same time, so that, given sufficient men, a positive hail of arrows could be directed at the enemy.[2]

Thirdly, and perhaps most importantly, the outer wall acted in the same way as a barbican in front of a gate: it prevented enemy troops from manoeuvring. If they overran the outer wall, they were trapped in a narrow open space; unable to advance, to find cover in the open-backed towers, or even to get back over the wall, they were at the mercy of the bowmen above. At that point, mounted knights could be sent out from the castle into the space between the walls; it then became in war what it often was in peacetime – a tilt-yard. All the

The mid-thirteenth-century walls and towers of Pevensey Castle's inner ward.

force of armoured men and horses was channelled against the helpless foot-soldiers: the result would be a massacre.

To transform the Tower into a concentric castle, first Henry III's recently dug moat had to be filled in to create a level earth platform round the whole castle. This cannot have been simple, even on the landward sides, but it was impressive engineering to claw back 12 or 15 metres (40 or 50 feet) from the river. When it was done, towers which once rose sheer from the Thames, like the century-old Bell Tower, stood on a sort of quay; those on the landward sides, previously washed by the moat, also stood on dry ground. A new outer wall was built, as thick as the main curtain of the castle, but much lower and almost without towers; numerous embrasures, rather irregularly disposed, were provided for the shelter of archers. Beyond the wall another broad moat was dug and flooded from the Thames.

The outer wall formed a concentric system of defence, but also blocked the old entrances to the castle itself. The former water gate, the Bloody Tower, no longer reached the river, so a new, grander one

London Castle, transformed into a concentric fortress under Edward III, 1275–85. ST: St Thomas's Tower, B: barbican (Lion Tower), BT: Beauchamp Tower. (*After English Heritage*)

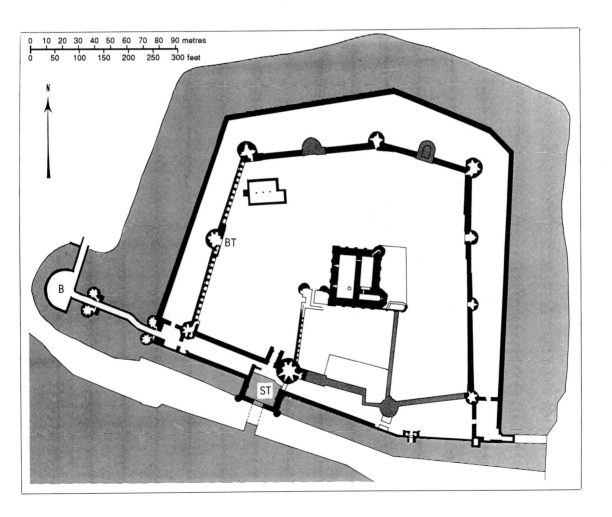

was built – St Thomas's Tower.[3] Unlike its predecessor, this interesting building jutted out into the river, and had an enclosed dock in its lower level. The floor above contained an apartment connected by a bridge to the Wakefield Tower, a further addition to the royal suite; the king withdrew from the commoners in the hall by one more step. The approach by water rebuilt, Edward turned his attention to the approach by land.

The existing gate was probably still on the site of the present Beauchamp Tower, but its condition after the collapse of 1240 is not known. In the event, Edward dispensed with it altogether, and made a complicated new entrance in the south-western corner of the site. Here a semicircular barbican, an island in the new moat, was made in front of a new twin-towered gatehouse, the Middle Tower; a causeway then led to the Byward Tower, a second, slightly larger gatehouse. Drawbridges, heavy doors, meurtrières and portcullises were multiplied along the route: nobody was going to get far unless permitted to. Once the main entrance was complete, the old gate was pulled down, along with the west curtain, which was rebuilt with embrasures for bowmen at ground level. The mighty Beauchamp Tower replaced the old gate and with its construction the major works were completed.

It is hard to recreate Edward's castle in the mind's eye: later kings and governments, with purposes often more unpleasant than his, have gradually altered the aspect of the Tower. As time passed and it seemed less and less likely that horsemen would have to charge along it, the narrow space between the walls was gradually given up to a clutter of lodgings and stores: a plan of 1597 already shows them, and by 1682 they had taken over. The old outer wall has been raised and

The Tower of London, showing the double walls and the mighty Beauchamp Tower, with the White Tower behind. Later buildings and restoration have marred the appearance of Edward I's castle.

even the huge Beauchamp Tower seems rather to peep over it, hemmed in on all sides by little buildings. Sash windows and uncrenellated parapets now belie the original martial purpose of the two gatehouses, and there is no water in the moat to reflect turret or tower.

Perhaps because it has changed so much, while the others have not, Edward's reputation as a castle builder rests not on London, but on the fortresses he planted to secure the conquest of north Wales: Builth, Rhuddlan, Aberystwyth, Flint, Conwy, Caernarfon, Harlech, Beaumaris – the list of new and rebuilt castles seems endless. Although they do not fall within the scope of this book, they demand some discussion because they are central to an understanding of Edward's impact on the development of the English castle.

They were built consecutive to the military campaigns of 1277 and 1282, and were the means of stifling future attempts by the Welsh to claim independence. Judged in those terms, the castles, and the new towns which they often sheltered, must be accounted successful. Architecturally, they are equally successful: mostly designed by a Savoyard mason, James of St George, they are as ingenious and as sophisticated as the new work at London, or indeed anything to be seen in Europe at that period.[4] They are as strong as any English medieval castle: Harlech, for instance, which saw more sieges than any, was the last stronghold to surrender during the Wars of the Roses and the Civil War itself.

No two are alike, though parallels exist. Harlech, Aberystwyth, Rhuddlan and Beaumaris all follow a concentric plan and the last, its square ward contained within an octagonal one, is the finest of the type in Britain. Caernarfon and Conwy, on the other hand, have two towered wards side by side, a choice perhaps dictated by their respective sites. Flint, Builth and Hawarden have, or had, keeps, though the gatehouse at Harlech and the Eagle Tower of Caernarfon could have fulfilled that role. It is clear, even from such brief descriptions, not only that each castle was a unique solution to the problems posed by its site, but that an inventive delight was taken in their design.

About half have survived in a condition which still reflects their original architectural refinement: the banded walls of Caernarfon, directly imitating those of Constantinople, are a well-known example. As important, though perhaps more subtle, are the satisfying proportions of the curved and flat masses which, particularly at Conwy, Rhuddlan and Harlech, stress the order and stability of the king's authority. Little turrets above towers are another particular feature; a triple set marks out the importance of Caernarfon's Eagle Tower, while the four towers of the inner ward at Conwy are similarly emphasized. Such turrets were useful rather than necessary, and seem largely decorative in intention, an echo of the angle turrets of Norman keeps; they break up the skyline and increase that great symbolic quality of the medieval castle, height.

In political, military and architectural terms then, Edward's works in Wales were successful. But questions arise on two counts: first that of their cost, and secondly, their influence. By 1300 perhaps £80,000 had been spent on them, a sum which would rise to over £100,000 by the time the exchequer gave up trying to finish them in the 1330s. It was an enormous sum for its day (compare again the £10,000 spent by Henry III over fifty years in London) and it provoked a financial crisis towards the end of the reign. Indeed, the cost of Edward's castle building contributed directly to the financial weakness which so disabled the Crown during the fourteenth and fifteenth centuries. The subjugation of Wales was achieved at an unnecessarily heavy cost: if a Harlech or a Rhuddlan could be had for less than £10,000, why build a Conwy or Beaumaris at £14,000, or a Caernarfon at £27,000?

The answer must be that Edward was not a man to settle for a destroyer when he could have an aircraft carrier. There is a greatness in Edward I: perhaps no other medieval king's actions, constitutional, military and political, had such far-reaching consequences – good or bad. Edward was intelligent, cultured, gifted, ambitious, but, most of all, imbued with a profound vision of kingship, the image of which, tarnished by the failures and compromises of his father's reign, he strove to restore. His interest in the legend of King Arthur (the round table in Winchester Castle hall probably reflects this), his encouragement of the burgeoning cult of chivalry, the splendid crosses built to mark the resting-places of his dead queen on her journey to London: all are intended to underline the sanctity of kingship.[5] It is paradoxical that the first king to co-operate effectively with Parliament should at the same time have exploited every available symbol which might reinforce his authority. The splendours of the Welsh castles, and indeed of the Tower, must be seen in this context: they were built to reflect power as much as to exercise it.

The nature of the influence exerted by the north Welsh castles on subsequent buildings also suggests that their purpose was only partly functional, for although they set a tone, they were never imitated in scale. In particular, what might be seen as the overkill of concentric fortification systems was effectively ignored by later builders: no other concentric castle was built in England after Beaumaris, except Edward III's Queenborough; the British castles which made even partial use of the system, and were not built by Edward I, can be counted on the fingers of one hand. Indeed the reigns of his son and grandson show little evidence of real castle building at all.

The truth is that in 1300 the English castle was slowly, imperceptibly dying; henceforth, though castles continued to be used, it was less and less for their military value. There are important exceptions of course, particularly in the north of the country, but the level and nature of castle building in the fourteenth century confirm Edward I as the last great castle builder in England. The castles he raised in Wales are the flare of a dying fire. Some were never finished; most lived out a crumbling existence of genteel neglect, their fading suites unused by monarchs who had no wish to visit this remote part of their land. And, thanks to what had been spent on them, many others joined them in a long decline.

While Edward was building in Gwynedd, there was neither the money, nor the workmen, to repair the royal castles in England. Some, favourite residences like Windsor and Nottingham, were kept in repair and a few, like London and Cambridge, were rebuilt; but the majority were ignored. Castles like Lincoln, Oxford, Hereford, Canterbury and Guildford became more and more dilapidated; many ceased to be considered royal homes, and simply functioned as judicial and administrative centres behind cracked walls and ditches encroached upon by tenements. Others, like Horston in Derbyshire, were granted away in the usually vain hope that their new lords would bear the cost of maintaining them. In 1300 there were simply too many royal castles for the exchequer not to look on many of them, their military role diminishing, as unprofitable assets.

In England, and Wales, the castle reached its zenith in 1300; thereafter no one would undertake work on such a scale again. The rest of the story is one of slow uneven retreat, probably not sensed by those involved, and of curious reflections; it is interesting in itself, particularly for the oddities it throws up, but less and less part of the story of the nation and its affairs.

High Tide

Harlech Castle, squatting high on its cliff with the mountains of Snowdonia behind, is the archetypal 'Edwardian' castle. Roughly square, it has a massive drum tower at each corner and a huge twin-towered gatehouse facing the most likely direction of attack; a narrow terrace and a low second wall surround the inner ward, making the defences concentric. In addition to the grand lodgings in the gatehouse, substantial domestic accommodation was ranged against the inner walls, including a large hall whose windows look out to the west, over the Irish Sea. That its regular plan (without the element of concentricity), angle towers and imposing gatehouse were to become the most common articulation of the English castle in the remaining century of its active existence, demonstrates not the orig-inality of the design (although it is very good), but the way in which the Crown, particularly when in the hands of a charismatic and suc-cessful king like Edward I, was able to set the fashion for noble society – a court style.

The key elements of Harlech were not new in themselves: in the 1220s the Earl of Chester had used regular planning, straight walls and D-shaped towers, massive gatehouses and even, at Beeston, mul-tiple (though not concentric) lines of defence, and there were numerous continental precedents, like Philip II's castle of Dourdan. But, because of the genius of his principal architect, as well as Edward's undeviating determination to build greatly, these elements now became almost synonymous with the castle itself: what had in Rannulf's time been fresh ideas among existing ones, became in Edward's the standard. The north Welsh castles, and uniquely Harlech, have become so well known that they have thrown their contemporaries into the shade, and it is a measure of the power of Edward's image that it has even eclipsed Caerphilly, the precursor, if not the model of Harlech and Beaumaris, whose huge and well-preserved ruins may still be seen in Mid Glamorgan.

At the close of the thirteenth century, the court style made fashionable by King Edward's fortresses in north Wales was, at least in the highest circles, the dominant architectural expression of the castles, and although few new ones were built in England under him – with war taken elsewhere, they were scarcely needed – a number were brought up to date by the use, in more or less coherent form, of the elements of the Edwardian castle. Among the most impressive and interesting of those to receive this treatment was the small but very strong fortress of Goodrich, on the banks of the Wye in Herefordshire. A castle, of which the tall and thin rectangular keep is the only survivor, was first established on this red sandstone outcrop in the twelfth century, and was succeeded by a towered enclosure, of which only fragments can be found in the present structure. But most

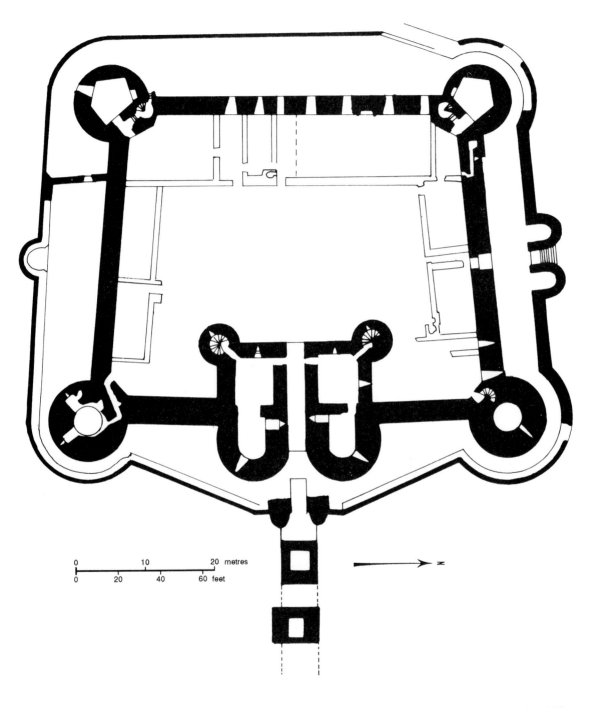

Harlech Castle, ground plan. (*After CADW, Welsh Historic Monuments*)

of Goodrich Castle is the work of a father and son, the Valence Lords of Pembroke, between about 1280 and 1320. They built a square castle with corner towers and a concentric outer ward on the two sides where the terrain permitted. The most obvious difference – clearly visible in the plans – between Goodrich and Harlech is the irregularity of the Herefordshire castle. Where the concentric castles of Edward I appear to have been drawn with a technical pen on graph paper, one might be forgiven for thinking that the plan of Goodrich had been roughed out with a Biro on the back of an envelope in the convivial atmosphere of a pub.

In fact this would be unjust to a castle which, if not perfect, is of exceptional quality. The differences are probably due to the genius of Edward's master mason, James of St George on the one hand, and the need to accommodate an existing site and buildings on the other. So at Goodrich the south wall is forced to make an odd acute angle in order to accommodate the existing Norman keep, apparently thought valuable enough to preserve in the new scheme. Likewise, the form of the south-western tower, which is larger and slightly more ovoid than those on either side, was dictated by the existing foundations of an earlier tower. The site itself, constrained by an older rock-hewn ditch, not only prevented the complete encircling of the castle by the outer ward, but also obliged the designer to place the gatehouse at the north-eastern corner, there being insufficient space elsewhere. None the less, the castle is, in all essential characteristics, identical with Harlech.

Behind the defences shelters domestic accommodation of considerable sophistication for, as was becoming more and more the case, towers, walls and living-rooms were united into a single building with an open space in the centre. Here, as might be expected, the space was quite small, a courtyard surrounded like a cloister by covered walks. It would appear that there were originally three separate suites, each comprising a hall and rooms in an adjacent tower, but it is no longer possible to be certain.

The case for seeing in William de Valence's reconstruction of Goodrich Castle in the adoption of a court style is circumstantial but strong. William de Valence, half-brother to Henry III and uncle to King Edward, was heavily involved in the struggle against the native Welsh since his acquisition of the lordship of Pembroke around 1247, and was Edward's chief lieutenant in the control of south Wales during his campaigns in the north.[1] He must have seen the works at Caerphilly and been involved in the planning and prosecution of the king's wars and the consequent developments in castle design and construction. It is also known that in 1280 and 1282 oaks were supplied for the work at Goodrich from the king's forest of Dean.[2]

In Edward I's court, there was an interest in, and a commitment to, the science of fortification, the level of which is only matched by that of Henry II. The uncomfortable entrance at Goodrich, with its single tower squashed into a corner of the site, reinforces this sense of the movement of ideas, for the approach to the castle was much strengthened, not long after it was built, by the addition of an enormous barbican clearly modelled on Edward I's Lion Tower at London.

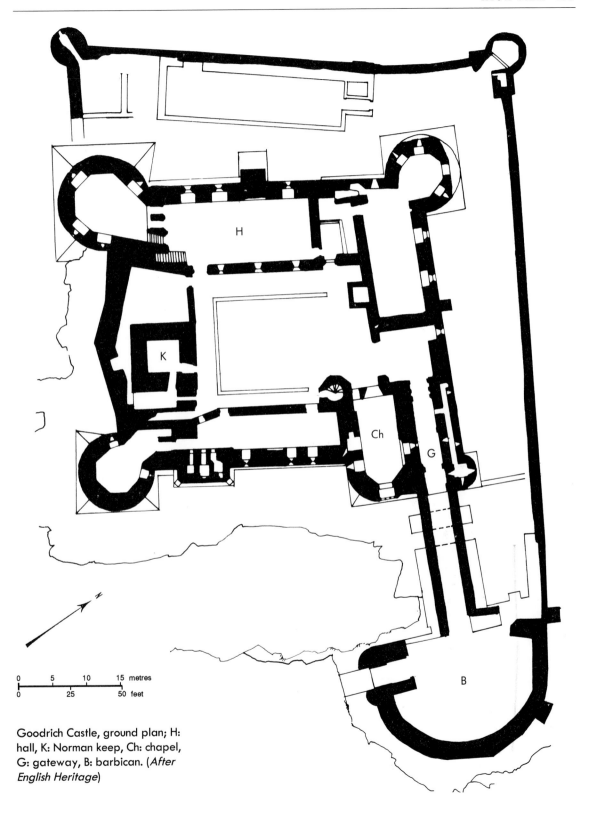

0 5 10 15 metres
0   25   50 feet

Goodrich Castle, ground plan; H:
hall, K: Norman keep, Ch: chapel,
G: gateway, B: barbican. (*After
English Heritage*)

The absence of a twin-towered gatehouse at Goodrich, due to the nature of the site, makes the castle an unusual example of its time, for the massive structure at Harlech is the most characteristic element of the Edwardian castle. At Harlech, Beaumaris, and a little earlier, Caerphilly, the principal gatehouse was designed not only to control access to the castle, but also to offer a high-quality suite and to serve, *in extremis*, as a keep, for it could be isolated by a portcullis at every entrance from both the outside and the inside of the castle. Where earlier twin-towered gatehouses, like those at London or Dover, protected a strong point behind them, these buildings were themselves the heart of the castle. The keep itself was still considered a valid element in the design of a castle: King Edward built keeps at Flint, Builth and Cambridge (though the last two have vanished), and at about the same time a huge D-shaped keep, Marten's Tower, was built at Chepstow Castle in Gwent. The siting of a tower at the point most vulnerable to attack had a long list of precedents, going back through Scarborough and Richmond to Exeter. Keep-gatehouses, as they have been called, were thus a new expression of an old idea. An exceptionally well-preserved example can be seen at Tonbridge Castle in Kent, where the huge gatehouse was probably built by Earl Gilbert de Clare shortly after his work at Caerphilly.

The Clare castle was a post-Conquest motte and bailey on the

The portcullis groove and meurtrières guarding the outer arch of Tonbridge Castle gatehouse.

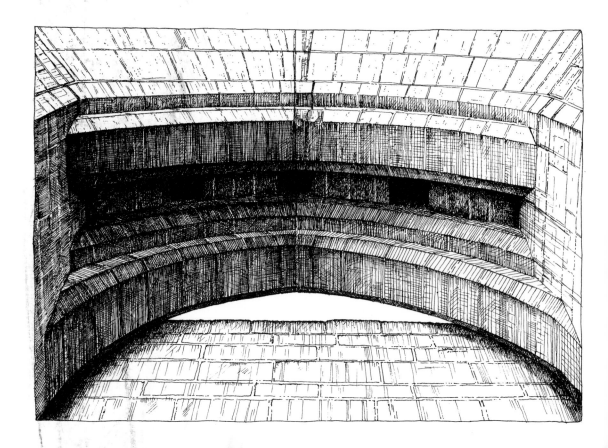

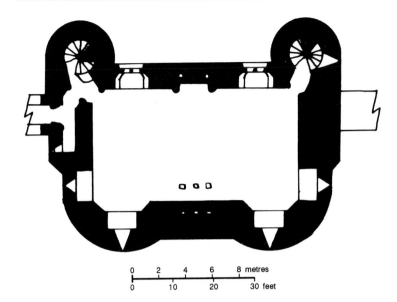

Tonbridge Castle gatehouse, second-floor plan. (*After Sidney Toy*)

0 2 4 6 8 metres
0 10 20 30 feet

north bank of the Medway, where it could control both the settlement of Tonbridge and the ford where the road to Hastings crossed the river. Today, continuous traffic rumbles down that road, oblivious to the guardian hiding in the trees. Although they stand in a public park, the ruins have almost escaped municipalization; withdrawn from the town, they preserve an atmosphere a little older than that of our own time. During the twelfth century, the castle was walled in stone and its motte provided with a shell keep, but little of this work, or of the domestic buildings in the bailey, remains; only the huge gatehouse, now missing its top storey and battlements, speaks of the great fortress this once was. It originally had three floors above the ground level, where the entrance to the castle itself passed between guard-rooms. Although it presents the curved faces, pierced only by mean-looking slits, of two massive towers to the outside world, in conception it is a single building, for above the first floor the apartments stretch from one side to the other, providing rooms some 17 metres (55 feet) long and 9 metres (30 feet) wide.

The approach from either the town or the bailey took the visitor under a machicolation, or meurtrière, a portcullis and through double doors to a dark and narrow passageway overlooked by arrow-slits and by meurtrières in the vault overhead. There were two small doorways into the tower itself: these, the only ground-floor entrances, were both provided with small portcullisses so that the tower could be sealed off not only from the town, but also from the bailey, should that be overrun. The top two floors were hall and chamber for Gilbert de Clare or, in his absence, his constable. They probably supplemented rather than replaced other, more spacious, accommodation in the castle, fulfilling the same role as King Edward's private apartments in St Thomas's Tower at London. The refinement of its architectural treatment implies that the new suite was used for the earl: as at Caerphilly, large traceried windows overlook the bailey and sculptors were employed to embellish both windows and the fireplace between them. The gatehouse must once have reached a height of 24 or 27 metres (80 or 90 feet) and transformed the aspect of the castle; its combination of living accommodation, powerful defences and the embodiment of lordship are the very stuff of the medieval castle, so it is unsurprising to find the fashion for such triumphal arches spreading.

The addition of such gatehouses to existing castles, while being relatively simple, strengthened the fortress and brought it fashionably up to date. Edward himself built powerful gates at Chester and St Briavel's, the castle of the Forest of Dean, but at Rockingham, another forest castle in Northamptonshire, he contented himself with the addition of curved fronts to an existing gateway, creating a structure which, while impressive from the valley below, was never capable of independent defence. The nobility, like the Camvilles who built a fine tower at Llanstephan in Dyfed, or the Bishops of Winchester at the castle in Farnham, followed the royal lead. A few years later, when he built a new castle to help protect Northumberland from Scottish invasion, Thomas, Earl of Lancaster, took the idea to its logical extreme by building at Dunstanburgh defences which consisted of little more than a towered wall across a promontory and a positive giant of a gatehouse giving access through it.

But Dunstanburgh also reveals the most telling insight into these hybrid keep-gatehouses, for around 1380, when the castle had come into the hands of John of Gaunt, the passage through the great gate was walled up and a new entrance contrived through the wall at its side. The gatehouse simply became an enormous keep, covering the entrance to the castle in just the same way that Henry II had planned the entrance and keep at Scarborough over two centuries earlier. This is a valuable reminder that the Edwardian style of 1300 is neither so new, nor indeed so dominant, as at first appears, but rather the ultimate refinement of a long chain of experience. The castles of north Wales appear today as the apogee of castle building in England for a number of reasons which are distinct from their actual quality. Not least among these are that they were built of a piece and on new sites, by an architect of genius with the resources to match his imagination, and that they have survived exceptionally complete. If, in these

Dunstanburgh Castle, Northumberland.

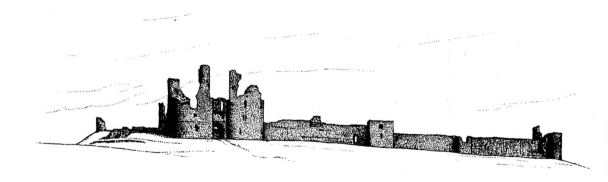

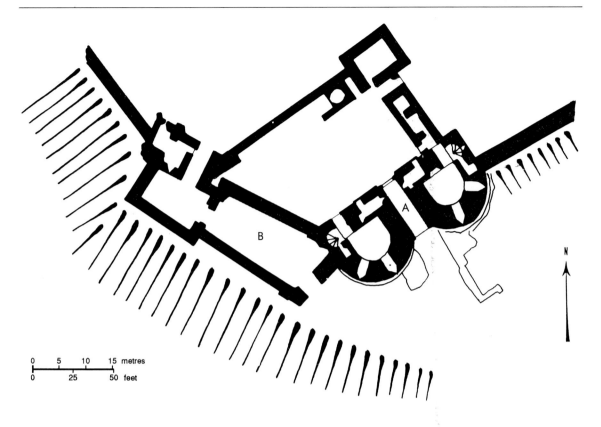

circumstances, they appear to be the supreme achievement of the English castle, it must be remembered that the ideas which they articulate have very long roots and that the subsequent development of those ideas is patchy and confused.

About 1300, at the very moment when the Edwardian ideas dominate, Robert Clifford rebuilt his castle at Brougham in Westmorland, but in spite of his experience in Wales and closeness to Edward I, Clifford used none of the defensive elements of Harlech. At Brougham, the irregular site is enclosed by long stretches of wall almost undefended by towers or turrets, while the massive square keep not only continues in use, but is heightened and a square gatehouse added to it: and yet, despite eschewing current styles, Brougham was never taken by siege. The great castles of the end of the thirteenth century are, in their time, paramount, but they remain none the less a part of the long and immensely complex story of influence and counter-influence, fashion, resources and need: the court style of Edward I was widely imitated and developed, but there were many men who, poorer than the king and with different needs and ideals, found other solutions to the problem of securing their families, property and homes from attack.

Dunstanburgh Castle, plan of the gatehouse area. A: original entrance, blocked by John of Gaunt, B: new entrance made to replace the former. (*After English Heritage*)

——15——
The Turning
————

The reign of Edward II saw, at least in its first years, a real falling-off in castle building compared with the previous decades, though there was eventually to be enough internal unrest and external assault to force many to reconsider their security. But Edward, who had inherited strong castles and a weak treasury from his father, had neither the need nor the resources which spurred most earlier kings, even had he been drawn to a life of war. So, apart from the desultory continuation of his father's works in Wales, the only important royal work which survives from the earlier years of his reign is the keep added to the Yorkshire castle of Knaresborough. Much of this tower stands today, together with scraps of walling and towers on a dramatic site overlooking the River Nidd. It formed a private suite for the king, like the gatehouse at Tonbridge, though, with a huge window at first-floor level, emphasis was on comfort and security rather than defence.[1] Money was spent on Knaresborough because the lordship had been granted to the king's current favourite, Piers Gaveston, and later in the reign it would be his successor, Hugh le Despenser, who would benefit from the king's generosity at his castle of Hanley in Worcestershire. But these works, with some at Carlisle and in Wales, are virtually the sum of Edward II's insubstantial castle building.[2]

In the case of baronial fortresses, the uneven survival of records makes the dating of remains more difficult than for royal castles. The reconstruction of Goodrich, for instance, has been ascribed to the period around 1300 largely on architectural and circumstantial evidence. The important castle of Raby in County Durham which, despite being licensed in 1378, appears on architectural evidence to have been begun earlier in the fourteenth century, provides a further example of the problem. However, the affairs of the castle of Pickering in North Yorkshire are well documented, and offer an insight into the everyday life of a minor castle.

The castle was founded by William I, probably around 1071. A good site at the end of a ridge was chosen and the bailey sandwiched between the cliff and motte; an outer ward formed a further line of defence on the more easily approachable side. The castle was strong enough, but was never in the first rank of royal strongholds, like nearby Scarborough, with which it sometimes had to share a constable. Its role was not primarily a military one; like Oakham it served to protect agricultural estates and forests and, until Edward I's ill-starred invasion of Scotland in 1298, the castle and its town enjoyed a quiet and prosperous existence.

In that year the honour of Pickering formed part of the estates of Thomas, Earl of Lancaster, a cousin of Edward II; it had been given to his father by Henry III in 1267 and was not repossessed by the Crown until Thomas's execution for treason in 1322. Its defences still consisted only of a shell keep on the motte and a stone curtain round the inner bailey. The lands were productive, supporting in 1314 about 600 sheep (a number which had nearly trebled eight years later), whose wool was stored in bales in the castle before sale.[3] The park had 1,300 deer and the hunting opportunities offered there and in the forest beyond were the earl's main reason for bringing his household to Pickering. In his absence, the castle was in the hands of its constable who, since he was expected to live there permanently, had lodgings in the bailey. This complex of timber-framed buildings included a hall and chambers, a buttery, pantry and kitchen, storehouses and a cellar.

In 1314 the earl's own accommodation was improved by the

Pickering Castle, ground plan. OH: old hall, NH: new hall, Ch: chapel, PT: prison tower, CL: constable's lodgings. (*After English Heritage*)

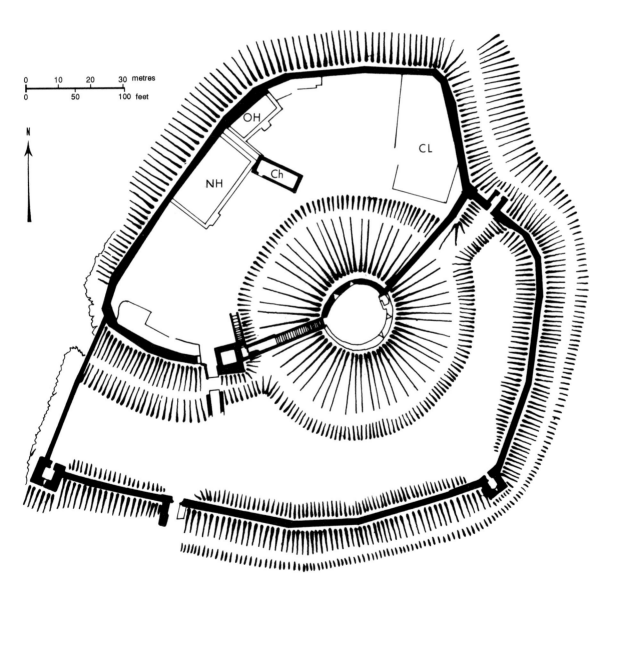

construction of a new hall in the bailey. It cost about £341, but that was easily covered by the year's revenues of almost £386. The Coleman Tower, which protected the gate, contained the prison where offenders against forest law were kept. The royal forests, which were such a conspicuous element of Norman England, had shrunk by the mid-fourteenth century to about two-thirds of their previous extent; of these, the forest of Pickering was one of the more important, and its severe laws were applied from the castle.

Apart from the constable, wages were paid to a chaplain, a porter and a bailiff; a park-keeper, a forester and four shepherds were also employed. The rest of the work was done by the manorial tenants in return for the land which they farmed. The revenues came from the wool and other farm produce, fines exacted in the forest court (held in the castle hall), rents from commuted service and pasture in the forest. To ensure the winter survival of so many animals, the principal crop was hay, so corn for the staff had to be bought in. Some weapons, including a springald, were stored in the castle. By 1314 Earl Thomas kept a small garrison there; men-at-arms tended increasingly to be hired men, rather than feudal tenants, and it must have seemed prudent in those troubled years to protect his manor by paying for a few guards.

Even without the political disturbances of Edward's reign, in which Thomas was deeply involved, the situation in Scotland was sufficiently threatening for castles in the north of England not to be left in the hands of a chaplain and four shepherds. Since the death of Edward I, the English had been pushed further and further south by Robert Bruce and his forces; abandoned by the new king, the English castles north of Berwick had fallen one by one to the Scots.[4] By 1314, when Earl Thomas's hall was being built at Pickering, only Stirling Castle stood against the Scottish armies. It was a characteristically medieval pact between besieged and besieger which finally brought Edward II to Scotland: they had agreed that if the castle was not relieved before mid-summer it would be surrendered.

Edward, forced to take up the gauntlet in the hope of regaining a degree of the authority he had lost, marched north at the head of a vast army of 2,000 mounted knights, and some 17,000 archers and foot-soldiers. By the side of a stream, called Bannockburn, outside Stirling, they were crushed by five or six thousand Scotsmen, of whom only 500 were horsemen; the loss of life was huge, and included many of the greatest English nobles.[5] The reasons for the Scots victory were, apart from English incompetence, that their troops had trained hard before the battle, that they had strewn the ground with caltrops (spiked iron balls which would cripple a horse's hooves) and that their infantry was formed into disciplined units, called 'schiltrons'. These might comprise up to 500 men who used their shields to protect themselves from arrows, while holding 4-metre (12-foot) lances out to the enemy; the English cavalry charges were turned by these foot-soldiers. The Scots won, in short, because they opposed the conventional tactics of chivalry with intelligence and imagination.

The immediate consequence of Edward's devastating defeat was that it opened the north of England to the Scots, causing the hurried refortification of castles as far south as Yorkshire. In the longer term, it marked the end of the period when cavalry – and particularly the heavy charge at the heart of medieval tactics – stood supreme in war: the Battle of Courtrai, twelve years before, had suggested that infantry could overcome a cavalry charge, but Bannockburn proved it decisively. Hastings had been won by horsemen, and for two and a half centuries they had been invincible in legend if not in fact; though a single battle changed neither legend nor fact, it looks now like the beginning of the end for heavy cavalry. The great English victories in France in the mid-fourteenth century were the triumphs of foot-soldiers over horsemen, and were played out in open fields, not over the walls of a castle. Any reduction in the importance of the mounted knight meant an equal reduction in the importance of the castle, its partner in warfare.

But Bannockburn's short-term effect was exactly contrary, for the defeat of English arms in Scotland opened the placid northern counties to the worst of medieval war – slaughter, rape, burning and thievery. Men, rich and poor, abandoned by a Crown unable to defend them, had to look to their own resources to save themselves: castles great and small were strengthened, ditches cleared, new towers built, timber replaced with stone. Major new castles, like Thomas of Lancaster's Dunstanburgh, were exceptional, but most great lords began to bring their castles up to date.

Alnwick, a Northumbrian Norman fortress with a shell keep between two baileys, was bought by the Percy family in 1309 and comprehensively rebuilt over the next century and a half. Not only did they add a series of powerful wall-towers, variously square and D-shaped, to the outer walls, they studded the shell keep with no fewer than seven great towers, making a Bolingbroke of it alone. Although the family has continued in residence and reconstruction since the fourteenth century, the castle retains much medieval work under the veneer of later times.

Not long after their purchase of Alnwick, the Percys acquired nearby Warkworth, another motte-and-bailey castle, tucked into a sharp bend of the River Coquet, and this too benefited from their attentions. The Clifford Lords of Brougham rebuilt their castles at Brough in Westmorland and Skipton in Yorkshire; the first in the simple, old-fashioned style of Brougham, the second as a strong cluster of towers on a cliff above the Eller Beck, to a design much closer to that of Harlech or Conwy. The powerful Nevilles began the fortification of Raby in County Durham and greatly strengthened their castle at Middleham in the Yorkshire Dales by encircling the Norman keep with new walls in a manner similar to Goodrich, though without strong corner towers.

But perhaps more typical of the area, and of the effect that warfare had on it, are the numerous small castles and towers to which people turned for protection. At the poorer end of the scale, these were no more than stone houses sheltering animals on the ground floor and people above, perhaps enclosed by a low wall; at the other, they were imposing towers, like the beautiful example at Belsay in Northumberland, offering good accommodation in a self-contained unit, its fine ashlar walls topped with battlements and turrets. Keep-

The Mill Tower added by Edward II
to Pickering Castle.

and-bailey castles, of a type no longer being raised in the rest of
England, can be seen in the far north of the same county at Etal and
further south in an architecturally distinguished example, at Edlingham. The keep at Edlingham was added to an existing lightly
defended hall-house, and represents a process which occurred all over
the north, where undefended stone houses were made more secure
against raiders.

Some attempt was made to protect the hall at Aydon, near
Corbridge, by the construction of low battlemented walls, but to no
avail: by 1323 when its owner, Robert de Reymes, died, it had been
taken twice by his enemies. Indeed, the description of his Northumbrian possessions at that time is sad evidence of the depradations of
war: apart from Aydon, his houses at Shortflatt and Bolam had both
been burnt by the Scots, his 122 hectares (300 acres) of arable land left
untilled, his meadows and pastures ungrazed, and his ten farms and
cottages untenanted. His annual income was reduced to 14s 7d.[6]

In 1322 the violence briefly reached as far south as the North and

East Ridings of Yorkshire, and Pickering Castle, now in the king's hands after Earl Thomas's final defeat and execution, was spared only on payment of a heavy bribe. The poor constable was taken away by the Scots and Edward had to appoint a new one; after peace was made the following year, the king spent time at Pickering and ordered the reconstruction in stone of the outer bailey. The resulting work, probably finished before the king's deposition in 1326, stands as a memorial to the fear of those times. With its square towers unprovided with arrow-slits for flanking, and large stretches invisible from any tower, it recalls the twelfth rather than the fourteenth century; Harlech and Caerphilly might never have existed. Simple and cheap to build, it might keep a Scottish raiding part at bay, but did not change Pickering's status as a minor castle.

Further still from the northern marches, the story is much less grim. Work tends to be more domestic in nature, neglecting improvements to the defences in favour of better living conditions. As often as not, this reflects a man's growing wealth or status, as in the case of Roger Mortimer who, as lover of Edward II's queen and with her the king's eventual murderer, effectively ruled England between 1327 and 1330. Mortimer built at Ludlow the vast residential suite which dominates the castle's inner ward, providing great hall and chamber, extensive lodgings, new latrines and a kitchen; this work was conceived and executed on a royal scale and, even in its ruined state, it still shows exceptional refinement. Further south, Thomas, Lord of Berkeley, began improving his motte-and-bailey castle by concentrating, once again, on the hall, chambers and service rooms in the bailey; while in Devon, the transformation of Okehampton Castle into a fortified palace by Hugh Courtenay was undertaken largely to underpin his role in national affairs and his claim, eventually successful, to the earldom of the county.

After Bannockburn, there is a north–south divide in the development of the English castle. While in most of the country there is a steady pursuit of increased comfort, though the appearance of strength, more or less real, continues to be valued, in the north the castle, often in its most primitive form and built by those, like clerics and farmers, unconcerned with war, continues in use for day-by-day protection. If its creation and development is shifting and complex, the pattern of the castle's demise is no less full of twists and paradoxes.

The Fifty Years of Edward III

Edward III ascended to his murdered father's throne in 1327, but took control of his kingdom only three years later. Roger Mortimer, the queen's lover and her co-conspirator in the deposition of Edward II, was executed, and Isabella herself sent into retirement at Castle Rising in Norfolk. The new king's situation was scarcely promising: the political landscape remained scarred by the difficulties of the previous reign; bad harvests had led to widespread misery, and the economic expansion of the thirteenth century seemed, at least in agriculture, to be stalling. Edward's answer to such difficulties was war: it was what he was best at; it was – particularly in Scotland – demonstrably necessary, and its activity and rewards offered a distraction to the nobility. His early campaigns were successful and saw victories at Dupplin Moor in 1332, and Halidon Hill in 1333; castles taken and destroyed by the Scots – Roxburgh, Stirling, Edinburgh and others – were rebuilt in what was to be almost the only such work of Edward III's to have a primarily military purpose. The ultimate failure of the Scottish campaign – by the 1340s England once again held only the castles of Berwick and Roxburgh – was masked by the successes which accompanied the beginning of Edward's new war, with far richer prizes, in France.

It might be expected that the fevered militarism of Edward's reign would have produced a group of castles as impressive as those created by his grandfather in the 1280s: in fact, in most of southern and central England, it produced almost no important castle-works. Edward III undertook a hugely expensive reconstruction at Windsor – at £50,000 it was the most expensive such programme of the entire Middle Ages – but the work was domestic in nature. At the time, it was said that no one could get craftsmen for the king had impressed them all, much as his grandfather had done to build castles in Wales. The money went on the creation of a new palace in the upper ward, with lodgings for the important household officers and officials, and a new collegiate church with its attendant buildings; the result was closer in spirit to the nineteenth-century work of Wyatville than to that of Henry II.[1] Sadly what survives of all this is too patched, altered and restored to be attractive. Apart from Windsor, work was carried out at London (the Cradle Tower), at Nottingham, Gloucester and elsewhere, but it consisted mostly of repairs. Most castles were barely maintained, and preserving their defences was often the area of least concern. Lincoln, Norwich, Northampton, Colchester, Devizes, Shrewsbury, Exeter – the list of royal castles in disrepair was long. At the same time, increasing amounts were being spent on unfortified houses, like Sheen, Eltham and later, Havering.[2]

The pattern of royal building is, to some extent, reflected in the work undertaken by the English nobility. Pontefract stands out as a major reconstruction of the fourteenth century, though only its excavated site is to be seen today; the use of great rectangular wall-towers may be a sign that convenience was sought as much as strength. Elsewhere in the north, refortification begun under Edward II continued steadily, with an equal emphasis on defensive and residential improvements, but no castle of the first rank was begun after Dunstanburgh. Where castles still had a residential or administrative role, they were maintained; elsewhere they were abandoned to squatters and the elements. At the same time, large houses, sometimes lightly fortified, began to be built by the nobility and by merchants like Sir John de Pultney of Penshurst Place in Kent. The cluttered site of the medieval manor was becoming more ordered, and during the fourteenth and fifteenth centuries it became usual to dispose hall, chamber, chapel and lodgings round a quadrangle, with ancillary buildings arranged in a second court, in a figure-of-eight plan: such a house, developed over these years, may be seen at Haddon Hall in Derbyshire. A real alternative to the castle, unmilitary but still capable of expressing high social status, wealth and power, was emerging in the courtyard house.[3]

The picture of neglect (except in the north), of improvements only to residential suites, and of few new foundations, is balanced by a group of second-rank castles belonging principally to the 1340s. Since the reign of King John it had been usual, before building a new castle, to obtain a 'licence to crenellate' from the Crown. The licence, verbal or written, allowed the recipient to add battlements and other specified defences to his home, and was sought not only for true strongholds, but also for houses such as Penshurst (licensed 1341) and Broughton (licensed 1405) which were never castles. Indeed, it is probable that licences were obtained in some cases as much for the cachet of nobility as from fear of the king's displeasure.[4] In the 1340s, licences were issued by Edward III for a series of buildings whose nature – whether castle or fortified house – is indistinct: the first was probably Mettingham Castle (Suffolk), licensed in 1342, followed by Westenhanger (Kent) in 1343, Chillingham (Northumberland) in 1344, Maxstoke (Warwickshire) in 1346, and Rotherfield Greys (Oxfordshire) in 1347.[5]

Enough of all these buildings survives to show that they were roughly quadrangular structures with corner towers and, as Leland sometimes put it in later years, 'builded castle-like' (indeed, he took the towers of Rotherfield Greys to be 'a manifest token that it was sume tyme a castle').[6]

Hindsight allows a more circumspect judgement. Maxstoke, the most complete of those listed above, has low curtains and towers which could offer no resistance to a serious assault; unlike the walls of earlier castles, which rose up to protect the roofs of buildings from missiles, these barely reach the eaves of the houses within. In short, the building is a strong house dressed up as a castle. Although inspired by the plan of Harlech, Maxstoke is like a poor photocopy: everything is there, but weaker, paler than on the original. The building aspires not to be a strong castle, but to appear to be one, and its plan has been adopted for domestic convenience, not military strength; this is not a fortress which could ever cause much nuisance to the king. Maxstoke and its cousins begin a line of quadrangular semi-castles characteristic of the fourteenth-century which reaches its climax in the troubled reign of Richard II at Bodiam in Sussex and Bolton in Yorkshire.

There is an apparent contradiction between the intense military activity of Edward III's reign and the minor castle building which took place, at least before the 1360s. Of course, as had been the case under Edward II, the major castles of king and barons stood in relatively good repair. Moreover, the focus of English politics had been internal during the previous three reigns, and warfare had occurred within the British Isles. With the expansion of trade, however, and the territorial ambitions of Edward III, it switched to the Continent. He had begun a war with France in part to protect English economic interests, but perhaps more to protect the status of the Crown, eroded financially under his grandfather and politically under his father.

Edward III, in the figure of a warrior-king, was popular, and his wars in France gave his barons opportunities for glory and wealth which they could not have hoped for at home. If the king's side-stepping of the conflict between ruler and ruled did not solve England's constitutional problems, it postponed them. Likewise, the defences of the realm could be neglected while England's soldiers took war abroad.[7]

Then again, as had become clear at Bannockburn, and was to be underlined at Crécy, Poitiers and Agincourt, battles were no longer automatically won by mounted knights, and warfare turned more on

A damaged corbel from the gate passage of Westenhanger Castle, near Folkestone in Kent.

open battles and the seizure of rich towns, than on the mere possession of castles.

But the most important reason for the decline of the castle under Edward III was also the most complex. English society was beginning to undergo the changes which would eventually lead it out of the Middle Ages. During the thirteenth century the ties of class interdependence had been loosened as both population and economy expanded, as education reached more people, and as government and culture became more sophisticated. The household of William the Conqueror, which had been the very Government of the realm, had long since developed into far more complex branches of administration and, though Edward II, Edward III and Richard II each attempted to create new departments subject only to themselves, power was slipping little by little into the hands of Civil Servants and Parliament. The concept of precedent, a mainspring of English conservatism, was beginning to have a restrictive influence on the king, who found himself obliged to act in accordance with accepted rules. The power of the merchant and manufacturing middle classes was beginning to make itself felt, and the simple society of the twelfth century, knitted together by its concept of God and man, and by a real interdependence, was ebbing away.

By many, the poet William Langland among them, these social changes were seen as dangerous, decadent and unjust. Even the aristocracy, which benefited most, seems to have looked back on earlier, and apparently simpler, times with some regret, and it is not coincidental that the cult of chivalry was most ardently pursued during the fourteenth and fifteenth centuries. It is as if, knowing that their traditional way of life was slipping out of reach, men clung to the only things they could control: its outward symbols. What had evolved as a system for mitigating the worst effects of feudal society on its weakest members, gradually became, under the three Edwards, like English art and architecture: something far more self-conscious.

In 1349, as the Black Death swept away thousands upon thousands of his subjects, Edward III was preoccupied with the creation of the first of the major orders of chivalry, the Order of the Garter. The business of being a knight, though retaining one foot on the solid ground of the battlefield, was to become more and more artificial, with a sophisticated literary and artistic culture to foster it.[8] Heraldry, originally a way of identifying knights whose faces were hidden by helmets, was developing into an elaborate ritual, and castles were maintained as much for their historical associations as for their strength, becoming the stages for complex ceremonies. Their architecture became increasingly mannered, retaining an appearance of military function, but really beginning to provide comfortable, and sometimes luxurious, homes for their owners. Windsor was rebuilt, partly as a palace for Edward III, but also to make it a suitable home for the Order of the Garter. The material standard of living had increased greatly and no one who could afford it was prepared to forgo the comforts now available, even if it did mean a lowering of the guard.

By the 1360s, the tide of war had changed; Edward had been unable to exploit his great victories, and the French were pushing

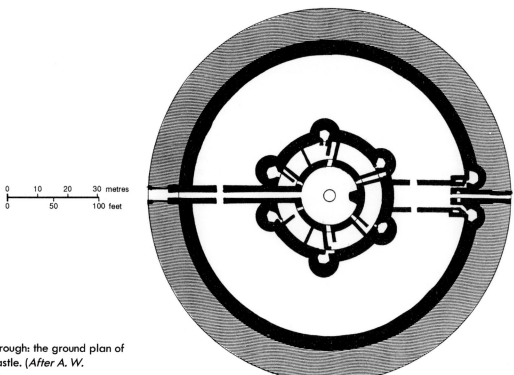

0   10   20   30 metres

0   50   100 feet

Queenborough: the ground plan of the lost castle. (*After A. W. Clapham*)

back hard, especially in the southern counties of England, which found themselves under attack from raiders. This, at last, prompted some military building in the vulnerable areas, but it is a sign of how much had changed that the defences of towns received as much attention as those of castles. By 1370 Edward was tired and old, and subject to moments of senility; most of the fortifications built to resist the French date from the years immediately after his death.

He did, however, order repairs to be carried out at Dover and at the crumbling castle of Rochester, where two of his mural towers survive. The only important project he undertook was the creation of a new castle and town at Queenborough, on the Isle of Sheppey in Kent. Though the castle was totally demolished in 1650, it is significant both for being the last new royal castle in England, and because it is clear from the plan that it formed an interesting experiment in concentric design. It had a round inner ward, defended by six towers, and surrounded by a circular outer ward; it resembles some of Henry VIII's later artillery forts, and was clearly the work of a designer of originality. It was a source of delight to the old king, who spent much time there, but whether it was more than a footnote in the story is debatable; certainly Richard II had no use for Queenborough since he granted it away ten years after it was built. Whatever its true military value, the perfection of its geometry and the grandness of its conception make it a fitting end to the long line of new castles built by the various kings of England.

By the time real defences were needed, Edward possessed neither the will nor the finances to erect them. The age of the feudal castle was dying around him, and in future there would be need only for strong houses, proof against raiders and thieves in the night. The castles of an earlier age were not beautiful enough to be wanted in time of peace – nor useful enough to be wanted in time of war – by the knights of the late fourteenth century. They built new homes for themselves in the next reign; homes quite different in spirit, if not always in appearance, from the feudal castle.

So, between Windsor, Hadleigh and Queenborough, with occasional stays in other royal houses, the old king spent his final, helpless years, as the political crows he had evicted at the beginning of his reign came home, one by one, to roost.

Hadleigh Castle.

Imitations

After the reign of Richard II, the story of the castle in England begins its uneven and protracted close: from about 1400, castles play, with the curious exception of the English Civil War, no role of importance in the history of the realm. They continue to be lived in, and occasionally, to be defended, but almost no new castle worthy of the name is built and repairs to defences are effected reluctantly, in response to severe threats like that of Owen Glendower in Wales.

In the last quarter of the fourteenth century, however, circumstances combined to create a final flowering of the art of fortification. What was created provides the link between fortress and country house – stylish and artificial, their nature springs from a blurring of appearance and reality: in their implicit claim to uphold an existing tradition of castle building, they conferred upon their owners a power disproportionate to the actual strength of the castle. In the 1380s, the castles of William the Conqueror were 300 years old, hallowed by legend and history – the very stuff of lordship. No surprise then that, if the newly rich, often newly ennobled soldiers returning from France wanted comfortable and beautiful houses, they also wanted them to look like castles. In the south of England, French pirates provided another incentive.

The political situation inherited by the child King Richard II was fraught with difficulties, and might have proved unmanageable even to a more politically cunning sovereign. The struggle for power between Crown, barons and middle classes had stood in abeyance during the reign of Edward III, because, so long as war provided outlets for the military ambitions of knights and the economic ambitions of merchants, the community's internal tensions seemed less important.

But at the beginning of Richard's reign, the wheel of fortune had swung in favour of the French who, having wrenched mastery of the seas from England, were bringing war to her coastal areas. Raiders pillaged and burnt ports like Rye and Winchelsea and temporarily occupied the Isle of Wight: for a while the English felt under threat of wholesale invasion. In counties which, save for one or two crises, had been blessed with a century and a half of relative peace, this was a severe psychological blow, the evidence of which survives in a rash of new fortifications across the south of England. But society and its conduct of warfare had changed since the last invasion in King John's reign, and as much effort went into the creation of communal defences as of private strongholds. Towns which were central to the economic prosperity of the region were hurriedly fortified and, among others, Southampton, Canterbury, Rochester and Rye retain city walls and gates erected in the hope of protecting their citizens from attack.

During these years, Richard and his officials were obliged to repair those royal castles on the south coast which had been allowed to decay in the preceding reigns. Substantial works were undertaken at Corfe, Rochester, Carisbrooke on the Isle of Wight, and at Southampton, where almost £2,000 was spent, excluding other works, on the construction of a new cylindrical keep on the motte. This tower, perhaps built to the design of Henry Yevele, struck Leland a century and a half later as 'the Glorie of the castle'.[1]

Not much of Richard's work has outlived him, but at Portchester Castle, on the coast between Southampton and Portsmouth, a pala-tial suite put up towards the end of his reign can still be seen. Built like Pevensey in one corner of a Roman fort, the castle was estab-lished early in the twelfth century. It had remained in use since then as an embarkation point for France; despite continuous attention, no attempt was made to bring its defences into line with Edwardian standards, and it retained its simple keep-and-bailey plan. Richard II improved the domestic accommodation, and the surviving parts of his great hall, chamber and service rooms form among the finest of their kind in the country. Pressure from France was matched, as was often the case, by increased pressure on the Scottish border, and the Crown also found it necessary to repair and improve such castles as Berwick, Roxburgh and Carlisle, at the last of which an impressive gatehouse survives.

As well as improving his own castles, Richard issued a large number of licences to crenellate to individuals in Kent, Sussex and elsewhere; they encouraged many who had won riches under Edward III to acquire castles reflecting their new social position. Men like Sir John de Cobham, Sir Thomas de Hungerford and Sir Edward Dalyngrigge, veterans of the French wars, disguised obscure back-grounds behind the imposing walls of castles. The lightly defended quadrangular castle of the 1340s suited the needs of this lesser nobil-ity very well and the new castles of Richard II's reign mostly follow the plan, with some local differences. They had square or round towers at the corners and, in the larger examples, further towers on the walls; while an imposing gatehouse, in a long tradition of ostenta-tion, tended to dominate the main approach. The principal difference between these and earlier castles is the unity of their construction: they were almost always completed in one build, often on new, level sites, and possess an architectural unity denied a castle which has evolved over three centuries. Occupying quite small areas, they gen-erally have only one defended ward, a single building uniting walls, towers, gate and residential accommodation around an open court. Among the finest and best known is the picturesque castle of Bodiam in Sussex.

Sir Edward Dalyngrigge had fought in France and returned much the richer for it. He bought the manor of Bodiam and settled into the existing house, like the Victorian colonists who returned to the home counties with their wealth. The River Rother was navigable as far as Bodiam in the late fourteenth century, and Dalyngrigge used the threat of French piracy to obtain a licence to crenellate in 1385; he abandoned the old manor-house and began a new castle beside the river. The result, ruined but unaltered, still rises in stately isolation

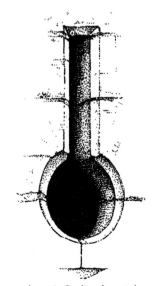

A gun-loop in Bodiam's gatehouse.

from the artificial lake which is its principal source of strength.

A lake, of course, was not an unmixed blessing, for it meant building in a hollow and leaving higher ground from which catapults might one day pound the walls. A castle surrounded by a moat could also be as difficult to get out of as to enter; even if Dalyngrigge had provided stabling for horses within the walls (which he did not), it would have been impossible for him to make a sortie to harrass his enemies. They would need only to defend the points where the two causeways crossing the lake reached dry ground to have Sir Edward caught like a fly in a bottle: the exposed causeways which allowed the defenders to cover the approach to the castle could, during a siege, be as effectively covered from the shore. But Bodiam was not designed for active defence: its towers are residential and have windows, not arrow-slits; its walls are thin and, although the main gatehouse with its machicolated parapet and two gun-loops is fashionably up to date, the simple postern tower on the other side of the castle offers an assailant a much weaker point of entry.[2] But it would be wrong to demand that Bodiam be Harlech for, although the castle could not have withstood a siege by the king's or any other army, it was not intended that it should. Dalyngrigge's enemies were pirates and his concern was to secure his home and manor against the depredations of an opportunistic raider who, faced with some resistance, would go elsewhere in search of weaker prey.

Bodiam Castle, seen across its broad lake.

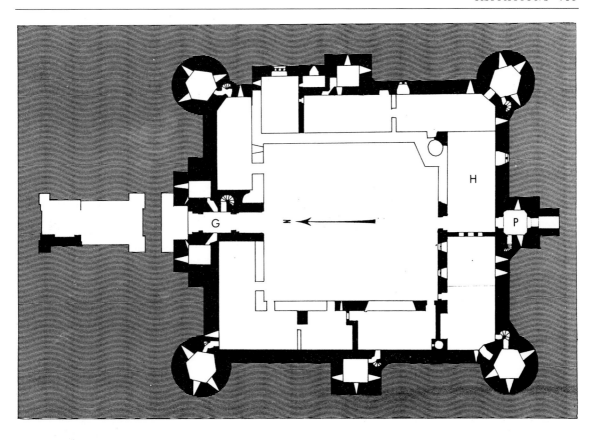

0 2 4 6 8 10 12 14 metres
0   10   20   30   40   50 feet

Bodiam Castle, ground-floor plan.
H: hall, G: gatehouse. P: postern.
(*After the National Trust*)

But if the military strength of Bodiam was no more than adequate, the castle's domestic facilities were ample: it was certainly a pleasant place in which to live. Unfortunately, little remains standing within those perfect walls and it is hard to be sure how all the rooms were used. There seem to have been two superimposed suites along the east side of the castle, the lower perhaps for the constable, the upper forming private accommodation for Sir Edward and his family. The southern range had on the ground floor, great hall, service rooms and kitchen, and above the latter, a formal great chamber. There were further self-contained suites on the west and north sides of the quadrangle; some occupied by servants and soldiers, perhaps with their own servants' hall, while others may have been intended for guests. Whatever the case, it is clear that the domestic planning of Bodiam was carefully designed to meet the needs of a society no longer living communally. The great hall, a mere 12 by 7 metres (40 by 24 feet), is like the dining-room of a Victorian country house, not a place where the household ate and passed its leisure hours, as it had at Oakham. Thirty-three fireplaces provide further evidence of the fragmentation of the household and its increasing wish for privacy.

The relatively obscure origins of Sir Edward Dalyngrigge (and most of his contemporaries in castle building) is the key to their castles. The wars of Edward III had provided spectacular opportunities for a man to rise, but there were other ladders to social

This elegant decorated window, from Wingfield Castle in Suffolk, dates from about 1380 and was old fashioned when it was made, for perpendicular architecture was already half a century old.

advancement. The royal administration, which had in earlier centuries been so dependent on the skills of clerics, was increasingly run by civil servants and lawyers, trained in a more secular educational environment. The activities of a merchant or financier might also open a door to the nobility, as in the case of William de la Pole, merchant of Hull, who founded the unhappy line of the Earls of Suffolk on the strength of his loans to the Crown, and built the castle of Wingfield in Suffolk.

This mushrooming nobility sought symbols of their arrival and found them in comfortable castles. The danger of invasion legitimized their construction: Sir Edward Dalyngrigge's licence to crenellate refers specifically to its role 'for the defence of the adjacent county, and the resistance to our enemies'.[3] At Cooling, Sir John de Cobham gave this sentiment pious expression by fixing to the outer gatehouse an inscription which reads:

> Knouwyth that beth and schul be
> That I am mad[e] in help of the cuntre
> In knowying of whyche thing
> Thys is chartre and wytnessyng[4]

But, though the threat from France was real enough, it may be unwise to trust fully the loyal protestations of these new men, and their patriotism should be offset against the vanity of self-inflation and a hard-headed fear of the peasant classes. In June 1381, the men of Kent and Essex had risen and brought the royal government almost to its knees; the radicalism of the Peasants' Revolt may have been defeated, but attacks on nobles and the lords of the Church multiplied under Richard II. John of Gaunt, the king's uncle and regent in all but name during his minority, had been obliged to flee from the London mob; while in the violence of 1381, the Archbishop of Canterbury himself was seized and beheaded on Tower Hill.[5] The climate of social unrest must have been as powerful an incentive for a rich man to secure his home as the declared wish to defend the kingdom. These factors combined to produce a number of Bodiam-style castles and examples survive, to a greater or lesser extent, at Cooling, Westenhanger and Scotney (Kent), Wingfield (Suffolk), Farleigh Hungerford (Somerset), Wressle, Sheriff Hutton and Snape (Yorkshire) and elsewhere; it would be difficult for their builders to make a good case for the patriotic necessity of a number of these.

Perhaps the most impressive of them all, and one where the domestic arrangements are better preserved than at Bodiam, is Bolton, in the North Riding of Yorkshire, which was started about 1379 by Sir Richard Scrope, Richard II's Steward. The castle is lofty, three of its towers still reaching 31 metres (100 feet) into the sky; while ranges between them, at over 18 metres (60 feet) are almost as tall as the towers of Bodiam. The hillside site is poor, for it has rising ground to the north, but the castle was not expected to withstand a full-blown siege. Like Bodiam, its function was to provide a secure house and to discourage raiders like Sir William de Bowes, who had broken into Sir Richard's parks, hunted there without leave, and carried away his deer and goods – an incident exploited by Scrope to justify the construction of the castle. He too was a rising star: from his origins as a minor noble, he attained, through faithful service to the Crown, a position of much greater wealth and power than that of Sir Edward Dalyngrigge. When he died in 1403, he was Lord Scrope and King Richard's chancellor. His castle has survived almost unchanged, save for the insertion of a number of unattractive Tudor windows, and its ruin is a monument to a man, his achievements and perhaps to their ultimate futility.

Bolton's square corner towers project only slightly beyond the walls and it has neither mid-wall towers (apart from two small turrets) nor gatehouse, so the visual impact is unlike Bodiam's water-mirrored breadth: here the impression is of height, rectangularity and compactness. Indeed, perhaps the most remarkable aspect of the castle is the way it compresses the spreading plan common in great houses of the period into a single unit: inner and outer courtyard, instead of lying side by side, are here superimposed. The ground floor is given over to those offices crucial to the fourteenth-century household, but which Bodiam largely did not bring within its walls: there were not only stables and guard-rooms, but a bakehouse, brewhouse, forge, stores and even a horse-mill; residential accommodation begins only at first-floor level. An air of menace lingers in the bare central courtyard: you feel like a mouse at the bottom of an empty swimming-pool. This is reinforced by blank walls and small doorways giving no clue to the principal entrance. The way to the great hall, whose tall windows overlook the courtyard, is through a door indistinguishable from the others. These defences are designed to secure the house against surprise assault and armed robbery; like the castle

Bolton Castle, Yorkshire.

entrance itself, each of the inner doors was secured by a portcullis, and those in the corners were also covered by machicolation: Bolton is notable for being as secure from within the courtyard as from without.

The castle was always a home and the fortunate survival of Lord Scrope's will permits the restoration, at least on paper, of some of its grandeur. The hall remained the formal centre of the household: it rose through first and second storeys on the north side of the courtyard, and like the old Norman halls, had a wall passage half-way up. The will, in describing the furnishings and property in the castle, mentions no less than thirty-five salt cellars, some of gold, some of silver, some with lids and one inscribed with the arms of Lord Neville.[6] The walls were hung with tapestries (a usefully mobile form of decoration for the itinerant households of great men), including a green one 'woven with griffins with my Arms worked in metal', and the boards spread with linen of a quality appropriate to the day and the table. Cutlery of gold and silver is mentioned, including 'one

Bolton Castle, ground-floor plan. H: hall (over), G: gatehouse, St: stables, Ki: kitchen (over), M: mill, S; service rooms, Ga: guardroom. (*After George Jackson*)

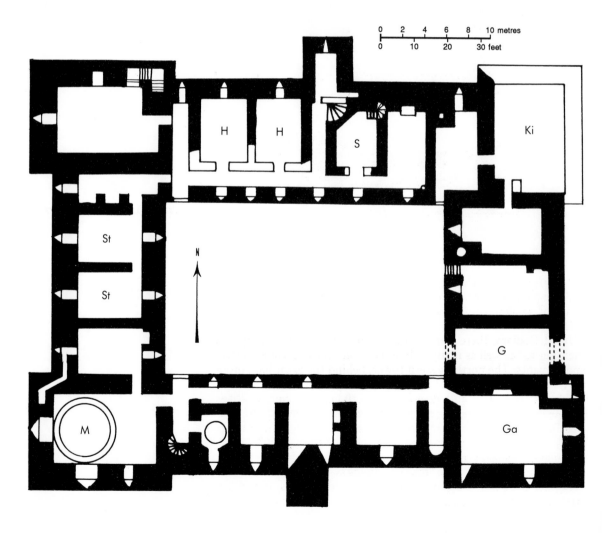

The piscina in Bolton Castle chapel.

round bowl of silver, twelve silver plates, two silver jugs for the upper buttery, [and] one paton with ewer which I had as a gift from the Earl of Arundell'. However dour the outward appearance of the castle – and it was much less so than today – the standard of living enjoyed within was of the highest.

As at Bodiam, there were a number of suites for the family and their guests, as well as many individual rooms for household officers and servants. The north-western tower, behind the great hall, probably contained the private apartments of Lord Scrope, while the north-eastern tower, now demolished, is thought to have held the kitchens; the north range thus follows the conventional pattern of chamber, hall, service rooms, and kitchen. The south-western tower contained lodgings for noble guests; while the south-eastern, together with part of the adjacent ranges, forms an almost independent unit apparently reserved for the steward and his staff.[7]

By the time that Bolton was built, the feudal basis of military organization had disintegrated. Edward I had been the last king to try to wage war with the feudal levy; thereafter, the commutation of military service for cash payments was so complete that paid soldiers formed the bedrock of Edward III's army.[8] A new class of professional soldier was emerging, a man who depended on military service for his day-to-day survival. The magnates of the fourteenth century drew in these mercenaries, establishing permanent retinues of armed men, some paid, some retained by a system of indenture, or contract, so that nobles like Richard Scrope could field, when required, small personal armies. Retainers, unlike the feudal levies whose ultimate loyalty was to the Crown, felt their duty to begin and end with their employer; this disintegration of social cohesion was to contribute to the endemic warfare of the following century. Such a change naturally had an impact on the design of the castle and, from the mid-fourteenth century onwards, space was allocated to house professional soldiers.

Perhaps the finest room which survives in Bolton Castle is the chapel, which occupies half the southern range on the second floor. It was endowed in 1399, as a chantry for six priests who were to pray for the soul of the murdered Richard II, Scrope's lord and benefactor. The chapel was dedicated to St Anne and was furnished with gold candlesticks, cruets and chalices. The best of these, together with the finest vestments, were left to the Abbot of Easby, near Richmond; this monastery had already benefited from the generosity of Lord Scrope and it was there that he was laid to rest in 1403. The second-best vestment was left to Roger, his heir, for use in the chapel at Bolton, together with 'my second missal, [and] my porteus which I used at the saying of matins and vespers'. Richard Scrope's life was not concerned only with the worldly occupations of politics and power, nor was his wealth expended only to material ends; his will speaks for him as well as his castle, and through it he may have the last word: among other legacies, he left his son Roger 'a pair of paternosters of coral, which once belonged to the Lord my father, and a gold cross which I used and bore with the blessing of Almighty God, of the most glorious Virgin Mary, the blessed St Anne and all the Saints and me.'

—18—
Towers for Gentlemen

Bolton Castle is the best preserved of a number of similar northern strongholds built in the later fourteenth century. Ruins of an even larger castle, built for the Nevilles of Raby, can still be seen at Sheriff Hutton, just outside York, and others exist at Lumley in County Durham and Middleham in North Yorkshire. A fine example was built for Sir Thomas Percy at Wressle, in the old East Riding of Yorkshire; although no more than two towers, the hall between them and a fragment of the entrance survive; the quality of the masonry and of the architectural details is still wonderful.

A characteristic difference between these northern castles and their southern counterparts, like Bodiam, Cooling and Farleigh Hungerford, is the considerably greater social status and actual power of the northern builders: the Nevilles, the Percys, even Lord Scrope, were men closely involved with the Crown's and the nation's affairs and, in the case of the first two, also great war-lords and the owners of numerous castles. They built splendidly to demonstrate their wealth and power and to offer appropriately lavish hospitality to friends, retainers, tenants and rivals, in the knowledge that their reputations, and their authority, depended on these visible manifestations of grandeur.

The solutions of lesser men to the problem of securing a home from potential or actual assault, while retaining a degree of convenience and comfort in domestic arrangements, and working to a smaller budget, created new expressions of the castle idea which are often as interesting as the larger courtyard castles. It could be said that, as far as the medieval castle was concerned, there were only two real concepts of defence – the ringwork and the motte and bailey – and that all subsequent developments constitute no more than variations on one or other theme: the ringwork becomes the enclosure and courtyard castle; the motte and bailey translates into keep and bailey and, in the north and west of the British Isles, pele tower and barmkin. Between Bolingbroke and Bodiam, the differences are of emphasis and architectural style, not of nature.

It is not surprising, then, that the idea of the tall, compact stronghold protecting a more lightly fortified bailey, not only fails to disappear during the fourteenth century, but actually increases in popularity and becomes the subject of a similar degree of ingenious planning as the courtyard castle. Straightforward keeps had been added, where necessary, to existing castles throughout the period (Cambridge, Pontefract, Knaresborough and Southampton, for example) and new castles based on a keep-and-bailey plan were also established.[1] At Dudley, in Staffordshire, a new keep of unusual plan was put up by the uncontrollable John de Somery shortly after 1300. On top of an existing motte, he raised a two-storeyed rectangular building with large round towers projecting boldly from each corner, and surrounded by a low wall. At Stafford Castle itself, and at about the same time, a keep of similar plan, but with octagonal towers, was also built; this survives only in fragmentary form under a nineteenth-century rebuilding.[2]

These towers, with new royal keeps like those at Flint in north Wales and at Knaresborough, signal a resurgence of interest in the idea of the keep after a long period of concentration on the defences of the bailey. All these examples are or were notable for the ingenuity with which they attempt to provide a suite of high-quality accommodation without diminishing the tower's security. They also possess the one great advantage of the tower over an enclosure castle – the symbolic association of height with lordship, exploited so deliberately in earlier centuries. New gatehouses, like those of Tonbridge and Dunstanburgh, explored the same idea in their own way, but the relative privacy of the keep clearly had its advantages over them, a point underlined by the conversion of the Dunstanburgh gatetower into a keep.

In the following years, a number of men, most of them in the lower ranks of the nobility, chose the keep and bailey rather than the courtyard plan for new castles. Nunney, in Somerset, and a close contemporary of Bodiam and nearby Farleigh Hungerford, is a simple example. Built by Sir John de la Mare, following a licence granted in 1373, it echoes Dudley in its tough rectangular block with towers set dramatically close together at the corners. The manor was small, held of the Earl of Hereford for just one knight's fee, and of no strategic value, so the castle must reflect only Sir John's importance in local

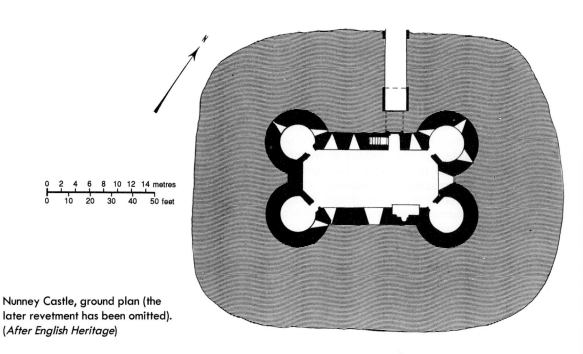

Nunney Castle, ground plan (the later revetment has been omitted). (*After English Heritage*)

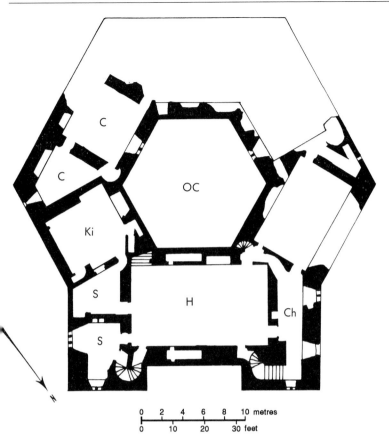

Old Wardour Castle, first floor.
H: hall, C: chamber, Ch: chapel, Ki:
kitchen, S: service room, OC: open
courtyard. (*After English Heritage*)

0   2   4   6   8   10 metres
0   10   20   30 feet

politics and his wish for an enhanced level of security. Nunney is actually a large house with hall, chambers, kitchen and storerooms superimposed within its walls and protected by a machicolated parapet around the summit of the tower. This feature, popular in fourteenth- and fifteenth-century France but exceptional in England, has led to suggestions of French influence, though there is no evidence that Sir John ever visited France. A lightly defended bailey, now gone, was the only other element of the castle.

Harewood Castle in Yorkshire, licensed six years before Nunney, is somewhat larger although, now hidden in woodland, its roofless remains are more difficult to appreciate. The main building is rectangular with square towers and only two storeys, to Nunney's four; hall, kitchen and service rooms are on the ground floor, with a chamber and other rooms above: a small chapel occupies one tower. The quality of the masoncraft, as at Nunney, is excellent.

One of the finest and most complex examples of this sort of latter-day keep is the castle of Old Wardour in Wiltshire, built by sanction of a licence granted to Lord Lovel in 1393. The tower is hexagonal, with one side much enlarged to accommodate both the entrance and above it the great hall; in the centre is a hexagonal court about 12 metres (40 feet) across – more than a light well but not enough to make this a courtyard castle. Part of the tower was destroyed during the Civil War, and the battlements and turrets which crowned it have gone; but for the most part, the structure and its use is easy to follow. It stood in the centre of a hexagonal bailey which presumably once held the ancillary buildings required by a great household.

The north façade, a broad recess between two towers, dominates the approach to the principal entrance (subsequently redesigned with Renaissance touches); high above stand the two enormous windows of the hall, sadly without their tracery. Having passed through a long vaulted passage, the visitor emerged in the court before ascending, via a broad stair, to the hall. This splendid room, though with a similar area to that at Bodiam, rises through three storeys, lit on both sides by great perpendicular windows; it was, and is, the centre-piece of the castle. Around it on the same floor were the usual kitchen, service rooms and chamber, while the rest of the castle's extensive accommodation served domestic functions and as lodgings for guests, household servants and garrison.

The quality of the masonry work at Wardour is remarkable: the walls are of perfect ashlar, interrupted only by string courses and a cornice with rosettes below the level of the battlements. At the summit of the corners project semi-octagonal bartizans, built out from the wall in a series of subtly graded steps, at once part of and

Old Wardour Castle.

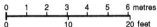

Belsay Castle, principal floor.
(*After English Heritage*)

supplementary to the castle. The hall itself, its windows appearing simultaneously to watch over the entrance and to hover aloof from the everyday business of the bailey, is an extraordinarily imposing room, the approach to which, through the tower, into the courtyard and back upon itself to the stairs, is calculated to create drama.

The castle, from its fashionable bartizans down to its frankly bizarre hexagonal plan, is a mannered creation, intensely self-conscious and concerned more with style than reality. There is nothing wrong with good masoncraft – where earlier builders could get it, they did – but here they are not made to serve the usual purpose of creating a well-built structure: they are the very reason for that structure. The quality of the details and the fashionable French style of the castle are what mattered to its builder, not its strength or even its convenience: what it said about him was the most important consideration. Without those aesthetic qualities – square, rubble-built and ill-lit – the tower would have been no more than a bolt-hole, like so many of the pele towers erected in northern England, Scotland and in Ireland; it would have revealed its builder as a small man afraid of others. Instead, its artificial recreation of a picture of a castle claims Lord Lovel's place in the aristocracy, as a knight and a leader of men, as one of those who do, rather than are done to.

In the northern counties such grandiose gestures are also found, though rarely with the willful originality of Wardour. At Belsay, in Northumberland, is an excellent example of the best sort of tower house being put up in the fourteenth century. The castle was built close to the main road from Jedburgh to Newcastle and, unlike Wardour, was clearly inspired by a real need to defend the manor and village from which it took its name. It stands today in a later park, connected to a seventeenth-century manor-house, but its original situation, whether surrounded by a walled enclosure or standing with other buildings, is not known.

The tower is a squat rectangle with three principal floors corresponding to kitchen, hall and chamber; numerous small rooms, some of them vaulted, were also provided in two short extensions to the main block. The battlements are Belsay's glory, for they survive almost complete, with bartizans on each corner and long stretches of machicolation between them; the extension containing the stair rises to form a turret not only taller but – a subtle touch – broader than the others. Throughout, the masonry and details (like the transomed two-light windows) are of the highest standard. Belsay was the

A corner fireplace in the first floor of Ravensworth Castle gatehouse.

residence of a knight built proudly for security and display, but it eschews the mannerist expression of Wardour: as befits a working castle in a troubled part of the realm, it is entirely sensible.

Keep-and-bailey castles were built throughout the Borders during the fourteenth century – at Etal, near the Tweed, for example, or the fine, ruined castle of Edlingham, standing in a lovely broad valley between Alnwick and Rothbury. Both of these have business-like keeps guarding sizeable and properly fortified baileys, but not everyone could afford such strongholds.[3] At the lower end of the social scale, where people had less cash for buildings, less to protect from robbery, and fewer pretensions to air, the simple tower house with its attendant yard or barmkin is commonplace. Two, three or more storeys high, pele towers are generally rectangular (though they also follow L, U and Z plans) with vaulted ground floors and an entrance above, and only small windows.

These structures, which litter the Borders, are akin to the fortified manor rather than the castle, for most have an exclusively defensive nature, whereas the castle united defensive and offensive capacities. Noble tower houses were built – like Belsay or Chipchase – in northern England, and still more in Scotland, where the idea was taken sometimes to quite fantastic lengths, but the majority are mediocre structures, interesting neither for their architecture nor for their background. Often unknown to history, the events they witnessed long forgotten, they seem bleak monuments to grim times.

Warkworth Castle, near Alnwick, and principal seat of the Percys, preserves an enormous late-fourteenth century keep with all the ingenuity and style of Wardour but in a castle which, in a troubled part of the realm and central to its lord's political ambitions, continued to have a very real military purpose. One of England's finest ruins, the extensive remains of an early motte-and-bailey castle were rebuilt in stone throughout the medieval period, and always with work of the highest quality. Warkworth guards a spur of land protected on all other sides by the River Coquet, and on which a small town was established. The approach from the north is unforgettable, for the road runs straight through the picturesque town towards the huge motte with its tower, before diverting sharply left to skirt the castle walls and escape to Amble. The town, river and the countryside beyond are surveyed from the keep, and it is possible to appreciate how the sheer scale of their houses distinguished the medieval nobility from the peasant, artisan or tradesman in their one- and two-storey homes below.

The new tower was the keystone of an extensive transformation of Warkworth Castle undertaken after 1377, when the Percys were granted the earldom of Northumberland. The earls planned the construction of a palace within existing bailey walls and towers, sanctified by a collegiate church and crowned by the keep. A good deal of their work has been destroyed, and some was never completed, but the tower of about 1400 survives entire but for the battlements. Its curious plan, square with chamfered corners and octagonal turrets projecting from the centre of each face, may have been suggested by that of an earlier keep, but the building standing today is, in the complexity of its domestic planning, entirely of its time.[4]

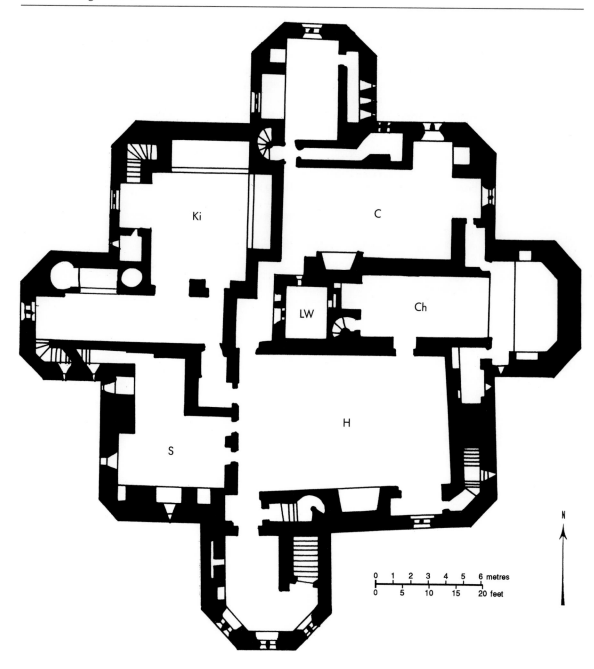

Warkworth Castle keep, principal
floor. H: hall, C: chamber, Ch:
chapel, Ki: kitchen, S: service room,
LW: light well. (*After English
Heritage*)

It provided self-contained accommodation which duplicated the much more spacious hall and chambers of the bailey but which, without the suites of lodgings provided at Wardour, was very much the lord's tower. The vaulted ground floor had thick walls and small windows and was given over to storage, but above it the tower's amenities become much more gracious. Large windows lit a hall and chapel which rose through two storeys to the roof, and the walls themselves are pierced with such a profusion of passages, stairs, rooms and alcoves that they would have been little help against the cannon which were being used increasingly in warfare. Indeed, when Henry IV came knocking at Warkworth's rebellious door in 1405, he had only to discharge his guns seven times at the castle to secure its surrender.

The Impression of Power

Further south, the surviving evidence of castle building is as ambiguous as at Bodiam, Wardour or Warkworth, and the complexity of
intention increases in proportion with social status, as is illustrated
by two great Warwickshire strongholds. Kenilworth Castle has been
compared to a burnt-out factory, and from a distance the garish and
grim red standstone ruin does not look promising. Sunshine, which
brings all architecture to life, is absolutely essential at Kenilworth,
for only then does the stone lose its damp, mildewed tinge and begin
to reveal the grandeur it actually holds.

Dalyngrigge was a lesser knight enriched by war, and Scrope an
ennobled civil servant; John of Gaunt, owner and rebuilder of
Kenilworth Castle, was the son of Edward III and, as Duke of
Lancaster, the possessor of wealth and power comparable only with
that of the Crown. The works which Gaunt undertook at Kenilworth
Castle stand with the highest architectural achievements of the age,
and reflect the sophistication both of its art and of its society. They
were entirely domestic in nature and, like his father's at Windsor,
transformed the Norman fortress into a Gothic palace.

Work began about 1389 under the direction of the mason Robert
Skyllington. Retaining only the massive keep, he rebuilt the entire
inner ward of the castle, providing a complete domestic suite, with
kitchens and service rooms, great hall and private chambers. Some 28
by 14 metres (90 by 45 feet), the new hall was conceived on a princely
scale – almost four times that of the hall at Bodiam. It stood on a
vaulted undercroft, and was approached from the castle courtyard by
a flight of stone steps. These have gone, but the arched doorway to
which they led still stands: it has seven orders of shafts, three of which
grow into carved foliage in the arch itself. The door opened on to the
low end of the hall, and it is likely that this bay was separated from
the rest of the room by a wooden screen supporting a gallery where
musicians could sit to play.[1] The next two bays had enormous perpendicular windows with stone seats (the height of fashion inci-
dentally, appearing concurrently in some of Warwickshire's most
prestigious churches). The lights themselves were fully glazed and
may have had heraldic painted glass in the traceried heads: its
north–south axis ensured that the room glowed with light all day.
The third bay had wall fireplaces on each side; the fourth, windows
like the first two; and the fifth, oriels to give extra light and emphasis
to the high table at which Gaunt and his Castilian queen sat.

That this was a remarkable room is still evident to the visitor; but
the impressive nature of its interior may not be. The hall was particularly dramatic because, although as broad as the twelfth-century hall
at Oakham, it was not divided by arcades supporting the ceiling. The
development of the hammer-beam roof had greatly increased the

width which could be spanned by unsupported timbers (indeed, as Gaunt was building at Kenilworth, his nephew, the king, was creating at Westminster a hammer-beam roof spanning some 21 metres/ 69 feet). Gaunt's new hall enclosed a single space of a size quite new to English domestic architecture; this majestic design must have been breathtaking in its time.

The exterior of the new building, facing the great lake which embraced the castle, was conceived as a symmetrical façade. Service rooms were provided at the north end of the hall, and here the building was extended westwards to form the Strong Tower, a series of lodgings for important members of the household. To match it, another tower, externally almost identical, was built at the southern end of the range, this time providing a passage to private rooms on the south side of the inner bailey. We have inherited from the last century an indistinct impression of medieval architecture as

Kenilworth Castle, the inner ward as rebuilt by John of Gaunt. K: keep, Ki: kitchens, H: hall, C: chambers. (*After English Heritage*)

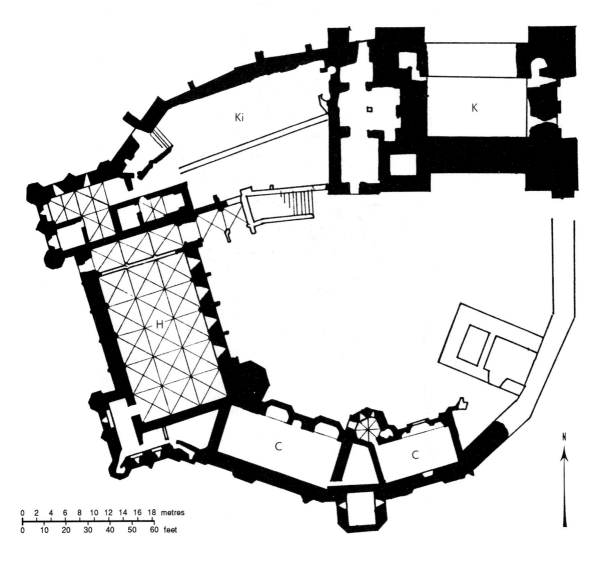

Perpendicular stone panelling in John of Gaunt's hall at Kenilworth.

rambling, asymmetrical and 'picturesque'. In fact, though it was not used in three dimensions as Leonardo advocated, symmetry commonly formed the basis of single-plane compositions like the west fronts of churches – indeed the demands of military architecture led to its use in buildings like Harlech. Robert Skyllington, clearly a designer of the first rank, created a façade for the new hall at Kenilworth as deliberate as even the eighteenth century might have wished; at dusk, seen from a boat on the mere, the new hall must have been a gorgeous sight, its crisp masonry glowing warmly and its vast windows turned orange by the setting sun.

These splendid buildings formed a comfortable residence in their own right, but they also served as a backdrop for stage-managed ceremonies which sought to reinforce an *impression* of power. Its actual transaction no longer took place in the great hall as it had done under Norman and Angevin kings: the room served only to reveal the outward signs of power, in much the same way that business corporations affirm their status with chrome-and-marble foyers today.[2]

In the Middle Ages, as now, much actual power depended on the confidence of lesser men in greater ones. At the end of the fourteenth century and throughout the fifteenth, it was necessary for a great man to appear magnificent and powerful in order to prevent dangerous rumours that his fortunes were on the wane. (An analogy has been made with modern financial markets which can be threatened by little more than panic about their soundness, and a consequent transference of capital.) The hall remained essential, because of its time-hallowed associations, as the principal stage on which the image of power could be created; but the reality was exercised discreetly in private rooms behind it.

The secrecy and suspicion of the Tudor court goes hand in hand with the multiplication of rooms in State palaces; the design of early medieval castles, and the communal life implied by that design, could never have produced such an atmosphere. The question of royal favourites had become more pressing throughout the fourteenth century and although some of the emphasis on them sprang from the diplomacy which made it wiser to criticize his advisers than the king himself, it was grounded in a feeling that the king met increasingly in private with chosen noblemen; that the party which had the king's ear was often in a position to determine who else had access to it, did nothing to stifle suspicion. Secrecy in politics fuels mistrust and factionalism, those characteristic elements of the Wars of the Roses. The chambers built for John of Gaunt at Kenilworth, if not private in the modern sense, clearly reflect these social changes. More emphasis was placed on the hall than ever before just because it was being used less for living in; as is so often the case, the architecture reveals as much about how people wanted to live, or thought they should live, as about the reality of their lives.

The romantic picture of late-medieval chivalry painted both at the time and in subsequent centuries is tenacious, and cannot be dismissed as mere fiction; however, to use an image which might appeal to that morbid age, it is, like a beautiful alabaster tomb, built round something far less wholesome. There was a dark side to the fourteenth and fifteenth centuries' obsession with chivalry. While John of Gaunt was building a palace at Kenilworth, his son was engaged in less inoffensive occupations.

Henry Bolingbroke – soon to usurp his cousin Richard's throne and to become Henry IV – was crusading in Lithuania with the Teutonic Knights.[3] This nominally religious order had left the Middle East in the early 1200s in search of infidels weaker than the Saracens. It found them in Prussia and Lithuania and by the 1380s the Order, now based at Marienburg Castle, was seen throughout Christendom as the noblest incarnation of the chivalric ideal. In truth, it had become a honey-pot to which the knights of western Europe – among them Chaucer's knight in *The Canterbury Tales* – flew in the hope of glory and wealth. If the crusades are a shameful and a sorry episode in medieval European history, they were motivated, in the beginning at least, by high ideals, producing moments of nobility as well as savagery; but the crusade against the Lithuanians, for all its Papal blessing, was without a single redeeming aspect and was recognized by contemporary writers, like John Gower and Geoffrey Chaucer, for the lawless banditry it was.

Knights fought in Lithuania only to make or enhance their reputations, and the chivalric rituals indulged in at Marienburg had slipped so far from the early religious concept of knighthood, that they were among the grounds for the charge of heresy eventually levelled against the Teutonic Knights.

Henry went to Marienburg in the spirit in which people went big-game hunting in the 1920s. The sport was not to be foregone on account of the acceptance of Christianity by the Grand-Duke of Lithuania, which he did five years before Henry Bolingbroke fought

The head of a king, probably Richard II, from the gatehouse of Thornton Abbey, Lincolnshire.

at Vilna where, on 4 September 1390, he participated in the massacre of 2,000 civilians.[4]

The splendours of the court of John of Gaunt, still reflected in the ruins of Kenilworth Castle, cannot obscure the link between such pageantry and the gradual debasement of the reality of knightly behaviour; the disintegration of central authority, and the presence of more and better armed men in the population, were to lead in the years after the death of Richard II to an increasing level of violence and lawlessness in England. Castles played little part in that fighting but they remained the bases for the fighters; the architecture, as always, reflects the time.

Curiously, there is little evidence that new lodgings took much part in the rebuilding programme at Kenilworth. Traces of fireplaces and windows remain on the outer curtain to show that timber-framed buildings once stood against it, and perhaps these and other vanished houses provided rooms for the vast retinue which John of Gaunt maintained about him at all times. Castles like Bolton were designed with individual rooms in mind, but Kenilworth and most older fortresses, originally the products of a different society, did not have such accommodation. In the earlier Middle Ages, great lords had not expected all their retainers to live permanently with them: on the contrary, each had his own estates, houses and castles, and generally attended his lord only at great religious feasts, or to fulfil his feudal duty of castle-guard. Thus Lincoln or Kenilworth were large enough to accommodate great gatherings for short periods, but not for the continuous residence of more than the handful of people needed to administer and protect the estates.

But John of Gaunt, and other magnates whose power increased as that of the Crown diminished, now kept permanent retinues clothed, housed and fed at their own expense. The bulk of these were composed of common soldiers who did not require any special treatment; but many were nobles who attached themselves to greater men by choice, and they had to be accorded the tokens of their rank. Sir Hugh Hastings, who contracted for life with John of Gaunt in 1366, was one such person: he received £20 a year (more in wartime), and when called to his lord's house he was to have board and lodging, along with his own retinue of six.[5] The dormitories of monks, once bare rooms with mattresses on the floor, were being partitioned into cells, while higher monastic officials had suites or even houses to themselves. What was expected by monks was demanded by the nobility. So a number of older castles were updated in the late fourteenth century by the addition of lodgings for important retainers. Warwick Castle, a day's ride from Kenilworth, was one of these.

Until a few years ago, Warwick could boast a period of continuous occupation since it was built in 1068 by William I, and so it presents a completely different face to its ruinous neighbour. The principal living accommodation has been rebuilt over the centuries, but the east front survives almost untouched; it is a masterpiece of late-fourteenth-century military architecture, as Kenilworth is a contemporary apogee of domestic building. Warwick consists of two huge towers with a gatehouse and barbican astride the curtain-wall which links them. No precise date is known, nor the order of building, but the whole castle belongs certainly to the second half, and probably to the last quarter, of the fourteenth century.

A hundred years earlier, the Beauchamp family, Earls of Warwick, had been among the poorest nobles in the realm, but their fortunes were, like those of so many others, improved by the French campaigns.[6] Thomas Beauchamp, a friend of Edward III and a founding member of the Order of the Garter, probably began the task of bringing the castle up to date, but it was completed after his death by his son, also Thomas, continuing until about 1395. The castle being rebuilt was old fashioned for the mid-fourteenth century: it had a motte with a shell keep at the western end of a rectangular bailey, which was ditched on three sides and protected on the fourth by a cliff falling to the River Avon. The domestic buildings stood above the river, having the advantage of its protection and of a southerly aspect. At that time, the east curtain overlooked the main road into Warwick from Banbury and the south, so it was at once the entrance and the most public part of the building.

The Beauchamps concentrated almost all their efforts on this part of the castle, their other work being confined to a water gate and the improvement of the accommodation overlooking the river. The scale

Warwick Castle, as drawn up by Robert Smythson in 1590. G: gatehouse, WG: water gate, GT: Guy's Tower, CT: Caesar's Tower, R: Richard III's unfinished tower, begun a century after the east front. (*From* Country Life)

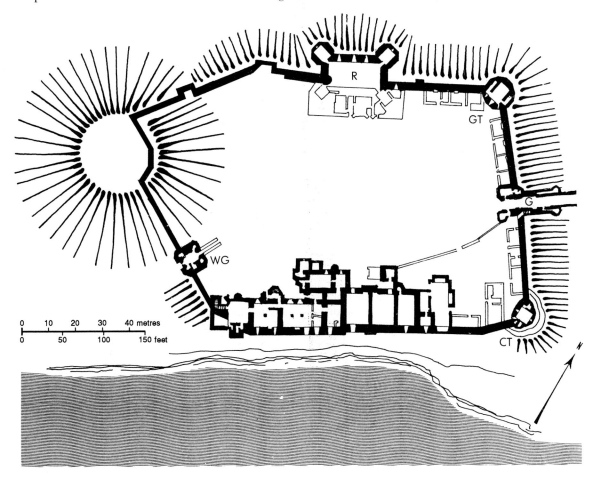

The great gatehouse of Warwick Castle.

of the new east front is huge, and it is not until the north and west curtains of the castle are seen that it is revealed as a façade; the north curtain – twice as long as the east – was defended only by twelfth-century towers until Richard III began his works there a hundred years later. It cannot be that the Earls of Warwick expected to be seriously besieged in their castle.

Apart from ostentation, the principal purpose of the two towers, Caesar's and Guy's, was to provide lodgings. In the mid-fifteenth century, the Earl of Warwick travelled with 400 men-at-arms, dressed in red livery at his expense, and if his immediate predecessors had fewer retainers, they still had many. Most did not expect lodgings as fine as the seven sets of rooms provided in the two new towers; ordinary men-at-arms and servants would have slept in timber-framed buildings more like barracks. The lodgings were for more important people, men like Sir Hugh Hastings, and were designed to provide maximum comfort. The two towers are of different shapes (one tri-lobed, the other twelve-sided), but show almost identical planning. They are stone vaulted throughout, with guard-rooms on their top floors, but, significantly, no arrow-loops lower down. On each floor is a suite comprising a sitting-room, a small bedroom and a latrine; the main rooms have fireplaces and single-light, ogee-headed windows. In each tower, a spiral stair rises from ground to battlements, giving access to the lodgings, while another connects the top with the wall-walk, so that a continuous *chemin-de-ronde* between towers and walls was created. Both were machicolated, and Caesar's has a second fighting platform above the first, creating the striking and aggressive profile belied by the tower's limited fire-power.

Astride the curtain between the two towers stands the gatehouse. Despite its powerful appearance, this building is no new departure in the art of defending castle entrances, but an excellent example of the continuity of thinking shown by castle builders. It uses the same ideas – albeit in a grander and cleverer design – as the west gate built at Lincoln 300 years before. It suggests a twin-towered structure in thirteenth-century style but, as the plan makes clear, it is really one rectangular tower with a passage through the middle.

A barbican of two parallel walls extends into the ditch in front of the gatetower, and it is closed at the end by two further turrets joined over an outer gateway. As at Lincoln, the ground between the barbican gate and the castle gate is left open to the sky so that an assailant can be trapped between the walls, exposed to arrows and other missiles from the wall-heads on every side. Two portcullisses and three sets of meurtrières completed the defences, together with a drawbridge across the ditch beyond the barbican gate. A particularly notable feature of this fine structure are the flying parapets which link the turret-tops of the gatehouse proper to form a continuous walk; however, it is also noteworthy that it was not provided, either at the time of its construction or later, with gun-loops.

Individually, the gate and towers make the public face of Warwick Castle enormously strong, but they could not, alone, make Warwick a strong castle; the earls did not follow their work through, preferring

The gatehouse and Caesar's Tower at Warwick Castle (*After Sidney Toy*)

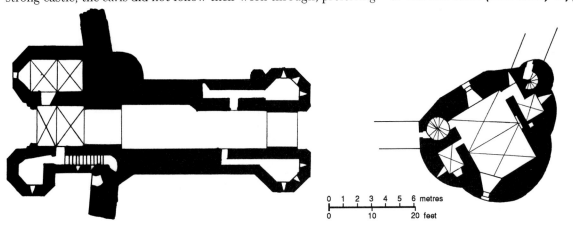

0 1 2 3 4 5 6 metres

0   10   20 feet

to rebuild the domestic buildings in equally grand style. The most convincing explanation is that they never intended their castle to be put to the test of war, but expected its show of strength to intimidate; it was a statement of power and wealth, but the extraordinary rhetoric of that statement should not deceive us into believing it. Like John of Gaunt at Kenilworth, the Beauchamp Earls of Warwick were erecting a stage set, very convincing, and yet with little more substance than the streets built in Hollywood to represent Dodge City. Today, a large blue clock-face adorns the gatehouse of Warwick Castle; at first sight it seems incongruous, but actually it is a piece of latter-day ostentation entirely in keeping with the spirit of the structure it sits on.

—20—
Diverging Paths

After the death of Richard II in 1399, the story of the English castle peters out. Some splendid castellated buildings were put up during the fifteenth century – Herstmonceux in Sussex, for instance, or Caister in Norfolk – but they were not castles: the century's contribution to the national architectural heritage lies in its manor-houses, colleges and churches. The *idea* of the castle, however, was tenacious and its architectural imagery lived on: turrets, machicolations and battlements found their way, through their association with power and authority, on to the most unexpected buildings, from abbey gatehouses to the new colleges at Oxford and Cambridge. Crenellations – the only aesthetic contribution of military to ecclesiastical architecture – even began to adorn churches, lending variety to the straight parapets associated with perpendicular roofs. Two houses, erected by the same man at the same time, define the stylistic – and conceptual – range of aristocratic builders during the fifteenth century: Tattershall Castle in Lincolnshire and South Wingfield Manor in Derbyshire. Both were the work of Ralph, Lord Cromwell, and were built during the last two decades of his life, between about 1434 and 1456.

The family came from the Nottinghamshire village which gave them their name, and rose to a position of wealth largely through judicious marriages. Ralph, a veteran of Agincourt, came into a substantial inheritance in 1419 and embarked on a political career, much of it in the government of the infant Henry VI who acceded to the throne in 1422, when barely 9 months old. Cromwell collected a number of lucrative appointments, including the charge of Nottingham Castle and Sherwood Forest, and in 1433 attained the Treasurership of England, a post which he held for ten years, and which put him in the centre of English politics at a particularly unhappy time.[1] Cromwell spent much wealth and energy on building projects intended to express his own view of his social position. Principal among these were the reconstruction of the thirteenth-century castle of Tattershall, together with the establishment of a college outside the walls containing one of the finest perpendicular churches in Lincolnshire. New manor-houses also rose at South Wingfield in Derbyshire, and Collyweston in Northamptonshire, and the churches of Wingfield and Lambley, in Nottinghamshire, were rebuilt (the latter because it was the resting-place of his parents). Of all this building activity, much has been swept away, and apart from the churches, only the great tower of Tattershall Castle and the ruins of Wingfield Manor survive.

The first castle of Tattershall had been built around 1230, in a similar style to nearby Bolingbroke, for it was a moated enclosure defended by a curtain with half-round towers. The Cromwell family acquired the castle in the fourteenth century, and it became their

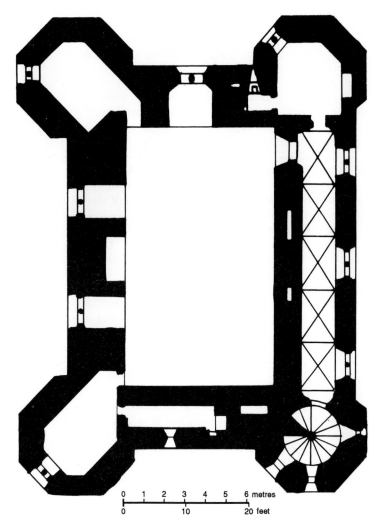

Tattershall Castle, plan of the audience chamber on the second floor. (*After the National Trust*)

```
0   1   2   3   4   5   6 metres
0          10          20 feet
```

principal seat. Few of the changes wrought by Ralph Cromwell at Tattershall survive today, but the huge keep-like tower he added is almost complete and gives us an idea about the quality of the rest. Rectangular, with octagonal corner turrets, the new building had five storeys, topped by a machicolated parapet and a double fighting platform; at 34 metres (110 feet), it was as tall as the keep of Rochester, and must have made the older mural towers seem puny at its feet.

It was built entirely of brick – an early use of the material on this scale – with windows and dressings of Ancaster limestone; red brick and white stone combine to produce a cheerful and rather unmilitary appearance. It now stands alone, but there was once a hall in front of it; the two were connected by a corridor and holes for its floor and roof timbers can be seen on the face of the tower. It was, thus, quite different to the self-contained towers of the fourteenth century, like Nunney, Belsay or Warkworth. Cromwell's tower formed a lavish addition to the existing accommodation in the castle, and the lower floors were designed to be used in conjunction with the old hall: the basement possibly as a servants' hall, and the ground floor probably as a parlour, or withdrawing room. This floor, like those above it, is provided with latrines and a fireplace whose chimney-piece bears carved heraldic arms and badges, including the Treasurer's purse and, punningly, the gromwell weed. The three remaining storeys, each of which has a large main room with smaller turret rooms off it, form a suite of private accommodation for Lord Cromwell, with a hall, then an audience chamber, and finally a private bedchamber below the battlements. The principal difference between these rooms and the hall and chambers built by John of Gaunt at Kenilworth is their vertical, rather than horizontal disposition.

Although, when seen from afar, it is diminished by the vast horizon and the empty Lincolnshire sky, and though it stands alone without the buildings which once huddled at its feet, Cromwell's tower impresses today as much as it can ever have done. And, of course, it was designed to impress rather than to intimidate, for though in scale and splendour it stands comparison with any of England's great keeps, in purpose it is altogether different. This up-ended palace could never have been a refuge in time of siege: it is full of doors and windows. No Norman keep ever had three entrances at ground-floor level and two on the first; the beautiful perpendicular windows

The roof gallery at Tattershall Castle, showing the two tiers of fighting positions.

overlooking the moat provide light, not security. There was a well in the basement, but no access to it from the upper rooms; even the aggressive-looking rows of machicolations were more about giving architectural emphasis to the building than about war.

The tower is a fifteenth-century vision of a twelfth-century reality, an interpretation of an earlier age by a later one. It is one of the first English buildings deliberately to attempt the evocation of a past society's finer qualities through an imitation of its architectural language; in this it is closer in spirit to the nineteenth-century work at Cardiff and Castell Coch, than it is to Rochester or Hedingham.[2] If Maxstoke, Bolton and their kind were the last of the castles, Tattershall was the first of the pseudo-castles. Indeed its suggestion of the chivalric past was apparently considered so successful that it was widely imitated in the half-century after its construction. Similar brick towers exist at Farnham in Surrey, Buckden in Huntingdonshire, Middleton in Norfolk and elsewhere. As late as the 1470s, Lord Hastings added an ugly stone tower to his existing fortified manor at Ashby in Leicestershire, and a decade later Richard III began, but never completed, a great tower at Warwick.[3]

Lord Cromwell had reason to indulge in a romantic revival of the

South Wingfield Manor.

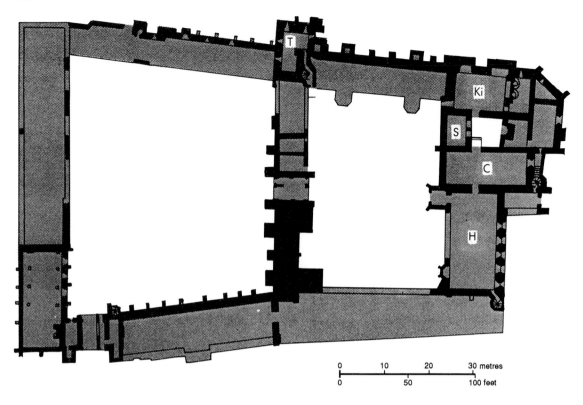

early Middle Ages at Tattershall, for his social roots were planted in
the little market town. The manor of South Wingfield, which he
acquired about 1440, was a place with no such associations and was
actually sold by Cromwell shortly before his death: there was no
reason to build anything other than a comfortable and secure country
house, and that was exactly what was done.

The tall, splintered ruins of that manor-house still crown the
Derbyshire hill he chose, visible from some distance away. The inac-
cessibility of the site was really all its strength, for it was designed as a
lightly fortified courtyard house in the style of Haddon Hall or the
Archbishop of Canterbury's house at Knole in Kent. Here there are
two courtyards – an echo of the castle's outer and inner wards – the
outer and more southerly apparently containing lodgings for
Cromwell's retainers, as well as the necessary offices and stables.

A gateway in the cross-range gave access to an inner court, which
has survived better than its neighbour. On the northern side of this
was the great hall which, though rather hacked about (it was once
converted into a two-storey house), was built to the highest standards, as the surviving porch and oriel amply demonstrate. Because
of the lie of the land, the hall was built over an undercroft and even in
this obscure part of the house the quality of workmanship is maintained: it is vaulted (at so flat a pitch that it is a real technical achievement) with bold ribs springing from short octagonal piers to large
panelled bosses. The remainder of the north range was occupied by
kitchens and service rooms; above the latter was the great chamber,

South Wingfield Manor. The
shading indicates the parts
originally roofed. H: hall, C:
chamber (over), Ki: kitchen, S:
service room, T: tower. (*After
W. Hawkesley Edmunds*)

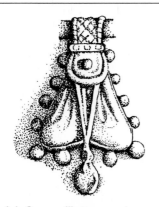

Ralph Cromwell's treasurer's purse.

lit by a large window overlooking the courtyard. On the west side were more lodgings, including a high tower of quasi-military appearance at its southern end; while the east range, which has completely vanished, apparently accommodated a parlour used in connection with the hall, and perhaps a chapel.

The whole of the inner court – which was built first – reflects the standards and taste of their builder, and everywhere, as at Tattershall, can be seen the arms of Lord Cromwell and the stylized purses, symbols of his office. But the conception of the two buildings could not be more different: one suggests the castle and power based on arms; while the other is a country house where a non-specific architectural idiom expresses power through the manifestation of wealth. Wingfield has no machicolations or wall-walks, no corner towers or drawbridge; the battlements on its porch are no more military than if they had stood on a church. The house was wisely made secure, for the times could be dangerous, but whatever strength it had lay in its position and the absence of large windows in the lower parts of the walls. Fundamentally, it does not try to *look* like a castle.

From these two buildings lead different architectural paths: Tattershall leads to Castell Coch, Wingfield to Hampton Court and onwards to the eighteenth and nineteenth centuries. Presumably Tattershall received its great tower because it was Cromwell's principal home, and it was there that he wished to claim association with the knights of old; Wingfield was just a modern house. In fact, the manor must have been the pleasanter home; its rooms are on a human, comfortable scale, and the site itself more attractive.[4] What Cromwell gained in grandeur at Tattershall, he lost in comfort; and the grandeur was itself short-lived: Cromwell died without heirs in 1456, his estates were dismembered, and over the next centuries, his houses fell one by one to abandon, and ruin. Perhaps the humble gromwell weed itself found a home in them.

—21—
Ruin

In August 1485 the undulating pastures of south-western Leicestershire witnessed the defeat of Richard III by the army of Henry Tudor, and the creation of a new royal dynasty in England. The Battle of Bosworth, unlike the Battle of Hastings, did not instantly transform the socio-political panorama: it was just the final engagement in a lifetime of civil war in England. It ushered in a new ruler but he did not, as William the Conqueror had done, bring with him a new way of life: the close of the Middle Ages in England was a gradual affair which unfolded slowly over the fifteenth and sixteenth centuries as social institutions were overthrown, changed, or just quietly faded away. Foremost among the last was the castle and, even as Henry VII seized the Crown, many of those described in the preceding pages were already derelict and half-abandoned, some reduced to mere grass-grown humps and a few scraps of wall.

The East Anglian fortress of Castle Rising, for example, was said in 1483 not to possess a building capable of keeping out rain, wind or snow, while nearby Castle Acre had been recorded as being of no value 100 years earlier. Richmond Castle stood neglected and unrepaired; Leland, travelling in the 1540s, described it as a 'mere ruin'. In 1537 Conisbrough was in the same condition, a large section of the southern curtain having fallen, as well as a floor in the keep, the gates and the bridge. Lincoln's walls were patched, and in succeeding years its ditches were sold, filled and gradually built over; it had for many years been used only for judicial purposes and, like Exeter and Oakham, it was preserved only for the sake of the courts which sat, and still sit, within the ramparts. Many other castles, once important strongholds on which depended the security of the kingdom, were abandoned as the threat or actuality of foreign incursion receded.

In the Welsh Marches, the fortresses of Beeston, Clun, Shrewsbury and Hereford were in ruins, while across the border, Carreg Cennen and Cardiff, among many others, were equally dilapidated; the great Caerphilly itself was all but abandoned with just one tower maintained for a prison. In the north, where the military threat continued until the union of 1603, the castles were generally in better order and some, like Wark-on-Tweed, Norham and Carlisle, were substantially strengthened under Henry VIII; still York, Mitford, Brougham and Appleby, once important bulwarks against the Scots, were ruined. Many of the castles which had once dominated the country's towns and cities found themselves abandoned, not worth the cost of maintenance either to the king or a thriving borough equipped with its own walls: thus Bristol, Norwich, Oxford, Totnes, Worcester, Reigate, Lewes, Bedford, Barnstaple, Guildford and others, once noble places, sank in varying stages of decay. John Leland's *Itinerary* is the most comprehensive survey we have of the English and Welsh

The battlements of Herstmonceux Castle gatehouse.

castles at the close of the medieval period. His descriptions, usually but not always of what he has seen, have been analysed by M W Thompson, who shows that, of the castles whose condition is described, barely a third were still in use, and in the rest the state of ruin was often complete.[1]

The castles which survived beyond 1500 were mostly great strategic fortresses, like London, Dover, Carlisle and Norham, or the comparatively modern buildings of the fourteenth and fifteenth centuries – Bodiam, Bolton and their like. Henry VII was a frequent visitor to the Tower of London and held a tournament there in 1501, but he was the last king to use the castle as a home. It had always been a State prison and under Henry VIII and his successors that was to be its paramount role, with subsidiary use as armoury, treasure house and mint: duties requiring substantial alterations, mostly damaging to the medieval fabric of the castle. Dover also remained important after 1500: Edward IV had spent at least £10,000 there but in subsequent centuries it seems, despite its position, to have been much neglected. In 1745 its conversion for the age of industrial warfare began, a process which demanded the reduction in height of both outer and inner curtains, numerous demolitions, and the insertion of 'bomb-proof' vaults in the keep; the castle saw active military service as late as the Second World War, and was garrisonned until 1958.

Carlisle was converted to the use of guns under Henry VIII and has remained, with periods of neglect, an important State garrison to the present day, a use scarcely compatible with the care of its medieval fabric. The accumulated dross of the centuries can make the attempt to see Dover, London or Carlisle dispiriting; that they retain a medieval aspect at all is a measure of their original greatness. Though Scarborough also remained a State fortress into the nineteenth century, and was attacked by two German cruisers as late as 1914, its wind-swept cliff-top is more atmospheric, probably because most subsequent building has been destroyed.

A number of other great castles, particularly those associated with the Duchy of Lancaster, were in good repair and sometimes improved during the fifteenth and sixteenth centuries. Among these were Lancaster itself, Pontefract, Knaresborough, Bolingbroke, Leicester, Warwick and Kenilworth.[2] The last of these received substantial additions at the hands of Robert Dudley, Earl of Leicester in the 1570s, on the occasion of a nineteen-day visit by Elizabeth I. Leicester's work, while less architecturally distinguished than John of Gaunt's, also sought to make the castle more comfortable while preserving it, by stylistic anachronism, as a setting for elaborate pageantry.

The late castles of Cooling, Bodiam, Sheriff Hutton, Wressle and Bolton were all still inhabited, in itself an indication that they were different in nature to the older fortresses. Yorkshire castles seem, in particular, to have shared the protracted life witnessed in more dangerous counties further to the north, and Leland saw a good number of stately piles, like Sheriff Hutton, serving as the homes of old families. But to these were added scarcely any new castles during the fifteenth century. Even discounting the ambiguous nature of the buildings for which they were granted, only one quarter of the licences were issued in the fifteenth as had been in the fourteenth century. The whole period can only show one true castle, the extraordinary Raglan in Gwent, with its massive hexagonal keep and machicolated towers; even in Northumberland and Cumbria, pele towers were virtually the only new fortifications.

For the rest, new buildings like Caister or Baconsthorpe in Norfolk, or Herstmonceux in Sussex, are but reflections of reflections, ever paler copies of imitation castles. Walls get thinner, towers slighter, and any attempt at providing for serious defence is abandoned in favour of a peacock-like display of martial bravura.[3] Brick, newly fashionable but structurally weaker than stone, is much the most common building material for these buildings. Little more than a moat and a strong door protects them from attack. Caister's brief resistance in 1469 was due more to the courage of its defenders and the nature of the assault than to the advantages of its design.

Almost the last two buidings to pretend to the status of castle were built in the 1480s by the same man, Lord Hastings. The earlier of the two was the keep added to his Leicestershire manor of Ashby-de-la-Zouch; this tower house, in itself a strong building, provided only for his own comfort and security in an otherwise barely defended house. Not far away, he began construction of a quadrangular brick castle at Kirby Muxloe in Leicestershire, a project which was cut short by his sudden execution, but whose remains, for all the gun-ports and battlements, are those of a manor-house. Inherently interesting and often attractive, these fifteenth-century variations on the theme may be, but they are not castles.

A summary of the state of English castles around 1500 reveals many to be abandoned if not ruined; some preserved for their strategic, judicial or administrative value; others, generally the most recent, still inhabited; and new buildings of greater pretension than strength – a confusing picture which demands explanation. It is certainly puzzling that a period of violent civil war, in which royal

Sheriff Hutton Castle.

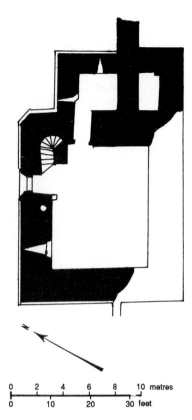

0 2 4 6 8 10 metres
0   10   20   30 feet

Ashby-de-la-Zouch, ground floor
of the new tower. (*After English
Heritage*)

authority was all but paralysed, should not have produced the rash of fortifications it had in King Stephen's time.

The development of cannon is the most obvious change in the nature of warfare in the fifteenth century, but the decline of the English castle can scarcely be attributed to this, for at the same period and throughout France, Italy and Spain, new castles were being built and old ones altered with the express purpose of facilitating their defence by guns. At Fougères in Ille-et-Vilaine, for example, two monstrous D-shaped towers were added to the curtain-wall, 21 metres (70 feet) high to the parapet, and 7 metres (23 feet) thick at the base; each had five vaulted storeys equipped with casemates for cannon, and was surmounted by a further two-storey building providing lodgings and magazine. Whole castles designed for the age of the cannon were built in France at Ham in Somme and, by the Spanish, at Salses in Pyrénées-Orientales, while equally impressive examples survive in Spain itself and in Italy.[4] The science of fortification in the age of artillery would progress rapidly during the sixteenth and seventeenth centuries, and an entirely new architectural idiom would be developed to cope with guns, but their initial impact on castles appears to have provoked adaptation rather than abandonment.

If the power of gunpowder did not, of itself, provoke the decline of the English castle, nor can the desire for better living accommodation be said to have done so, for the quality of the halls and lodgings sheltered behind these massive walls was often at least the equal of that offered by England's undefended courtyard houses – places like South Wingfield Manor. A man who could afford to build the castles demanded by the age of gunpowder, not only expected the highest quality in his home, but had the resources to pay for it. There is no sense of the bunker in the late-fifteenth century castles of France, but rather a lavish display of wealth: they prove that it was thought possible, for a while, to adapt the castle to the age of guns while simultaneously providing living-quarters of unprecedented splendour. In the end, of course, the guns became too effective and new defensive systems, all earth banks and angles and irreconcilable with the idea of the castle, were developed, but in 1500 that revolution was still some way off.

Clearly, anything which could be built in France could equally well be built in England. The two major factors for change – the growth of guns in warfare, and the desire for better living accommodation – affected English society as much as they did French and yet, with the exception of Raglan, there is simply nothing in England to compare with Fougères, Salses, Rambures or Coca. The idea of the castle clearly became discredited in England at least a century before it did in continental Europe, for reasons which must be local rather than general, and which, since they concern social and political attitudes, are more difficult to discern than the effect of artillery on stone walls.

The English medieval castle, given its importation from France and its role in the transformation of English society under Norman rule, was a fundamentally feudal institution. But the feudal structures of English society had begun to erode even in the fourteenth century as the balance of political and economic power shifted from the Crown to the barons and the emergent middle classes. In purely military terms, the concept of a feudal army had long been replaced, and the mounted knight himself was but an expensive element of armies which included trained foot-soldiers, armed with crossbow, longbow and, increasingly, with guns of all sizes and calibres. Consequently, the knight's castle was less and less relevant to the conduct of warfare: in a symbiotic relationship, the decline of one partner necessarily brings about the decline of the other.

In all the violence and slaughter of the Wars of the Roses, there was scarcely a siege: the issues were debated in desperate struggles at St Albans, Wakefield, Mortimer's Cross, Towton, Barnet and Bosworth. Such sieges as occurred were generally short, often reversed, and of no

The great tower added by Lord Hastings to Ashby-de-la-Zouch manor-house, in Leicestershire.

consequence to the progress of the war: the assault and capture of Caister was motivated by no more than robbery. Since the larger paid armies could campaign more consistently than the feudal levies, buying time with fortifications now had little value. What mattered was to control the towns and the people, the mechanism of government, and that was more effectively achieved in open battle than in protracted sieges: as long ago as 1264–5 it had become clear that a decisive battle could quickly transform a political situation and the experience of civil and national war since then had only confirmed it.

At the same time, the professionalization of warfare had had its effect on castles. In Stephen's time, an earth-and-timber castle could be a powerful military tool, but with the rise of larger forces, better equipped and protected with body-armour, such strongholds had long been outclassed by their stone successors. Many knights, unable or unwilling to keep pace with the financial escalation, had dropped out of the medieval arms race, their once-strong castles either abandoned for more comfortable quarters, as at Tretower in the Welsh borders, or simply allowed to decline to the status of a fortified manor. The gap between the upper and lower ranks of the nobility was also increasing steadily. More power – more lands and more castles – was concentrated in the hands of fewer men, lords who neither wished to, nor could, use and maintain all their castles. So, many deteriorated, while one or two became favourite residences and, like Kenilworth, were improved to meet new requirements of opulence.

Symptomatic of these social changes was the splintering of the castle's original role – home, fortress and administrative centre – into its constituent parts. The dynamic of the medieval castle lay in the tension between these principal, and other lesser, functions and as they separate it becomes clear that the castle, as a building rather than an idea, loses its relevance in English society. Scarborough and Dover were maintained only in their military role, no longer as royal houses; if, on the other hand, Bodiam or Kenilworth were still occupied, it was despite, not because of, their military qualities. At Lincoln, the administration of the law justified basic maintenance, while London survived for its usefulness as a prison and armoury. As the royal – the State – administration had been obliged by its own growth to abandon the simple structure of hall, chapel and chamber, so the increasing sophistication of English society produced a divergence of the functions it had been once able to combine in the castle.

Henry VII assisted this fragmentation both by chance and by royal policy. On his accession, he united the resources of the Crown – including about forty castles – with those he already possessed as Duke of Lancaster; to these he added further by acquisition and confiscation, so that in 1500 by far the greater number of serviceable castles were in royal hands. Even had the Crown possessed the resources to do so, it lacked the will to maintain unnecessary buildings, and so preservation depended on usefulness: where, like Conisbrough or Richmond, they had no real purpose, they were allowed to decay. The gathering of so many castles under royal control, where they could safely be left to moulder, also assisted Henry in his need to reduce the power of the nobility. He imposed controls on private retinues: impressed by the large numbers of liveried servants who had attended him when he stayed at Hedingham Castle, he nevertheless fined their lord 15,000 marks for exceeding the permitted number of retainers. Such crushing penalties transferred wealth to the State and extinguished any lingering desire to erect castles; those mighty subjects who still yearned to display their power contented themselves with the palatial houses characteristic of the sixteenth century.

The Elizabethan country house has its roots in Bodiam, and develops through Herstmonceux and Caister, before finally abandoning the pretence (if not entirely the style) of fortification in the triumph of conspicuous consumption that was Burghley House. The manor-house, low and comfortably disposed over a large area, has clearly had a peculiar attraction in England, and it may be that the growth of a national identity in the fourteenth and fifteenth centuries also helped make a move away from the castle more acceptable. English castles, always the articulation of an alien form, had been, like English cathedrals, less soaring than their French counterparts, preferring to spread comfortably on the land than to touch the hem of heaven. It is possible that there is something in the pragmatic English psyche which contributed to the earlier abandonment of castles in England.

A window at Kirby Muxloe Castle.

With the decline of feudalism, the defence of the realm became the responsiblity of a centralized State, and while it was many years before that responsibility ceased to be identified with the monarch's person, it may not be coincidental that the Tudor period saw the first English queens since before the Conquest. The fortifications of the sixteenth century – most notably the artillery forts built by Henry VIII to guard the coast from Yorkshire to Cornwall – were for the use of a professional army, and have more in common with the Martello towers erected against Napoleon than with castles. These utilitarian buildings, often architecturally impressive in their ingenious symmetry and distinctly post-medieval details, nevertheless lack human interest, for they were never homes; intellectually satisfying, they are emotionally barren, stripped of the tension which characterizes the castle. They underline, however, the age's continuing search for a solution in stone to the problems of cannon, and demonstrate that the English could build forts for guns even though they did not, like the French, wish to live in them.[5]

But for many castles, a final appearance in the footnotes, if not the pages of history beckoned: war between Charles I and Parliament began in the summer of 1642, on a scale as yet unknown in England. Although the outcome of the Civil War was decided by the sieges of towns like Oxford, Bristol, Newark and Hull, and pitched battles like Marston Moor and Naseby, many of the old fortified places of England were fought over once again, in actions which were often not less bloody and drawn-out for being local and irrelevant. Some of these sieges were brief: the walls of Lincoln Castle were scaled by Parliamentary troops one day in May 1644, under a cascade of rocks as its defenders resorted to primitive techniques of siege warfare. However, some were long and Bolton, South Wingfield and

Scarborough were among many castles which underwent bitter sieges.

Unlike the civil wars of the Middle Ages, the wars of 1642–8 were truly national and involved large numbers of ordinary citizens, perhaps because the issues were perceived, in a fervently religious age, as being of conscience. Thus there were adherents of both parties in every shire who, inexperienced in warfare and unconscious of national strategy, rushed to fortify places against one another and to hold them for king or Parliament. They were reacting to a military crisis not as the hard-bitten war-lords of the Wars of the Roses had done, but according to instinct; the idea of the castle, of the fortified place, touched a deep chord, and they responded to it. But, as has been said, the castle had found almost no place in English warfare since the fifteenth century and if it was neglected by the late-medieval tacticians, it was unlikely to be of real use 200 years later. Only where a castle stood in the centre of a town of importance, as at York or Colchester, was the outcome of the siege a matter of consequence to either side, and here it was the town which was under attack, with the castle merely forming a citadel within it.

So if this period has left tales of great sieges, it must be remembered that the castles were mostly being fought over by small forces, and the loss or gain of a remote fortress, like Bolton or South Wingfield, could make little difference to the outcome. Moreover, neither side in these engagements usually possessed cannon. When guns were set against medieval masonry, which after all was not built to withstand them, it fell; the royalists who had held South Wingfield Manor for many months in 1644 were obliged to surrender within hours of the arrival of Parliamentary guns: the damage inflicted by cannon on Scarborough keep in the course of a large-scale five-month siege is obvious. But because artillery was scarce and difficult to move, many sieges were conducted in medieval fashion, with muskets instead of bows, and so the greatest factor in the castle's strength, the spirit of its defenders, was often put to the test.

The re-use of these crumbling fortresses undoubtedly prolonged the fighting, complicated the development of the war, and caused many unnecessary deaths. Parliament decided that such a number of defensible places in the kingdom was a permanent threat to civil peace, and from 1646 began passing orders for the deliberate demolition, or slighting, of castles taken.

Kenilworth, Tonbridge, Pontefract, Bolton, South Wingfield, Wressle, Bolingbroke, Nottingham, Newark and Sandal are but some of the dozens of castles slighted after the Civil War; indeed so thoroughly was the task eventually done that it would be quicker to list the castles which escaped destruction. However, the slighting itself varied in degree: at Nottingham the work of demolition has left barely one stone upon another; but at Newark, despite its three-year

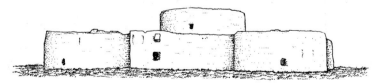

Camber Castle, near Rye in Sussex.

intermittent siege, the gatehouse, curtain and three towers survived. At Kenilworth, the castle was bought by a Parliamentary officer who transformed it into a home; only the north wall of the keep and the north curtain were brought down, though the great mere which protected the rest of the castle was drained.

The slighting of the castles had one major benefit for the historian and archaeologist: as with the abrupt death of the monasteries, it has kept them free of the accretions of later ages. Both monasteries and castles, each in their way so particularly medieval, have reached us unaltered by generations out of sympathy with their original spirit. A look at the depressing state of the castles which continue in regular use today confirms the advantage of the building abandoned at the end of its useful life, even though that abandonment has meant ruin. Some inhabited castles have preserved parts of great value – Warwick is an obvious example – but most, like Windsor, Alnwick and Arundel, are of primary interest to the historian of the nineteenth century not the Middle Ages. With one or two exceptions – Castell Coch and Cardiff, for instance – they have none of the purpose which can still be sensed at Rising, or Tonbridge, or Kenilworth; they are unsubstantial, often mean-spirited things suffused with the vanity of their builders. They reflect, like all architecture, the spirit of their age, and the nineteenth century was not at its most admirable in its castle building; in railway stations, industrial and public buildings, and often in churches, we should seek the better traits of the Victorian character, not in castles, restored or new-built.

But the reinterpretation of the medieval castle by subsequent generations is too long and too complex a story for this book. It begins certainly with Tattershall, and perhaps before, and spreads in ever more curious shapes to the beginning of this century. The buildings include toy castles like Bolsover, which might have appealed to Toad himself, follies like Edgehill tower, hulking brutes like Penrhyn, the inspired vision of Castell Coch, and the final purified subtlety of Lutyens' Castle Drogo. If our own time is the first not to have taken much part in the story, it may be because we are expending more, in care and in cash, on maintaining the real thing than any of our predecessors; we have, in any case, devised our own idioms to express overweening arrogance.

Buildings reveal attitudes, and the castles we have built and not built since the end of the Middle Ages reflect the highly charged and contradictory nature of the symbol. Writers and historians, painters and politicians have, as they will, taken the past and twisted it into some sort of order, some attempt at meaning. All that they have felt and given us, all the mixed-up ideas of pageantry and imprisonment, nobility and torture, fuse into a double image, which, given the dual nature of the building, is rather appropriate. The castle is a symbol of oppression and dominance, a storehouse of evil, and at the same time a place of refuge and safety, a protection against enemies: it depends so much on whether we are inside or outside its walls. Today the ivy which smothered ruins a century ago is being cleared; walls are excavated, lawns laid and knowledge extended; we know more about castles than did Byron or Wordsworth, though probably less than we think we do. We have formulated our own, twentieth-century idea of

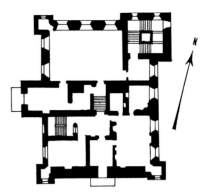

Bolsover Castle: plan of the 'Little Castle' of *c.*1620, no more than the suggestion of an idea. (*After English Heritage*)

Dreaming of castles: the medieval castle of La Rochepot, Côte-d'Or, extensively restored in the nineteenth century.

the buildings and the people who used them, but we are still the children of our parents, as they of theirs; the roots of our ideas reach back and, far from shaking off the contradictory fascination of the castle, we just shape the living idea with myths of our own.

The bones of the kingdom, in the end, seem to have served it well, for they held the realm together while more durable and subtle frames of law were forged to take up the burden. A man's house became his castle not because the king had allowed him to embattle its walls, but because the law, at least in principle, made it so.[6] The invisible idea replaces its visible expression: we are in the modern world, where ideas can be more powerful than weapons, though power is still not truth, and weapons still kill.

England's Castles
A visitor's list

The following list attempts only to point the reader towards the more rewarding castles to visit, and includes a fraction of the 1,500 to 2,000 sites in England. The selection is based principally on the extent and accessibility of the remains: those sites with no surviving masonry are rarely mentioned, though the minor ruins are often more atmospheric than the Alnwicks and Windsors, and the delight of discovery is one of the lasting pleasures of hunting down castles. For those who wish to find the more obscure sites, D J Cathcart King's two-volume *Castellarium Anglicanum* is the best starting-point. The historical English counties (i.e. before local government reorganization in 1974) form the basis of the list partly because when Roger de Somery built Weoley Castle he did so in Warwickshire, not in the West Midlands, but more importantly because most books describing medieval buildings (and crucially *The Buildings of England*) refer to the old counties. However, county changes affecting castle locations are noted below.

An asterisk (*) after a name indicates that the site is in the care of English Heritage. These are generally open daily from 10 a.m. to 6 p.m. in summer and to 4 p.m. in winter, though they may close for lunch between 1 and 2 p.m: a copy of the English Heritage handbook is an invaluable guide to anyone planning a visit. A cross (†) denotes that the castle is in private care, but is open to visitors at regular times; since these arrangements tend to alter, it is best to check details of opening, facilities, and access for disabled people in one of the publications which annually provide such information. Many lesser sites are on private land, and this should be assumed to be the case where there is neither asterisk nor cross.

Bedfordshire

Of about twenty-five castles which are recorded in the county, none survives except as earthworks: of these Yelden is a particularly fine motte and bailey.

Berkshire

Windsor† is an important and much visited castle, but the late-fourteenth-century gatehouse at Donnington* is in its way as rewarding.

Buckinghamshire

The gatehouse of a fortified house or castle at Boarstall† survives, otherwise there are only the earthworks of over twenty castles.

Cambridgeshire and the Isle of Ely

Once again, only earthworks, including the site of the important castle of Cambridge itself.

Cheshire

Beeston* is much the most impressive castle in Cheshire, though there are remains of the castle and the walls of Chester* itself; otherwise, Cheshire is strangely empty of castles for a border county.

Cornwall

Cornwall preserves an excellent motte-and-bailey castle with an unusual round keep at Launceston*, and a fine shell keep at Restormel.* Otherwise Tintangel* is impressive more for its site and associations than its architecture, and the shell keep at Trematon is not open to the public. In common with most south-coast counties, Cornwall has Henrician (and earlier) artillery forts.

Cumberland (now Cumbria)

The principal fortress was always Carlisle,* of which there are substantial remains, but other castles include Egremont* (early Norman gate and walls), the extensive remains of Cockermouth (not open to the public), and Penrith,* a much-ruined fourteenth-century communal shelter. Numerous pele towers exist in all conditions: Pevsner saw fifty-eight in the county (and thirty-two in Westmorland) and expected that he had overlooked some. In addition to these are a number of minor fourteenth-century castles, generally a tower with one or more ranges (Naworth, Greystoke, Muncaster) but nothing to compare with Bolton.

Derbyshire

The small castle of Peveril* in the north of the county is the only substantial masonry survival, though there are also slight remains at Codnor and Duffield.†

Devonshire

The most enjoyable castle to visit is Berry Pomeroy,* a castle of about 1300 which shelters ruined sixteenth-century buildings, and is tucked into a wooded valley near Totnes,* which also has a castle, a perfect, but slightly characterless, fourteenth-century shell keep and bailey. The gatehouse and walls of Exeter† can be seen, as may a simple square keep at Lydford,* and a complex site, largely representing a fourteenth-century reconstruction, at Okehampton.* Minor castles exist at Gidleigh (private), Tiverton† and Plympton,† and of a number of fortified houses, the well-known Compton Castle† should perhaps be mentioned.

Dorset

Corfe,† an almost unbelievably dramatic sight, takes precedence despite the treatment of Parliamentary gunpowder; it has a splendidly white rectangular keep, high-quality domestic ranges and a thirteenth-century enceinte. At Sherborne* the ruins of the episcopal castle may be seen, and at Christchurch,* in the suburbs of Bournemouth, there is a fine Norman hall and a small keep.

Durham

The episcopal castle still guards Durham,† but perhaps the most interesting and enjoyable castle in the county is at Barnard Castle,* a site with extensive remains, including a fine round keep, which was occupied from the eleventh century to the end of the medieval period. The other main castles belong to the fourteenth and fifteenth centuries: Raby† is the most important, but remains exist also at Lumley (a hotel), Hylton* (an impressive gatehouse, now in Tyne-and-Wear), Brancepeth (private), and Witton-le-Wear (a caravan site and hotel).

Essex

Most of the remains are early, including splendid keeps at Colchester† and Castle Hedingham.† Other masonry remains are slight (a shattered keep at Saffron Walden† and two towers at Hadleigh*), but the scale of earthworks, like Ongar and Pleshey, is often impressive.

Gloucestershire

Berkeley Castle,† which is still a home, is the most important, with a fine shell keep and a full range of fourteenth-century domestic buildings. St Briavel's* (in the Forest of Dean) has a fine gatehouse of about 1300, and at Beverstone (private) are substantial later remains.

Hampshire and the Isle of Wight

Pre-eminent is Portchester,* originally a Roman fort to which were added a Norman keep, and a suite of domestic buildings for Richard II. The hall of the royal castle at Winchester† is complete, and there are parts of the episcopal castles at Wolvesey,* Bishop's Waltham* and Merdon. At Odiham, the shell of King John's octagonal keep may be seen. Carisbrooke,* with a shell keep, fourteenth-century gatehouse and domestic buildings, is the only substantial castle on the Isle of Wight.

Herefordshire
(now amalgamated with Worcestershire)

Goodrich,* on the Welsh border, dates principally from about 1300 and is exceptionally well preserved; beside it there is nothing of major importance in the county, though there is a round keep at

Longtown,* and lesser ruins at Clifford, Wigmore and Bronsil. Croft,† Treago and Brampton Bryan, all late-medieval castles, are still inhabited.

Hertfordshire

Though there is stonework at Berkhamsted,* it is the earthworks which impress; otherwise there is only the modernized gatehouse at Hertford,† and scant masonry at Bishop's Stortford.

Huntingdon and the Soke of Peterborough (now Cambridgeshire)

The best thing is not a castle at all: Buckden Palace,† residence of the Bishops of Lincoln, was built in the later fifteenth century in imitation of Tattershall and has largely survived; otherwise only earthworks, including those in the county town.

Kent

Kent vies with Northumberland for first position in any list such as this, and only brief details can be included. The most important stone castles are, for the twelfth century, Canterbury,† Chilham,† Dover,* Eynsford,* Rochester;* for the thirteenth, Allington,† Tonbridge* and Leeds;† and for the fourteenth, Cooling, Saltwood† and Scotney. There are also masonry remains at Leybourne, Shoreham, Stone, Sutton Valence,* Thurnham, Westenhanger and West Malling,* as well as numerous earthworks. Whether the buildings at Hever† and Lympne† should be included is open to question.

Lancashire

The most impressive part of Lancaster Castle,† the late-fourteenth-century gatehouse, may be seen from the road; the castle, though open to the public in part, continues to be a court and prison. A small square keep survives at Clitheroe,† and an interesting early-fourteenth-century castle with keep, inner and outer wards, on Piel Island,* near Barrow-in-Furness (now in Cumbria). There are a number of pele towers.

Leicestershire

Apart from fragments of the castle in Leicester, and the late-fifteenth-century works at Ashby-de-la-Zouch* and Kirby Muxloe,* there are only earthworks, like King John's Sauvey.

Lincolnshire

Lincoln,† Bolingbroke* and Tattershall† are the most important sites; otherwise stonework exists at Grimsthorpe† and Somerton, where towers are incorporated in later buildings, and at South Kyme, where a fourteenth-century tower remains in what was a moated site.

London and Middlesex

Today there is only the huge Tower of London;* the capital's two other castles, Baynard's and Mountfichet, vanished in the thirteenth century, the former to be replaced by an unfortified building of the same name.

Norfolk

There are important early keeps at Norwich,† Castle Rising,* Castle Acre* and New Buckenham,† and other Norman remains at Weeting* and Mileham. Caister† and Baconsthorpe* are slight fifteenth-century courtyard castles, while at Middleton there is a brick tower perhaps inspired by Tattershall; Oxburgh Hall† is a fine moated manor.

Northamptonshire

The county's most important surviving castle, Barnwell, is open to the public only rarely; it was begun about 1266 and forms a rectangular enclosure with corner towers, but it has been suggested that it was never finished, for it was sold to Ramsey Abbey ten years later. Otherwise there is only Rockingham,† with a late-thirteenth-century gatehouse in a motte and bailey obscured by later building, and numerous earthworks.

Northumberland

It is impossible to list all the castles, fortified houses and pele towers in Northumberland, but the finest are probably Warkworth,* Alnwick,† Dunstanburgh,* Norham,* Prudhoe,* Newcastle† and Tynemouth* (the last two now in Tyne-and-Wear). More fragmentary remains exist at Mitford, Etal,* Berwick-on-Tweed,* Morpeth, Edlingham,* Cartington and in many other places. Bamburgh† is best seen from four or five kilometres away, and though its view of the coast and the sea is fine, the castle itself is of little architectural interest. Aydon Castle,* near Corbridge, is an attractive fortified house. Among sites which are not open to the public are Bywell and Bothal (which both have impressive gatehouses) and the remains of a large quadrangular castle at Ford. Probably as fine as any of the county's numerous pele towers is Belsay* which has the additional attraction of beautiful gardens and an exquisite early-nineteenth century house.

Nottinghamshire

A poor county in the Middle Ages, Nottinghamshire never had many castles; its finest ruin today is at Newark† which has a gatehouse and curtain of about 1140, as well as towers and alterations of later periods. Nottingham† preserves slight remains on an impressive site, but otherwise there are only a dozen earthwork sites.

Oxfordshire

Of a number of early castles, there are only slight remains in the county town, including a tall twelfth-century tower. Of the fourteenth century are Rotherfield Greys,† Shirburn and Bampton, the last two of which are not open to the public.

Rutland (now Leicestershire)

Rutland has only Oakham† which, if its aspect is no longer very military, remains beautiful and evocative, and some slight earthworks.

Shropshire

Ludlow, with remains dating from the period of the Conquest to the seventeenth century, is much the most important site in the county, but there are a number of interesting lesser castles, including Clun (keep),† Hopton, Shrewsbury,† Bridgnorth (fragment of keep),† Moreton Corbet (keep),* and Whittington (gatehouse). At Stokesay* and Acton Burnell* are two very different fortified houses dating from around 1300.

Somerset

There are two contrasting late-fourteenth-century castles at Farleigh Hungerford* and Nunney,* the first quadrangular, the second a large tower house. Apart from these there are much altered remains at Dunster† and Taunton,† and lesser fragments at Stogursey (overgrown walls) and Bridgewater (a water gate). The Bishop's Palace at Wells† is moated and lightly fortified. At Bristol (now in Avon), the once-important castle has left only slight remains of its keep and other fragments.

Staffordshire

Dudley† (now in the West Midlands) has a keep and extensive domestic ranges in a site 'adapted' to modern use as a zoo, and Tamworth† has a large shell keep whose internal buildings are occupied by a museum. Tutbury,† on its huge hill, has interesting fourteenth-century remains, and Chartley is visible from the road; Stafford† completes the list of important sites.

Suffolk

The county's best-preserved sites are close to one another: Orford* and the slightly later towered curtain of Framlingham.* Bungay's† keep and curtain is overgrown but interesting, and there are later gatehouses and curtains at Wingfield† and Mettingham. Earthworks, as in the other East Anglian counties, are often impressive.

Surrey

The county has the remains of an interesting keep amid later buildings at Farnham,* while another battered example survives a little incongruously in the centre of Guildford, the county town.

Sussex

Perhaps because its coastline afforded few good harbours, Sussex never had as many castles as Kent or Hampshire; moreover, many of its important fortresses have suffered badly over the years. Still, Arundel,† Bodiam,† Herstmonceux,† Lewes,† and Pevensey* all preserve important remains, while lesser sites include Amberley, Bramber,† Hastings† and Knepp. The town defences of Rye† and Winchelsea† are worth seeing.

Warwickshire

Apart from the major sites at Warwick† and Kenilworth,* and a lesser privately owned castle at Maxstoke, the county has only fragments to show at Weoley,† Caludon† (both now in the West Midlands) and Hartshill and, among many earthworks, the fine motte and bailey at Brinklow.

Westmorland (now Cumbria)

There are important castles, all with rectangular keeps, at Appleby,† Brough* and Brougham,* and another, later and in a less well-preserved condition, at Kendal.† Pele towers, with or without adjacent ranges, are common, and include Sizergh† and Yanwath.

Wiltshire

Early castles exist at Old Sarum,* Devizes and Ludgershall (very ruinous),* but the most architecturally rewarding is undoubtedly the tower at Old Wardour.*

Worcestershire
(now amalgamated with Herefordshire)

Virtually nothing survives of any of the county's few castles.

Yorkshire

As with Northumberland and Kent, the following is but a selection of the most important castles. The remains of York castle itself, a keep also known as Clifford's Tower* and two wall towers are rather overshadowed by the city walls.

East Riding (now Humberside)

Masonry survives only at Wressle, of a late and weak quadrangular castle, but there are a number of earthworks, including Skipsea.*

North Riding

The most important castles are, for the eleventh and twelfth centuries, Bowes (rectangular keep, now in County Durham),* Helmsley,* Middleham (keep),* Richmond,* and Scarborough;* for the thirteenth, Scarborough, again with its barbican and walls; and for the fourteenth, Pickering,* Bolton,† Ravensworth, Sheriff Hutton, and Snape.

West Riding

Some of the castles of the West Riding were once very important, but great fortresses like Pontefract† and Sandal† have suffered dreadfully over the years. More impressive are the twelfth-century fortresses of Conisbrough* (and Tickhill), thirteenth-century Skipton,† and fourteenth-century Knaresborough† and Harewood.

Glossary

ALLURE   See wall-walk.

ASHLAR   Stone laid in even, dressed blocks with very narrow joints.

BAILEY   Originally the defended yard adjoining a motte, but applied generally to the area(s) enclosed by castle walls.

BALLISTA   A heavy crossbow, mounted on a stand.

BARBICAN   A defensive work built in advance of the castle gate, often intended to constrain the area available to an attacker.

BARMKIN   The small walled yard attached to a pele tower.

BARTIZAN   A small turret projecting from the summit of a wall or parapet, generally covering an angle.

BATTER   The outwardly sloping base of a wall caused by a thickening of the masonry.

BERM   The flat and narrow piece of ground between a moat and castle wall, where these do not rise sheer from the water.

CAPITAL   The head, often decorated, of a pillar.

CHAMFER   The surface left when a corner is cut across at an angle of 45°.

CHEMIN-DE-RONDE   French term for a wall walk, particularly associated with the continuous circuits of late-medieval French castles.

CRENEL   The space between merlons (see below) on a battlemented wall, also known as an embrasure.

CURTAIN   Stone wall between towers, from which it may be said to hang like a curtain.

DONJON   Most common medieval term for keep.

DRESSING   Worked stone used for windows, doorways, angles – all features of a stone building.

EMBRASURE   See crenel.

ENCEINTE   A fortified enclosure

FOREBUILDING   Structure attached to a keep and serving the same function as a barbican.

GALLERY   In larger keeps (and churches), a passage running through the thickness of the wall and opening on to the principal space.

GARDEROBE   Properly a store-room for valuable items, but generally applied since the last century to latrines in castles and medieval houses.

HAMMERBEAM ROOF   Late-medieval form of roof supported on horizontal beams (hammerbeams) projecting from the walls; it enabled the central span of the roof to be open.

HOARDING   Timber structure projecting externally from the face of a wall and permitting a soldier to see the foot of the wall without himself being seen.

KEEP   The strongest single element of a castle, capable of independent defence, generally a tower of wood or stone.

LIGHT   Compartment of a window.

LOOP   A narrow slit, either admitting light to a basement or stair or, as in arrow-loop, designed for shooting.

MACHICOLATION   A structure similar to a hoarding, but built of stone and hence a permanent defensive feature; generally more common in continental castles than in English ones.

MANGONEL   A large stone-throwing engine, operating on the principle of torsion.

MERLON   Solid, upright part of a battlemented parapet offering shelter to a soldier on the wall-walk.

MEURTRIÈRE   An aperture in the roof or walls of a vaulted passage, through which an assailant can be safely attacked; also known as a 'murder hole'.

MOTTE   The large earthen mound on which a castle's keep once stood and which often forms the principal relic of England's early castles.

PELE TOWER   Isolated keep-like tower, built during the later Middle Ages in northern England, but more commonly in Scotland and Ireland.

PIER   A pillar of other than round section.

POSTERN   Small doorway useful for entering or leaving a castle after the main gates have been closed; sometimes also usable as a sally-port (see below).

QUOIN   The cornerstone which the builder did not reject.

SALLY-PORT   Postern used for making violent sorties from a castle under siege.

SERVICE ROOMS   Buttery (where drink was kept) and pantry (for dry goods, including bread) are often found at the low end of the hall, either side of the passage to the kitchen.

SOLAR   A term applied to the more private inner living-room of a castle or medieval house.

SHELL KEEP   The term created to describe circular stone keeps, generally with timber buildings within, which often crowned mottes.

TREBUCHET   Large and effective catapult.

VICE   Spiral stair.

WALL-WALK   The flat pathway protected by battlements on the summit of a castle wall, also known as the allure.

WARD   A castle courtyard.

End-Notes

Chapter 1

1. The red stone of the knoll gave the castle its name, Rougemont (red hill); a rare occasion, as Fuller observed, of an English castle not being named after the settlement it protected.

2. The joust, that enduring image of the Middle Ages, started life as a violent form of military training; only later in the period, as the cult of chivalry developed, did it acquire the more refined entertainment imagined by twentieth-century myth-makers. Stenton (1965) p. 82 ff.

3. The Bayeux Tapestry shows William building a castle at Hastings before the battle, a clear indication of his military priorities.

4. For early French castles, see Anderson (1970), Châtelain (1987) and Salch (1987).

5. *The Tower of London* guidebook (Brown and Curnow 1984) p. 5.

6. Cf. Brown (1989) p. 32; Salch (1987) p. 133. The word basement is used throughout to indicate that there was no direct access from the outside; keep basements are rarely actually below ground level.

7. Stenton (1965) p. 22 ff.

Chapter 2

1. By 1087, when *Domesday Book* was compiled, the king retained a fifth of the country in his own hands, the church held a fourth, and the dozen greatest magnates another fourth. Of course, lands were held by lesser men from these great landlords.

2. The reference to *Castelli nostri de Acra* (our castle of Acre) in the charter of foundation of Lewes Priory, in 1088, indicates that the word castle could be applied to structures which were militarily quite weak; see Armitage (1912) p. 124.

3. Armitage (1912) pp. 89–90, quoting the *Historia Ardensium* of Walter de Clusa.

4. King (1988) p. 42.

5. It is possible that other castles could be attributed to him, though the great motte at Thetford is no longer thought to be his work: see Brown (1989) pp. 213–14.

6. The explanation may lie in an agreement whereby Lewes was returned, during a crisis in 1079, to the king, who gave de Warenne extensive Norfolk estates, where he raised Castle Acre, in exchange. It is possible that a second motte was built at this time to permit both the king and the long-term holder of the castle to have his keep.

7. Brown (1989) pp. 1331–2; this castle, abandoned in favour of a new, stone-built one in the town of Montgomery, is now known as Hen Domen.

8. The account of the siege of Le Puiset by Louis VI of France in 1111 draws a vivid sketch of an assault on such a castle: at first the defenders sallied out to attack the royal forces, only to be pushed back to the gatetower, which Louis' troops then attempted to burn down using a typically revolting combustible mixture of pigs' fat and dried blood. At the same time a diversionary attack on another part of the bailey was repulsed by the defending cavalry, who rode out and cut down the attackers as they tried to get up the scarp of the ditch; the bailey was finally taken when the besiegers chopped at its timber walls with axes and broke through. See Anderson (1970) p. 82.

9. *Castle Acre* guidebook (Coad 1984).

10. Wilson (1985) p. 9.

Chapter 3

1. Rowley (1983) p. 47.

2. William and his two sons created few earls. The confusing proliferation of the title occurred under Stephen and Matilda, who created nine and six respectively, compared with only the seven existing in 1135: Poole (1955) p. 157.

3. King (1988) pp. 93–6.

4. Hassall (1957) pp. 49–50.

Chapter 4

1. It was at this siege that William de Warenne, newly created Earl of Surrey, sustained his fatal wounds.

2. Only in Normandy can much of Henry's work still be seen. There he was responsible for work on the great castles at Rouen, Caen (where he built the keep), Gisors, Falaise, Arques and Château-sur-Epte (a sophisticated motte and bailey) among many others: Châtelain (1983), Colvin (1963), and Salch (1987).

3. Robert spent the rest of his long life in unhappy confinement, ending at Cardiff Castle, where he may have composed a surviving poem in Welsh lamenting the fate of a man too young to die.

4. Even in AD390 Vegetius had recommended the provision of chutes over gates to permit defenders to douse such dangerous fires: Toy (1939) p. 85.

5. *Lincoln* guidebook (Elliott and Stocker 1984).

Chapter 5

1. It is not known for certain how the rooms in the keep were used, so this description is to some degree conjectural. One of the mysteries of the keep – as with the White Tower – is the absence of any obvious kitchen, like the ones that can be seen in the keeps at Castle Rising or Norwich.

2. The holes in the inner face of the north wall were for pigeons: a society so close to the sources of its food was provident.

3. Bishop Nigel rebuilt the Conqueror's motte and bailey at Ely (and possibly that at Willingham), only to lose it to King Stephen: Armitage (1912) p. 149; Renn (1968) p. 89.

4. Wood (1965) p. 166.

5. *Sherborne Old Castle* guidebook (White 1971), quoting the *Itinerary* of John Leland, ed. L. Toulmin Smith (1910), vol. 1, p. 154.

Chapter 6

1. John of Ford, *The Life of Wulfric of*

Haselbury: from *The Cistercian World* translated by P. M. Matarasso; (Penguin Classics, 1993. Copyright P. M. Matarasso 1993. Reproduced by permission of Penguin Books Ltd.).

2. *Castle Acre* guidebook (Coad 1984).

3. Church and cathedral building seems to have continued during the period. It has been suggested that the splendid west front of Castle Acre priory was going up at the same time as the nearby keep. Important work also continued during these years at the cathedrals of Norwich and Ely, and the abbey of Bury St. Edmunds, among others: Musset (1983) p. 243 (Norwich), pp. 269–74 (Castle Acre priory); Pevsner and Radcliffe, *Suffolk* (1974) p. 132 ff (Bury St Edmunds).

4. *Gesta Stephani* (Poole 1955) p. 51–3.

5. *Castle Rising* guidebook (Brown 1978) p. 11.

6. The dating of the medieval remains at Arundel is unclear but, given the extent of de Albini's other castle-works, it is probably that the shell keep and other early Norman work are due to him; cf. Brown (1989) p. 40.

7. The use of timber stockades alongside high-quality stone building was not uncommon. The keep at Bowes (once in Yorkshire, now in Durham), which is of similar if more spartan design, was never defended by more than a palisade, while the other ward at Pickering retained its timber defences until 1326.

8. *Lincoln Castle* guidebook (Elliott and Stocker 1984) p. 11.

9. According to *Gesta Stephani* (p. 121), Rannulf had, in 1145, added by force of arms so much territory to his own that he controlled a third of the kingdom.

10. *Lincoln Castle* p. 6, quoting Sir Francis Hill's *Medieval Lincoln* (1948); the original story is told by Odericus Vitalis.

11. In his introduction to *Gesta Stephani*, Poole argues that 1140 rather than 1149 (as often stated) is the true date of this important pact.

12. *Gesta Stephani* p. 121.

Chapter 7

1. Other Norman castles where the

strongest point is also the entrance include those of Newark and Ludlow.

2. The inner arch of the old gateway has since been reopened.

Chapter 8

1. Castle Acre had come to William of Blois on his marriage to Isabel, the de Warenne heiress. Thetford was a huge motte and bailey, whose earthworks remain. But the site of Walton has been lost to the sea; Framlingham was so thoroughly rebuilt in the 1190s that few traces of the first castle can be seen. Bungay, however, has interesting ruins which include the lower part of a keep similar to Hedingham and Scarborough, closely ringed by a later wall.

2. Round church towers are relatively common in Norfolk and Suffolk, the former county possessing no fewer than 119, while the latter has 41. Holy Trinity, in the castle town of Bungay, has an eleventh-century example: most of these towers date originally from the Norman period, and developed because good stone for corners was rare.

3. Purpose-built prisons are rare in English castles: prisoners were not detained in vast numbers, and their accommodation seems usually to have been provided in basements or towers. Newark Castle preserves a bottle dungeon, that awful unlit place into which unfortunate people were lowered by means of a trapdoor.

4. The right taken by feudal overlords to choose husbands for their tenants' female heirs arose from a wish to keep control of their lands. The lord's co-operation might sometimes be purchased, but rich women had to wait until Magna Carta to obtain the right not to be married against their consent.

5. *Castle Acre* guidebook (Coad 1984) pp. 12–14.

6. In this poorer part of the kingdom, and throughout Scotland and Ireland, the plain rectangular keep continued for several centuries in the form of the tower house; but these structures, built as a refuge from marauders rather than as a base for aggressive action, where the poor counties' equivalent of the fortified manor and not the castle.

Chapter 9

1. See King (1988) p. 96.

2. Single-tower gateways never fell completely into disuse: they were built, for instance, at Framlingham (1190–1200), Helmsley (1200), Allington (1290), Middleham and Pickering (fourteenth century). However, a number of gatehouses, especially in the later Middle Ages, were intended to look as if they had twin towers, but actually did not: Warwick and Maxstoke, in the same county, are of this type. Town and monastic gates continued to be accommodated in single towers: examples among the former include those of York, Southampton, Beverley and Winchester; and among abbey gates, those of Cleeve, Bury St Edmonds, Colchester, Thornton and Roche. The twin-towered idea was echoed in the lodges so characteristic of the eighteenth- and nineteenth-century country house.

3. It is not known whether the inner or the outer curtain was built first, a problem not eased by the advanced design of this tower, and the rest of Henry's outer wall.

4. Two other castles still existed in London at the end of the twelfth century, Baynard's on the river near St Paul's, and Mountfichet at Addle Hill, but both were destroyed early in the next century; the site of Baynard's Castle was subsequently used for a Tudor palace which took the same name.

Chapter 10

1. Its most forward-looking idea was contained in the last clause, which laid a duty on a group of twenty-five barons to 'distrain and distress' the king by seizing his castles, lands and possessions and by any other means short of attacks upon his person or his family, should they consider him to have transgressed the rights given him in law. This idea, so un-feudal in concept, shows the extent to which the English constitution had developed since 1066: the concept of a king held in check by the law, as interpreted by the majority of an assembly of barons, was radical.

2. A starving garrison would eventually be obliged to surrender, however strong and well designed the castle. In 1266, having been reduced to eating their horses, the rebels besieged in Kenilworth Castle capitulated; that castle was then as strong as any in the kingdom, but Henry III had been prepared to wait the six months it took to exhaust its defenders' supplies and courage.

3. This medieval artillery was of two main types, the mangonel and the trebuchet. The former was probably in use at Rochester; its power came from torsion and it could be temperamental in damp weather, as well as being difficult to set a range for. The trebuchet was the latest technology, probably first used in England during these wars, and worked on a simple system of counterweight; one advantage it had over the mangonel was that by adjusting the counterweight, it was possible to adjust the range of the shot.

4. Warren (1961) p. 247.

5. A mark was two-thirds of a pound: 13s 4d (67p). The defeated knights at Rochester were themselves held to ransom: William de Albini, the commander, was released only on payment of a colossal fine of 6,000 marks, and William de Eynsford, of nearby Eynsford Castle, did not finish paying his fine until after the death of King John.

6. The situation was obviously quite different in the border counties of the north and west and, to a lesser degree, on the south coast, where castles were often kept at a higher level of readiness, saw more action, and were used for longer than their inland counterparts.

7. Poole (1955) p. 18.

8. MacGregor (1983) p. 41.

9. To surrender a castle could have repercussions after the cessation of hostilities: the constable of Appleby and twenty-five others were fined sums ranging from 500 to 2 marks by Henry II for abandoning the castle to the Scots in 1174.

Chapter 11

1. Sauvey was built around 1210 as a motte and bailey, an interesting late survival of the type, which was, however, still in use in Scotland, Wales and Ireland at least as late as this.

2. Much of the castle was destroyed to its foundations after the Civil War, but the whole plan is clear; the towers do not seem to have been well designed for

defence by archers.

3. He was the grandson of the Rannulf who seized Lincoln Castle in 1141.

4. One of the towers is now octagonal, with five faces to the field: it was rebuilt between 1451 and 1456, at a cost of £271, excluding the stone.

5. For Leland, see Thompson (1987) p. 171; for Holles, see Colvin (1963) p. 571.

6. See Lawrence (1936) p. 87. For the siege of Krak, see Fedden (1954) pp. 51–2. Chastel Pélerin is also known as Athlit.

7. Nor did Henry II, that other innovative castle builder, even go on crusade, despite his promise to do so in expiation of his part in the murder of Thomas Becket.

8. Rannulf, and his fellow Earls of Leicester and Pembroke, were the three greatest English landlords in Normandy after the king: Warren (1961) p. 103.

9. See Châtelain (1984) pp. 281–5, 304–17 and 340–7, and Salch (1987) pp. 52–4; Boulogne would appear to succeed rather than precede Bolingbroke.

Chapter 12

1. *Sir Gawain and the Green Knight* translated by Brian Stone; (Penguin Classics, 1974. Copyright Brian Stone 1974. Reproduced by permission of Penguin Books Ltd.). pp. 50–51.

2. The medieval Lanthorn Tower was burnt out in 1774; the present structure is a nineteenth-century building on a slightly different site.

3. The vault is little more than a century old, but replaces a medieval, possibly wooden, original.

4. Colvin (1963) pp. 713–15. One of Henry's surviving orders is for the construction of a hoarding at the top of the south face of the keep, in order that the soldiers might better see the foot of the wall. The provision of such a hoarding on the most protected side of the keep implies that similar ones existed on the other three sides, and is firm evidence for such works on rectangular keeps.

5. Harvey (1959) pp. 97–9.

6. Colvin (1963) p. 759.

7. The Flint, Brick, Constable and Lanthorn Towers are modern reconstructions, as is the wall between the latter and the Salt Tower.

Chapter 13

1. The lesson was understood by Edward who ensured that all his castles in North Wales (except Builth) could be relieved by sea.

2. This was not the only means of obtaining such fire-power. At Caernarfon, galleries in the thickness of the curtain provided additional arrow-loops below the battlements, and the west curtain at London was pierced by twenty-three embrasures.

3. This has since acquired the more sensational label of Traitor's Gate. Most of the names ascribed to the wall-towers of London, Dover and other castles are post-medieval and often misleading.

4. For the attribution of the work to James of St George, and the Savoyard origins of some of the castles' details, see Taylor (1985) pp. 1–44.

5. For the association of Edward I with the round table, see *Winchester Castle* guidebook (Biddle and Clayre 1983) pp. 36–41.

Chapter 14

1. Powicke (1962) pp. 422, 441.

2. King Edward contributed directly to the construction of a number of baronial castles in Wales and the Marches in an attempt to reinforce the ability of the local nobility to resist Welsh rebellion: among these was the castle of Denbigh and probably those of Chirk, Holt and Hawarden, all in Clywd.

Chapter 15

1. It is possible that the arch opening at first-floor level was a door rather than a window, though this would not accord well with the internal arrangements.

2. Edward II also raised a number of pele towers in Yorkshire and Northumberland in the not entirely vain hope of deterring Scottish incursion: Colvin (1963) pp. 235, 671.

3. *Pickering Castle* guidebook (Thompson 1958).

4. This campaign, fought with particular savagery (witness the massacre of prisoners at Castle Douglas in 1307 or Forfar in 1308), was notable for the ingenious use of rope ladders by the Scots to effect surprise assaults by night.

5. Among them the Earl of Gloucester, son of Gilbert de Clare, who was barely 20 years old, and Robert Clifford, the builder of Brougham and Skipton Castles.

6. *Aydon Castle* guidebook (Dixon 1988).

Chapter 16

1. Henry III spent £15,000 on Windsor, and Edward III £50,000; George IV gave Wyatville over £1 million. Even allowing for the changing value of money, it is unsurprising that, St George's Chapel aside, the castle is of primary interest to the historian of the nineteenth century.

2. Sheen was demolished on the orders of Richard II after his wife died there – a touching piece of late-medieval theatre; it stood on the site of what is now Richmond Palace. Eltham survives as a moat and a fifteenth-century hall, hidden away in south-east London. Havering has gone.

3. Thompson (1988) p. 43 ff.

4. A licence to crenellate is no more certain evidence of the date of a building than of its nature, for they were often sought after the event.

5. To these may be added the Berkshire castles of Aldworth and Beaumyss, begun about 1338 but completely destroyed, Ford (licensed in 1348) and others in Northumberland.

6. Leland (1910) vol. 5, p. 72.

7. While they were abroad, England's king and nobility had, in any case, little opportunity to rebuild their castles, and it was only upon their return, if they were fortunate enough to have enriched themselves, that, like the Earls of Warwick, they looked to their castles.

8. The manuscript of *Sir Gawain and the Green Knight* makes a clear reference to the Order of the Garter itself by concluding with its motto, *Hony soyt qui mal pence.*

Chapter 17

1. Colvin (1963) pp. 842–3.

2. It is worth comparing Bodiam with the contemporary west gate at Canterbury: here gun-loops on three levels point in four different directions from each tower. It is during this period of fortification that gun-loops make their first appearance in England, simultaneously in Richard's gatehouse at Carisbrooke and at Canterbury. Firearms had been purchased regularly by the English Crown from the mid-fourteenth century and were, by the 1380s, getting larger and more effective. At this time, their limitations probably favoured the static needs of a castle's defenders than its attackers.

3. Johnson (1978) p. 132.

4. Harvey (1944) p. 39. The inscription is on a copper tablet fixed to the right-hand tower (as seen from the road). It should be said that the verse, which has a ring of the sixteenth century about it, may well be later than the castle itself.

5. Goodman (1977) p. 177 ff.

6. *Bolton Castle* guidebook (Jackson 1984).

7. Barley (1986) pp. 94–6.

8. After a long gap, the feudal levies were called up for the last time in history to meet the threat of French invasion in 1385.

Chapter 18

1. At the end of the thirteenth century, the Bishop of Bath and Wells built a very interesting two-storey castellated house at Acton Burnell in Shropshire; while in 1307 the Percys raised a similar building at Spofforth in Yorkshire: these were simply strong houses, but they underline the continuing validity of the defensible stone hall.

2. There are a number of Irish examples of rectangular keeps with round corner towers, of which the oldest, at Carlow, is thought to date from the early thirteenth century: Leask (1946) pp. 47–51.

3. Powerful gatehouses which, like Tonbridge's, had all the attributes of the self-contained keep, were also built in the north and excellent examples survive at Carlisle and Tynemouth.

4. A keep was built to a similar plan about 1200 at Trim, in County Meath, by Hugh de Lacy, Henry II's justiciar in Ireland. It was square, like Warkworth about 20 metres (65 feet) on each side, with square towers attached to the centre of each face, and survives almost complete. Another of this odd family exists at Castle Rushen on the Isle of Man.

Chapter 19

1. Music was important to the wealthy households of the fourteenth century not only for entertainment, but also to mark the day's various activities. In 1379, some ten years before the building of the new hall at the castle, John paid for the installation of a parquet floor for dancing at Christmas in the priory hall at Kenilworth. Dancing was increasing in popularity and may be further evidence of a ritualization of life within the English aristocracy.

2. Commercial empires, of course, are particularly notable for the erection of huge towers; symbolism can be primitive even in the modern shiny world.

3. Henry was born at Bolingbroke Castle in Lincolnshire, one of many held by his father, and so acquired the name by which he is known in Shakespeare's *Richard II*.

4. Jones (1980) p. 49 ff. Bolingbroke's son, Henry V, also stands accused of causing the deaths of 12,000 refugees from Rouen, whom he refused to allow to cross the English lines; cf. Harvey (1963) p. 174.

5. Goodman(1977) pp. 147–8.

6. Thomas extorted £8,000 in ransom from the Archbishop of Sens after the Battle of Poitiers, and presumably this contributed to the rebuilding at Warwick.

Chapter 20

1. One of his earliest duties was to assess the financial position of the Crown, which would be presented to Parliament in the hope that it would grant a substantial sum towards the deficit. This document goes far to explain the weakness of the Crown during the fifteenth century: unavoidable annual expenditure exceeded available revenue by some £20,000, without allowing for the prosecution of the war with France; while ancient debts were estimated at £110,000. These debts shifted the balance of power between the Crown and the great magnates. See Goodman (1977) p. 268.

2. Both castles were rebuilt by William Burges for the Marquess of Bute in the later Victorian period, the results being perhaps the most successful of all such work. Their importance in this context was the mutual attraction, which motivated and informed all their work, to the spirit of medieval society of both architect and patron. Less attractive, because less genuine, retrospection can be seen in the surface neo-classicism of today.

3. Hastings knew Tattershall, for he was also building a brick castellated house at Kirby Muxloe, near Ashby, and sent his mason to study the Lincolnshire castle.

4. That the manor was both comfortable and convenient may be inferred from the fact that it was lived in until the middle of the eighteenth century, long after most castles had been abandoned.

Chapter 21

1. Thompson (1987) p. 104.

2. In 1478 Warwick came into the hands of Richard of Gloucester (later Richard III) and he began construction of a huge tower which, in plan at least, had affinities with Cromwell's work at Tattershall. It was built on the vulnerable northern side of the castle and had the only gun-loops evident at Warwick, but survives only in truncated form as the Bear and Clarence Towers with a later gateway between them.

3. The walls are as little as 0.5 metres (2 feet) thick in places at Caister, while those of the tall tower which makes the building's principal claim to be considered a castle are a mere 1.25 metres (4 feet); similar flimsiness also appears at Kirby Muxloe and Baconsthorpe. When compared with the contemporary thickening of walls which occurred on the Continent in the face of the threat of artillery, the unsubstantial nature of these 'castles' is underscored.

4. See Salch (1987) pp. 116, 230 and Thompson (1987) p. 39 ff. Other French examples include Rambures (Somme), Bonaguil (Lot et-Garonne) and Chaumont (Loir-et-Cher); in Spain there are, among others, Coca (Segovia) and La Mota (Valladolid).

5. Carisbrooke Castle, on the Isle of Wight, is notable as a rare example of a medieval castle subsequently surrounded by seventeenth-century artillery bastions and ditches.

6. The phrase was coined by Sir Edward Coke, the great Stuart jurist, in Chapter 73 of the *Third Institute*. Coke was also one of the first men ever to undertake conservation of a medieval ruin, for in 1615 he spent £60 repairing the battlements and other parts of Castle Acre. The law takes over precisely at the time when the institution is so dead as to be worth preserving as an antiquity.

Select Bibliography

All books about castles consulted in preparing *England's Castles* have been listed, both in acknowledgement and as a pointer to further reading. Guides to individual castles have also been listed, if they have been used, though these are sometimes without author or date, or both, where those details are not known. Of books other than those about castles, only the ones which have had the most direct bearing on the present work have been included.

Books about castles

Anderson, W. (1970) *Castles of Europe* (Paul Elek, repr. Omega Books, Ware, 1984)

Armitage, E. S. (1912) *The Early Norman Castles of the British Isles* (John Murray, London)

Auvergne, E. B. D' (1911) *Famous Castles and Palaces of Italy* (T. Werner Laurie, London)

Auvergne, E. B. D' (1926) *The English Castles* (T. Werner Laurie, London)

Avent, R. (1983) *Castles of the Princes of Gwynedd* (HMSO, Cardiff)

Bottomley, F. (1979) *The Castle Explorer's Guide* (Kaye & Ward, London)

Braun, H. (1947) *The English Castle* (Batsford, London)

Breffny, B. de (1977) *Castles of Ireland* (Thames & Hudson, London)

Brown, R. A. (1954) *English Medieval Castles* (Batsford, London)

Brown, R. A. (ed) (1980) *Castles, A History and Guide* (Blandford Press, repr. New Orchard Editions, Poole, 1985)

Brown, R. A. (1984) *The Architecture of Castles* (Batsford, London)

Brown, R. A. (1989) *Castles from the Air* (Cambridge University Press, Cambridge)

Châtelain, A. (1983) *Châteaux forts, images de pierre des guerres médiévales* (Union REMPART, Paris)

Châtelain, A. (1987) *Châteaux forts et féodalité en Ile-de-France du XIe au XIIIe siècle* (Créer, Nonette, France)

Colvin, H. M. (ed) (1963) *The History of the Kings' Works* (HMSO, London)

Cruden, S. H. (1981) *The Scottish Castle* (3rd edition, Spurbooks, Edinburgh)

Cullen, P. W. and Hordern, R. (1986) *Castles of Cheshire* (Crossbow Books)

Davis, P. R. (1988) *Castles of the Welsh Princes* (Christopher Davies, Swansea)

Deschamps, P. (1964) *Terre Sainte Romane* (Zodiaque, La Pierre-Qui-Vire, France)

Eydoux, H-P. (1970) *Châteaux Fantastiques* (2 volumes, Flammarion, Paris)

Fedden, R. (1950) *Crusader Castles* (Art & Technics, London)

Forde-Johnston, J. (1979) *Great Medieval Castles of Britain* (Guild (BCA), London)

Forde-Johnston, J. (1981) *A Guide to the Castles of England and Wales* (Constable, London)

Gascoigne, C. and B. (1975) *Castles of Britain* (Thames & Hudson, London)

Gies, J. and F. (1974) *Life in a Medieval Castle* (Abelard, London)

Gifford, P. R. (ed) (1982) *Resist the Invader* (Essex County Council, Chelmsford)

Guy, J. (1980) *Kent Castles* (Meresborough Books, Gillingham)

Harvey, A. (1911) *The Castles and*

Walled Towns of England (Methuen, London)

Illingworth, J. L. (n.d.) *Yorkshire's Ruined Castles* (Burrow, London)

Johnson, P. (1978) *The National Trust Book of British Castles* (Weidenfeld & Nicolson, London)

Kemp, A. (1977) *Castles in Colour* (Blandford, Poole)

Kightly, C. and Chèze-Brown, P. (1979) *Strongholds of the Realm* (Thames & Hudson, London)

King, D. J. C. (1983) *Castellarium Anglicanum* (Kraus-Thompson, New York)

King, D. J. C. (1988) *The Castle in England and Wales* (Croom Helm, Beckenham)

Lawrence, T. E. (1936) *Crusader Castles* (Golden Cockerel Press, London, repr. Michael Haag, London, 1986)

Leask, H. (1946) *Irish Castles and Castellated Houses* (W. Tempest, Dundalk)

Lindsay, M. (1986) *The Castles of Scotland* (Constable, London)

MacGregor, P.(1983) *Odiham Castle* (Alan Sutton Ltd, Gloucester)

Mildren, J. (1987) *Castles of Devon* (Bossiney Press, Bodmin)

Morley, B. (1976) *Henry VIII and the Development of Coastal Defence* (HMSO, London)

Morshead, Sir O. (1957) *Windsor Castle* (Phaidon, London)

Muir, R. (1990) *Castles & Strongholds* (Macmillan, London)

Oman, Sir C. (1926) *Castles* (GWR, London, repr. Beekman House, New York 1978)

O'Neil, B. H. (1954) *Castles* (HMSO, London)

Ortiz Echagüe, J. (1956) *España, Castillos Y Alcázares,* (Publicaciones Ortiz-Echagüe, Madrid)

Panouillé, J-P. (1984) *The City of Carcassonne* (Ministère de la Culture, Paris)

Platt, C. (1982) *The Castle in Medieval England and Wales* (Secker & Warburg, London)

Price, M. and H. (1980) *Castles of Cornwall* (Bossiney Press, Bodmin)

Reid, A. (1973) *The Castles of Wales* (George Philip, London)

Renn, D. F. (1968) *Norman Castles in Britain* (John Baker, London)

Ross, S. (1973) *The Castles of Scotland* (George Philip, London)

Salch, C-L. (1987) *Les plus beaux châteaux forts en France* (Publitotal, Strasbourg)

Salter, M. (1988) *The Castles and Moated Mansions of Shropshire* (Folly Publications, Wolverhampton)

Salter, M. (1988) *The Castles and Moated Mansions of Staffordshire and the West Midlands County* (Folly Publications, Wolverhampton)

Sellman, R. R. (1954) *Castles and Fortresses* (Methuen, London)

Simpson, W. D. (1959) *Scottish Castles* (HMSO, Edinburgh)

Simpson, W. D. (1969) *Exploring Castles* (Routledge & Kegan Paul, London)

Simpson, W. D. (1969) *Castles in England and Wales* (Batsford, London)

Somerset Fry, P. (1974) *British Medieval Castles* (David & Charles, Newton Abbot)

Somerset Fry, P. (1980) *Castles* (David & Charles, Newton Abbot)

Tabraham, C. (1986) *Scottish Castles and Fortifications* (HMSO, Edinburgh)

Taylor, A. J. (1985) *Studies in Castles and Castle Building* (Hambledon Press, London)

Thomas, R. (ed) (1982) *Castles in Wales* (AA/Wales Tourist Board, Cardiff)

Thompson, M. W. (1989) *The Decline of the Castle* (Cambridge University Press, Cambridge)

Toy, S. (1939) *Castles: a short history of fortification from 1600 BC to AD 1600* (Heinemann, London)

Toy, S. (1953) *The Castles of Great Britain* (Heinemann, London)

Tranter, N. G. (1935) *The Fortalices*

and Early Mansions of Southern Scotland (Moray Press, Edinburgh)

Tranter, N. G. (1962) *The Fortified House in Scotland* (5 volumes, James Thin, Edinburgh, repr. 1977)

Turner, H. (1970) *Town Defences in England and Wales* (John Baker Ltd, London)

Wilkinson, F. (1973) *The Castles of England* (George Philip, London)

Other works consulted

Barley, M. (1986) *Houses and History* (Faber & Faber, London)

Brown, R. A. (1984) *The Normans* (Boydell Press, Woodbridge)

Defoe, D. (1971) (ed. Pat Rogers) *A Tour Through the Whole Island of Great Britain* (Penguin, Harmondsworth)

Fiennes, C. (1983) *The Journeys of Celia Fiennes* (Futura, London)

Goodman, A. (1977) *A History of England from Edward II to James I* (Longman, London)

Harvey, J. (1944) *Henry Yevele* (Batsford, London)

Harvey, J. (1959) *The Plantagenets* (2nd edition, Batsford, London)

Hassall, W. O. (1957) *They Saw it Happen* (Blackwell, Oxford)

Hassall, W. O. (1962) *How They Lived* (Blackwell, Oxford)

Jones, T. (1980) *Chaucer's Knight* (Weidenfeld & Nicolson, London)

Leland, J. (ed Lucy Toulmin Smith) (1910) *The Itinerary of John Leland* (5 volumes, George Bell, London)

Musset, L. (1983) *Angleterre romane* (Zodiaque, La Pierre-Qui-Vire, France)

Myers, A. R. (1966) *England in the Late Middle Ages)* (Penguin, Harmondsworth)

Pevsner, Sir N. (1951–) *The Buildings of England* (Penguin, Harmondsworth)

Poole, A. L. (1955) *From Domesday Book to Magna Carta* (Oxford University Press, Oxford)

Potter, K. R. ed (1955) *Gesta Stephani* (Nelson, London)

Powicke, Sir M. (1962) *The Thirteenth Century* (Oxford University Press, Oxford)

Ross, C. (1976) *The Wars of the Roses* (Thames & Hudson, London)

Rowley, T. (1983) *The Norman Heritage* (Routledge & Kegan Paul, London)

Rowley, T. (1986) *The High Middle Ages* (Routledge & Kegan Paul, London)

Stenton, D. M. (1965) *English Society in the Early Middle Ages* (Penguin, Harmondsworth)

Stone, B. (1974) *Sir Gawain and the Green Knight* (Penguin, Harmondsworth)

Thompson, M. W. (1981) *Ruins, Their Preservation and Display* (Collonade Books, London)

Warren, W. L. (1961) *King John* (Eyre & Spottiswoode, London)

Wilson, D. (1985) *Moated Sites* (Shire Publications, Princes Risborough)

Wood, M. E. (1965) *The English Medieval House* (Bracken Books, London, repr. 1983)

Guides to individual English castles in State care

Acton Burnell (C. A. Ralegh, Radford, 1966)
Ashby-de-la-Zouch (T. L. Jones, 1953)
Aydon (P. Dixon, 1988)
Baconsthorpe (S. E. Rigold, 1966)
Barnard Castle (D. Austin, 1988)
Beeston (J. Weaver, 1987)
Belsay (S. Johnson, 1984)

Berkhamsted (Sir C. Peers)
Bishop's Waltham (J. N. Hare, 1987)
Bolsover (P. A. Faulkner, 1972)
Brough (W. Douglas Simpson, 1982 and J. Charlton, 1986)
Brougham (J. Charlton, 1985)
Carisbrooke (Sir C. Peers, 1982 and R. Chamberlin, 1985)
Carlisle (J. Charlton, 1985)
Castle Acre (J. G. Coad, 1984)
Castle Rising (R. A. Brown, 1978)
Christchurch (M. E. Wood, 1974)
Donnington (M. E. Wood, 1964)
Dover (R. A. Brown, 1985 and C. Platt, 1988)
Dunstanburgh (C. H. Hunter Blair, 1936 and 1988)
Eynsford (S. E. Rigold, 1964)
Farleigh Hungerford (1979)
Farnham (M. W. Thompson, 1961)
Framlingham (F. J. E. Raby and P. K. Baillie Reynolds, 1959)
Framlingham and Orford (D. F. Renn, 1988)
Goodrich (C. A. Ralegh Radford, 1958)
Hadleigh (1971)
Helmsley (Sir C. Peers, 1966)
Hylton (B. M. Morley, 1979)
Kenilworth (M. W. Thompson, 1977 and D. F. Renn, 1973)
Kirby Muxloe (Sir C. Peers, 1957)
Launceston (T. L. Jones, 1959 and A. D. Saunders, 1984)
London (R. A. Brown and P. E. Curnow, 1984)
Lydford (A. D. Saunders, 1982)
Middleham (Sir C. Peers, 1965)
Norham (C. H. Hunter Blair and H. L. Honeyman, 1966)
Nunney (S. E. Rigold, 1957)
Okehampton (R. A. Higham, 1984)
Old Sarum (H. Shortt, 1965)
Old Wardour (R. B. Pugh and A. D. Saunders, 1968)
Pevensey (Sir C. Peers, 1953 and D. F. Renn, 1970)
Peveril (B. H. O'Neil and P. R. White, 1979)
Pickering (M. W. Thompson, 1958)
Porchester (S. E. Rigold, 1965, D. F. Renn, 1972 and B. Cunliffe, 1984)
Prudhoe (1986)
Restormel (C. A. Ralegh Radford, 1980)
Richmond (Sir C. Peers, 1981)
Rochester (R. A. Brown, 1969)
Scarborough (1980 and R. Bush, 1981)
Sherborne Old Castle (P. White, 1971)
Spofforth (R. J. Bunnett, O. J. Weaver and R. Gilyard Beer, 1965)
Tintagel (C. A. Ralegh Radford, 1939)
Totnes (S. E. Rigold, 1979)
Tynemouth (R. N. Hadcock, 1952)
Warkworth (C. H. Hunter Blair and H. L. Honeyman, 1954)
Wolvesey (M. Biddle, 1986)
York (D. F. Renn, 1971, ed. R. M. Butler, 1973 and B. H. O'Neil, 1979)

Guides to English castles in private ownership

Allington (1983)
Appleby (L. Chandler)
Arundel (J. H. Robertson)
Bamburgh (1989)
Banbury (P. Fasham, 1973)
Barnwell (B. Giggins, 1986)
Berry Pomeroy
Bodiam (C. Morley, 1981)
Bolingbroke (Sir R. Somerville and M. W. Thompson, 1985)
Bolton (G. Jackson, 1984)
Bristol (M. W. Ponsford)
Bungay (H. Cane)
Caister (E. D. Smith)
Colchester (D. Clark, 1985)
Corfe
Dudley (H. Brakspear and A. A. Rollason)
Durham (D. Bythell, 1985)
Hastings (J. E. Ray and W. H. Dyer)
Hedingham (1983)
Hever
Knaresborough (J. Symington, 1975 and M. J. Kershaw, 1987)
Lancaster (J. Meakin, 1988)
Leicester (G. A. Chinnery, 1981)
Lincoln (H. Elliott and D. Stocker, 1984)
Ludlow (1987)
Newark
Newcastle-upon-Tyne (B. Harbottle, 1988)
Norwich (R. Teather, 1985)
Nottingham (A. Hamilton)
Oakham (T. H. Clough, 1981)
Pontefract (1985)
Rockingham (T. Stock, 1984)
Sandal (1985)
Skipton (1986)
Shrewsbury
South Wingfield Manor (W. Hawksley Edmunds)
Stokesay (J. F. Mason, 1986)
Tamworth
Tattershall (M. W. Thompson, 1981)
Taunton (R. Bush, 1988)
Tutbury (Sir R. Somerville, 1978)
Walden (1986)
Warwick (M. Binney, *Country Life*, 1982 and P. Barker and R. J. Unstead, 1983)
Winchester (M. Biddle and B. Clayre, 1983)
Windsor (1986)
Wingfield
Witton (1980)

Index